The Settler's Cookbook

The Settler's Cookbook

A Memoir of Love, Migration and Food

Yasmin Alibhai-Brown

To Jeannette
with Best wishes
Yasmin Alibhai-
Brown
March 2011

Portobello
BOOKS

Published by Portobello Books Ltd 2008

Portobello Books Ltd
Twelve Addison Avenue
Holland Park
London
W11 4QR

A CIP catalogue record is available from the British Library

2 4 6 8 9 7 5 3 1

ISBN 978 1 84627 083 3 (hardback)
ISBN 978 1 84627 200 4 (export trade paperback)

www.portobellobooks.com

Text designed and typeset in
Bodoni by Patty Rennie

Printed in Great Britain by
MPG Books Ltd, Bodmin, Cornwall

For Jena, my mother (1920–2006), who was feisty and tender.

She gave me mettle, a wakeful conscience, a few gold bangles

(rarely worn, for she was a simple woman) and a precious

supply of inventive recipes that tell our stories.

For London, city of feasts and commotion,
now my terra firma, my cause.

'I am filled with nostalgia for something I never had...'

Tamar Yellin

Contents

Acknowledgements

I AM INDEBTED TO all those people from East Africa, now global citizens, who shared their experiences and feelings about our old homeland. It is a truism – but completely true in this case – that without them there would be no such book of memories. Unlike some others in the business who couldn't see why a political columnist should want to write a food memoir, my publisher, Portobello, saw possibilities. Tasja Dorkofkis understood what I wanted to write from the first time we met for a coffee, and Philip Gwyn Jones was wonderfully enthusiastic. I thank them both. And my beloved husband Colin, who started off unusually chary as I embarked on this project but who came round after scoffing the dishes detailed in the book. Ari, Leila and Liz are my nearest and dearest. They should understand this heritage one day and be proud of it. Finally, thank you to those relatives and good friends of all backgrounds who never give up on me, even though my journalism and waywardness must try their patience.

Prologue

OUR FAMILY TREE IS puny, barren in large part. The roots don't go down deep enough to produce a plenteous crop of ancestral stories or fruity relatives. The few memories hanging on are losing colour and juice, soon will wither and fall away.

The human urge to trace long, biological bloodlines is strong. But our far past was swept away by careless fate impetuously carrying off my folk across the seas, away, away to new beginnings. They took little and left behind even less. Like many other East African Asians whose forebears left India in the nineteenth century, I search endlessly for (and sometimes find) the remains of those days. Few maps mark routes of journeys undertaken by these migrants; hardly any books capture their spirit or tell the story. Then Africa disgorged us too, and here we are, people in motion, now in the West, the next stopover. There is no place on earth we can historically and unequivocally claim to be ours, and so we have become adept wayfarers who settle but cautiously, ready to move on if the winds change.

Ayar Ata, a Kurdish refugee in London, writes an ode to capture the global drifter's attachment to bits and pieces – portable, potent reminders of loss and gain too:

Under my bed there it was my seemingly little suitcase

inside it my few precious belongings.

A present from my Grand mum, an evenly shaped

light blue stone with white spots spread all over it, a familiar

piece of early morning sky with stars twinkling in the palm of my hand

A photo of my mother smiling at me in despair

waving and wondering

A broken watch with frozen hands.[1]

I carry around with me unfashionable bags holding too many things I don't need but might, just in case: extracts of the Koran in Arabic and English, an old photograph of my university in Uganda, a hanky used to mop up tears when I married Colin, a pill box and rosary that belonged to my mother, hospital notes, job references – an exile's survival kit.

In my sunny, high-tech kitchen, one small cupboard keeps cooking paraphernalia I brought over from Kampala in 1972, the year we Asians were cast out of Uganda by the sadistic black nationalist Idi Amin. I had arrived in Britain a few months before his expulsion orders and was never to return to my old homeland. Into a storeroom back home went a box with my precious vinyl collection – Cliff and Elvis, Chuck Berry, the Supremes, Ray Charles, Marvin Gaye, Mary Wells, Helen Shapiro (where did she go?), Martha Reeves and the Vandellas, Jimmy Ruffin, the Beatles, Jim Reeves, Millie, Sandie Shaw, Pat Boone, Connie Francis, Ravi Shankar, Bismillah Khan, Hindi song discs by Lata Mangeshkar, Mohammed Rafi,

Talat Mehmood and Mukesh, and poorly recorded Congolese jigs which always incited my buttocks to quiver. Also placed in storage (never reclaimed) were my Eng Lit books, a painstakingly assembled canon of the greatest writers. Many were gifts from eager educators who had drawn this avid pupil into poetry, drama and the novel. Almost all my photos, wrapped tenderly, catalogued then arranged in a small, red suitcase, were entrusted to a friend who then had to join the exodus. No time then to think of photos.

Why I transported old pots and pans to England I cannot explain. I try but am unable to throw them away. The motley collection has had several stays of execution. During cleaning fits, I chuck them into a box to be dumped, and they return back to the house, just in time.

There is a wooden contraption for grating hairy, brown-shelled coconuts. The device has not been used on these shores and is mummified with paper and layers of oil to keep it from cracking and rusting. Two slabs of wood are cleverly put together to make a folding stool. A flat, oval, rusting metal blade sticks out in front, like the head of a tortoise.

The coconut was broken, its sweet, cloudy juice drained into a glass which always went to the favourite child in the extended family, always a boy, always over-weight and a bloody nuisance. Then the kitchen servants sat astride the grater as if on a saddle, except it was so low their knees come up almost to their shoulders. With both hands they rolled the half-sphere over the blade with a zigzag edge. Sometimes, they slashed their hands and harsh employers abused them for what they thought was native idiocy. Or for contaminating the white flesh with their inferior blood. Boiling water was added to the grated coconut, and the mixture was then poured into a straw basket shaped like a long sausage to be squeezed. Imagine the agony. The burning, pitchy hands added a sweetness you can never reproduce.

Then there is a Formica *chapatti patlo*, a round board with small legs, previously made of grainy wood to roll out various Indian breads. The new model (1970) was made by Mr Desai, a compulsive modernizer who went from house to house in a tweedy, dank-smelling suit to demonstrate the easy-clean properties of this very latest 'British' material. My mother bought an FP, as they were known, then had to pay for it in pitifully small weekly sums. I use it often. One day in 1988 it helped me capture the heart of my Englishman, four months after my Ugandan Asian husband flew the nest, taking his best clothes and irreplaceable, lived recollections of our old land and of England as it was when we had come.

A brass device came too. Shaped like a mug, it has a circulating handle at the top and plates you insert and secure at the bottom. One plate has holes the size of match heads, another has tinier perforations, another a star. Made by M. S. Chava, whose name is burned into the brass, it was used to make savoury Indian snacks. The 'mug' was stuffed with a spicy, thick gram-flour mix then held over boiling vats of oil, the handle turned by a fearless hand. Thin or thick threads looking like wet noodles fell in and were flash-fried. Almira, a neighbour in Kampala, used to make bright yellow spiral towers of thin *sev* and thick *gathia* which would then sit on newspapers, seeping oil until they were cold and dry enough to store. Though a matchless cook, Almira slowly wasted away. Brought over from India to marry into the family next door, she was palely beautiful and inconsolably sad. Her in-laws beat her often because she didn't try to look happier than she felt.

Some eccentric items I carried over were made by a crooning artisan who called himself Mr Harry Belafonte the Third. The singer has left his song in his handiwork. My rimmed aluminium bowl shaped like a scarecrow's hat capers merrily when you put it on a flat surface, and a huge stainless-steel *karai* – an Indian wok – bops on the cooker as the heat warms it. On the coldest days of winter, torpidity appears to enter these metals; the rocking slows down.

Abdullah, a fat and agile man who could bend right down and walk on all fours, made the colander I brought over, with a handle nearly a foot long. It was noisily hammered out on the street one afternoon. My mum had sent me and my cousin, Alnoor, with exact, memorized instructions for the dextrous metal-beater, who knew her and knew too that she wouldn't pay him if he didn't make her his best. This was in 1958, when food at home was still cooked on a Primus stove. The walls of our small kitchen were black, and my clean school uniforms often caught the soot if I forgot to be careful.

Eight years old, Alnoor and I waited patiently, sitting on wooden crates eating slices of sour, unripe mangoes dipped into a concoction of chilli powder, salt, sugar and Eno's Fruit Salt (a universal remedy for stomach upsets). Abdullah handed out small white-paper packets of the mix to his favourite kids, a forbidden pleasure. It fizzed in our mouths before the chilli set fire to the tongue as we bit into the mangoes. Sometimes I accidentally put one finger into an eye, spreading into it the potent dust. If I cried, Abdullah laughed and said I was being a baby.

We were the sugar children – *mtamu mototo* in Swahili – stuffed with the sweet foods believed to be essential for a happy childhood, our plump cheeks affectionately pinched by adults. Our soft tongues and lips, however, were kept from extreme savoury tastes. In the 1950s 'vernacular' food had been condemned as dangerous for growing kids by awesome white health experts who recommended plain English grub instead. (And they wonder why I detested British rule.) Subversive children rebelled against these boring injunctions, sought out food that hurt, drew tears.

I sucked on tamarind beans until my tongue bled, stole *paan* from my mother's handbag and hid it in a tin on a bed of pencil shavings. *Paan* helps to clear the breath and move on digestion. It is a special leaf smeared with a flavoured paste then filled with betel nut, desiccated coconut, various seeds and whole cloves, sometimes tobacco, sometimes hash, the last two sold only to men. The leaf is folded into a samosa shape and chewed slowly.

When Alnoor was seven, he turned into a compulsive onion eater. His nervy mum fed him too much plain broth to build him up so he fought back with raw onions, stole them from the larder, beat them on stones, opened them to look like heliotrope flowers, peeled off the layers and bit into the sharp taste, snuffling with pleasure. He carried the stench on his breath, his hands and his uniforms. The armpits of his white shirts turned lilac. His mother's laments grew more plaintive: this child must have sold vegetables in the last life and cheated customers, so Allah is punishing him. Who will touch him? A boy who smells like an uncooked biriyani? Allah, Allah, what will happen to my youngest boy?'

Abdullah was what we rudely called a *chotara* – a black/brown mix, the son of an old Asian trader and his teenage African servant girl who warmed his body before a proper wife, Suraya, arrived from India. Suraya immediately sacked the willing maid, a mother by then of coffee-coloured babies – three in all. Suraya, who looked perpetually pregnant, remained barren and turned sullen. Abdullah boasted that his father was a fabulously wealthy sugar-cane plantation owner who *would* claim his street son one day. His clothes were frayed, his eyes droopy and drippy from working hours every day over a white-hot fire.

He wrapped his creations in newspaper, and we knew my mother would find fault with them and send them back at least twice. My own transported relics were also wrapped in newspaper. Over the years I had to throw out the old papers as they disintegrated – copies of the *Uganda Argus*. The pages carried many accounts of petty criminals beaten or burned to death by crowds of excited men, women and laughing children. In the grainy photos, some of the proud slayers had their feet on the pulped prey, just like the white bwana hunters with their trophy lion and leopard scalps.

Until I was twelve, we lived in a small flat above the main marketplace in Kampala. I remember ululations rising up, the calls of a gathering crowd as a thief was spotted grabbing a handbag or, more commonly, fruit or bread from some vendor. Sometimes the person was innocent, just an unfortunate who met a surge of violent action. I would try to hide under the beds with pillows over my ears until it was all over. Sometimes curiosity overcame fear, and I made myself stand on our balcony to watch, peering through the lattice walls. The mob included honest folk and sprightly felons hoping it would never be their turn. The petrified quarry was almost always strangely silent and curled up small. They kicked him softly, burned his arms with matches, pushed in his face and eyes. Then a gang of big men finished him off. The pack of the poor and disenfranchised briefly exerted power as cruel custodians of virtue.

Other newspaper pictures were of the latest high-cost government folly, posed tableaux of staged political rallies and ministerial weddings, adolescent brides smiling nervously in white bri-nylon gowns. Festooned between the dense print appeared adverts for Royal Baking Powder, Kenya butter, Bird's Custard and Instant Whip, Coca-Cola, Omo washing powder and GEC ovens. Eno's adverts were ubiquitous: a white hand wearing white cuffs and a gentleman's cufflinks cradled the slogan 'The Line of Life'.

Our past has been fading faster than *Argus* newsprint. Words, languages, faces, images, landscapes are drifting away. Sometimes I struggle to summon them back. The other day an old auntie from Mombasa gave me some *ubani*: 'Here, take, you liked it so much when you were small, always chewing, even in mosque.' I stared at the amber nuggets – edible resin – and wondered what they were. That naughty girl in mosque exists in the memories of others, gone from mine.

What was I then and there? Is any of that left here and now? After so many years in Britain, speaking posh English, shaving off bits that offended or provoked disdain, time erasing the rest, I can feel a fake, at times a clanking composite of ill-fitting parts.

Some of the deceased men and women I knew as a child come back to jostle for space in my head, calling from the other side. Particular foods remind me of individuals. During the forty days of mourning after they were sent off to their graves, their favourite dishes were brought to mosque by relatives. After prayers, the sacred victuals were bought for a nominal sum by the poor, lonely, ill and hard-pressed whose pleasure upon eating would be transported to the tongues of the departed as they entered the forgiving gates of paradise, so we believed.

I see my Maami in my sleep, my maternal uncle's wife, eating her coriander omelette every morning with two thick slices of white toast followed by rough bran dissolved in sweet tea to prevent heart attacks. She was the kindest, jolliest person I ever knew, even though her life had been hard as a widow with many wayward children. At night after dinner, she sucked on wedges of sharp, acidic oranges, to break open the clogged arteries, she said. Her heart gave up anyway, and she lies cold and alone in a cemetery in New York, where her youngest son had moved on to after many years in Britain.

I dream of Roshan Auntie, a family friend. Unusually tall for an Asian woman, she had the grace of a gazelle. Her husband, Nazar, adorned her long neck with many strings of creamy Japanese pearls. She made dainty, crisp samosas small enough to be eaten in one bite. I see her in her kitchen, in her pearls and pink quilted house-coat, humming quietly as she rolls out the samosa pastry. In one dream she insists it is time I made these for myself. I know, and have tried without real success. My generation buys ready-made frozen samosas from expert pensioners who supplement their incomes selling foods that take time and patience. That skill will pass into the void within a few years, and we will make do with factory-produced spring-roll pastry.

The dough is simple enough: hot water, salt and white flour kneaded well. Eight pieces are broken off and rolled to the size and shape of saucers. They are layered, one upon another, with flour and oil smeared between them. Then the rolling begins again, gentle, coaxing, until the circle grows to the size of a big platter. The pastry is slapped on to a hot *tawa*, or flat iron pan, and turned over again and again by hand. Like fire-walkers, experts are immune to the scorching heat. They peel off layers of pastry as it blisters, then wrap the paper-thin sheets in a tea towel. These are cut into thin strips and folded like posh napkins, stuffed with spicy mince or vegetables, and finally sealed tight to be fried in a vast bubbling wok of oil big enough to bath a newborn.

Roshan Auntie always made a separate batch for children without green chillies. What a lady. We sat on tablecloths on the spotless red floor polished daily with coconut husks by the servants. Freshly fried batches arrived, scalding our small fingers. A bowl of icy water was placed in the middle and a jug of sweet, minty, fresh lime juice. My once-cherished ex-mother-in-law made excellent samosas too, and nobody ever made mince kebabs like Kulsum, my cousin's wife, and my mother's coconut dhal is famous in the Diaspora from Vancouver to Cape Town.

In 1978, on the 207 bus going up Uxbridge Road from Shepherd's Bush to Ealing, my mother was told to get off by a conductor because she smelled like a 'curry pot'. She replied (without budging), 'Sir not to mind. You must come and taste it one day, my curry. You people love it, isn't it?' She *was* stinking, having gone out in the same cardi she wore when cooking. 'But our food is not like those Bengalis and Gujaratis, or English. It smells so nice, these people don't know us

African Indians,' she said indignantly when telling us what happened. There you have it, our confusing identity carried on her sleeve.

I am often invited by true-born bigots to fuck off back where I came from. Where would that be then? Kampala, where I was born? Or Karachi, where my father hailed from but left forever at seventeen to come to his beloved England? Or Porbandar in the Gujarat in India, whence my maternal grandfather was dispatched as a small boy? Or Dar-es-Salaam in what was Tanganyika, where my mother was born and raised? And do my blue-eyed English husband and our gorgeous hybrid daughter have to leave too? What about my English-rose daughter-in-law and son, a proud Briton whose skin is dark caramel?

Samuel Pepys lamented 'the absurd nature of the Englishman who could not forbear laughing and jeering at anything that looked strange'.[2] As the British Caribbean writer Caryl Phillips has observed, 'The mongrel nation that is Britain is struggling to find a way to stare into the mirror and accept the ebb and flow of history that has produced this fortuitously diverse condition and its concomitant pain.'[3]

Initially Ugandan Asians only added to that pain. Our presence in Uganda and eventual ejection were intimately tied in with the fortunes and misfortunes of Empire. During the expansionist period of Rule Britannia, indentured Indian labourers – replacements for slave labour – were transported to build the East African Railway from the coast to the interior. Many lost their lives. But that didn't put off small entrepreneurs and adventurers who crossed over to the untapped continent, lured by beguiling promises of untold prosperity. Others took off to escape the callous policies of the Raj and catastrophic famines between 1870 and 1890. Lord

Lytton, the viceroy appointed by Queen Victoria (because she liked his poetry), decreed that shipments of cheap grain from India to the UK had to continue and outlawed relief efforts. Twenty-nine million people died. A journalist witnessed 'bony remnants of human beings begging for grain... their fleshless jaws and skulls were supported on necks like those of plucked chickens'.[4]

The first migrants travelled in sprightly dhows to the inviting coastline of Mombasa, thence to the unfathomable interior. And just as we struggle to hold on to the remembrance of a land lost, so did they, only in their case it was India. Real links did weaken, but the mythical India kept a hold and has followed us here.

In Britain the locals still enquire, politely, 'Where are you from? How come you speak such good English?' The questions – 'well meant' – are upsetting. Spectral fears flicker and flare, then subside. What if we are deported out of here too, just as we were from our beloved Uganda? (Should I take my kitchen utensils on to the next place?)

We are trying our very best, you know, striving to be good, to impress. We have blossomed and made places bloom. In the Midlands alone, East African Asians have created more than thirty thousand jobs and regenerated dying localities. We are in the millionaires' lists, top of educational-achievement tables, increasingly influential in mainstream political parties eager for cash and cachet. But we still cannot really belong and have to clutch at throwbacks and fantasy connections just as we did in Africa.

Bollywood films insinuated the subcontinent into our hearts and do so today. Mosques, temples, churches and *gurudwaras*, extended families, childhood tales and teachers took us and take us back to an idealized subcontinent. Like black Americans seeking a past in old slave ports and white Americans who come seeking Scottish and Irish ancestries, we yearn to belong to the ancient civilizations of the Ganges and Indus – futile quests by people nervous about their own condition. Sometimes I long to be an authentic somebody – a rooted Sikh, say, with a green plot of land in the Punjab handed down over generations, or a proper Karachi expatriate like so many of my friends who can always return there when the going gets impossibly tough here. Many other East African Asians and their children feel the same emptiness, historically and geographically disconnected.

There are no films about our old lives. East African Asians have been wary of written words and records which, once set down, can hold you to ransom, come and get you. When I was fifteen, I came home from school to find my dark green box had gone. It was where I hid my diaries, often full of frustration and anguish because my family was unpredictable and volatile. There were letters too, tied into bundles with red ribbons, sweet proclamations of love from my first secret boyfriend, and small gifts he had given me, including a dried rose smelling of the Old Spice he used even though his face had less hair than mine. My father, going through a particularly malevolent time, had rummaged through my things, found the box, set fire to it. I was both afraid and inconsolable. No conversation followed this act of vandalism. He just said, 'It is for your own good name.' After my mother was buried, relatives warned me not to write about the family because I would bring them shame. Words, words, how they fear the power of words.

Pragmatism has served us well yet also contributed to this culture of trepidation and philistinism. For practical, enterprising folk, too busy doing and making and moving, there is no space for self- or group reflection. Artistic expression or the life of the imagination is thought a foolish waste of time. 'You have not used your brain correctly at all,' lectured my millionaire uncle, nicknamed Mercedes Masa. 'Can you eat books or put them in a bank? Should have listened and become a doctor or accountant, gone into business with me. Could have three big houses in Harrow by now.' Snorting contemptuously, he blamed my mother for not training me right. They always said we were the Jews of East Africa. And yet, unlike the Jews, we have barely any keepers of our stories. As Paul Theroux noted in the 1960s, 'The amount written about Asians in Africa is pathetically small. There are perhaps five thin books, with unusually large typography, concentrating on kinship and nation building and faded pictures of fundis working on the railroad.'[5]

Cynthia Salvadori, an Italian anthropologist who has gathered invaluable testimonies of Kenyan Asians, wrote that she was provoked into publication by the fact that although there existed a flood of books about whites in Kenya,

it was as if Indians hardly existed. In the multitude of old books about Kenya by European adventurers, settlers and officials, there are passing references to 'banyan' traders and generic 'Indian dukas', to ubiquitous Goan clerks and cooks, 'babu' stationmasters and postmasters, to transporters and Sikh 'fundis'... the lack of information about Indian pioneers is due not only to the non-Indians' disinterest (and often hostility). It is due also to the Indians' own lack of interest in writing about themselves.[6]

The only novelist of merit to come out of the East African Diaspora, M. G. Vassanji, has suggested that Asians belong to very closed, and very close, communities, and to be able to write about them would require a tremendous sense of detachment, which they do not have.[7]

To my son and daughter, I am from a sad place in Africa where there are big beasts, safari jeeps and spectacular views, but too much butchery and poverty for their refined Western sensibilities. They feel detached from my complicated upbringing, and when I insist on reminding them of it they switch off or rebuke me sharply. I speak four non-European languages and tried to pass them on with no success. In her last years, when my mother found it harder to communicate in English, my children never got to know what she said and how she really felt. Perhaps they are apprehensive that to accept their cluttered heritage is to thin down their entitlement to be truly, purely, deeply British.

They are gluttons for East African Asian foods though. Favourites are fried *mogo* (cassava) and *kuku paka*, a coconut-chicken dish originally from Zanzibar. When my daughter was a toddler, I made her what I had been fed as a child: 'red rice' – boiled basmati mixed with tomato purée, garlic and butter – which she loves to this day. My adult son makes his own version of chilli and sour cream to eat with what we call fish cutlets – the old English fishcake recipe only 'fixed and much better', as my mother used to put it. The next generation does pick up this baton at least. While they eat I reminisce, linking the dishes to times and places, so that when I am gone, my voice will echo in their heads to remind them who they are.

Perhaps the lack of a homeland is a deliverance, an emancipation from the bounds of zealous, unseemly nationalism. Although there are times of immense dislocation and sadness, I now understand that our nomadic history has made us into enthusiastic, incorrigible cosmopolitans, winners in a globalized world. Our food bears testimony to this dynamic existence – creative, sometimes impertinent and playful blends of Indian, Pakistani, Arab, African, Chinese and English, now Italian and American too, forever in flux. Living in the UK, our food is constantly updated, adapted, altered, recast; much is borrowed. Other British Asians are becoming similarly dynamic, but we were the first to embrace the ceaseless movement of modernity. In the twenty-first century, during Ramadan in the UK, fasts can start with 'English' breakfasts: eggs, halal sausages, beef bacon, chillied baked beans and *parathas*.

Food is intrinsically connected to economics, politics, communication, knowledge, marriage, trade and the movements of peoples. Once upon a time, East African Asian food expressed both desperate nostalgia and hardship. Happiness then was eating a mango (two if you earned more than barely enough working in factories, hospitals or for British Rail) or adding an aubergine to spicy potato and making dhal less watery. I can make ten different potato dishes – all invented when I was a poor postgraduate at Oxford.

Then came the small savings which built up to bigger piles. East African Asian corner shops became sustainable; more imports were flown over faster. Families began to dress in their best and venture out to cafés selling Indian snacks. Food in the home grew varied and more luxuries were added, the same cycle our ancestors in East Africa went through from deprivation to abundance.

Prologue

Ugandan Asians love bargains and fresh culinary ideas, and they get them aplenty in areas with highly competitive small Asian businesses. Most of us consider it immoral to spend huge amounts of money on food and pride ourselves on being able to turn wilted vegetables and the cheapest cuts of meat into delightful dishes. We are canny and know where to get vine tomatoes for 12 pence per half-kilo, six bunches of fresh, aromatic coriander for a pound, boxes of Alphonso mangoes for a fiver, inexpensive sacks of rice, dhals, *chapatti* flours, gram flour, rice flour and fresh pickles made by local women. As we become time-poor we take short cuts: ready-ground spices and pastes, frozen *parathas*, yam, *bhindis* and *karela* (bitter gourd), crushed garlic and ginger and green chillies. We have adapted to the tastes of younger generations. An unprecedented number of our women are entering all the professions, rising up the ladder and making their mark. Extended families are passing away. Ambitious young wives and mothers seek out new tricks to cook good food well and fast.

If we transformed Britain, Britain moulded and transfigured us too. So here is our tale. Here are the dishes that carry our collective memories and imagine our uncertain future.

1 *Enticing Blightie, 1972*

I FLY INTO HEATHROW in March 1972 feeling blessed by the angels. I am about to start my postgraduate studies at Oxford and marry my own True Love (TL), who has been there for a year. The place is full, he says, of wise men and, to his delight, girls in very short skirts on bikes. He is a zoologist, embarked on a DPhil recording the reproductive habits of voles in nearby Wytham Woods. I don't know what voles are. They look like rats in the photos he has sent me. Plain voles in safe woods, after the wild, roaming beasts of Africa, must feel like domesticated science. But heck, it is *Oxford*. His stout father (who died an anorexic in Canada in 1988) never could describe what his son was studying but used to boast to one and all, 'Do you know? My son, number four, he's in England, *Oxford*, first-class university in the world, he is *there*, sons of kings and prime ministers are there.' Vainglory comes easily to Ugandan Asians. And until we were disabused, we believed that England was an orderly, eternally genteel haven, the antithesis of African mayhem.

In the 1960s, when all East African Asians were offered British citizenship, some politely refused and registered as nationals of their liberated countries if only to ensure that they were not discriminated against by the black governments. My family rushed to become Her Majesty's subjects, unaware that we were volunteering for abysmally low status within a strict caste system. The decision would sorely test our loyalties. In February 1962, Papa obtained the necessary forms, filled them out in a day, led us to a studio for passport photos and instructed us to look seriously worthy of the honour.

My mother, Jena, and I then took the forms to the High Commission, queuing outside in the hot sun day after day. My wheaten skin turned darker, causing my mother great consternation. Dark skin was a blight. We got there earlier and earlier, but a long queue of other Asians was always there before us. Jena brought on her high blood pressure to jump the queue, to no avail. Melodramatic scenes were played out all over the lawn – people fainted, wept, begged, threw themselves at the feet of the flint-faced guards, got their children to wail (quiet pinching was most effective), organized commotion Bollywood-style. The drama of desperation played to an indifferent audience.

Over five miserable days, doors shut before Mum and I could squeeze in. On the following Monday, we finally made it to the counter, only to pay 35 Ugandan shillings each and put up with official insolence. Our interrogator, a Scotsman with a wild red beard and profuse eyebrows, suddenly asked us to get our applications signed by yet another worthy; three professional men of good name were not enough. He explained that the same referees had signed too many forms and so were discredited: 'Can't trust you lot, charging for their signatures I'm sure. Money, money, money, that's all you brownies care about.' He sounded like a rotary trimmer. Mum pretended to faint and sank to the floor. Black security men lifted her into a chair (she squirmed when they touched her), and I started to bawl. A long lunch break loomed. The red devil decided we were too much trouble and stamped the papers. We thanked him excessively, as was expected. On the way out, my mum whispered to me in Kutchi to remember that he never washed his bottom; whites never did. 'And they eat pigs, you know, so their sweat smells bad and they are always heartless. Something in that pig meat makes you heartless so Allah told us not to eat it.' Our blue-black passports arrived three weeks later, beautiful to look at and touch. Papa wrapped them in red velvet and locked them away in a bank vault.

As Ugandan independence had approached in October 1962, thousands of Asians, faithful foot-soldiers of the colonial power, had taken up British citizenship. Kenya and other ex-colonies also had many such loyalists. This virtual empire assuaged British national vanity as decolonization accelerated. The rulers lost the lands but kept the subjects. Some Asians believed that British citizenship gave them security. Black Africans took this to be a sign of disloyalty.

Animosity between black and brown Ugandans intensified. Implacable racial and class divisions between indigenous Africans and settler Asians were a fact of East African life and had been encouraged and institutionalized by the British. Asians had come to believe that their lighter skin and middle-class status made them superior to blacks, who now had power in their unforgiving hands.

Racist, elected black politicians began to scapegoat Asians. 'Kenya will not tolerate these people, these Asians who practise cat and mouse friendship,' warned Jomo Kenyatta in 1967. His deputy, Daniel Arap Moi (one of the most corrupt African politicians ever), added his own invective: 'Asians, listen, one leg should not be in Kenya and the other in India. We will not tolerate that.'[1] Black politicians

demanded bribes from Asian businesses and then regularly abused them in public.

These were the Cold War years when Marxist socialism was gaining influence across

East Africa. Public service jobs were 'blackenized'. Asians propped up the economy

and infrastructure, but they lacked political skills, and many nurtured anti-black

prejudices. Those who could began to emigrate to Britain, and as numbers grew

Enoch Powell condemned the influx. His popularity soared. In 1968 a tight quota

was set to limit the entry into the UK of East African British Asians. The law

was cruelly specific. Only those with indigenous British ancestry had the right to

enter freely.

On the flight over, the plane is packed with Asians who consider themselves unbe-

lievably lucky to have got the right to enter their own country under the quota

system. They know they must be grateful for these small mercies. They look relieved

and anxious at the same time, hopeful and hopeless. Life for Asians in East Africa

has become perilous; my fellow passengers, a canny lot, have fled before they were

pushed. Some, travelling for the first time on an aeroplane, have dressed as if they

are going to a formal sundowner for *topiwallahs*, their teasing word to describe

colonial masters who always wore stiff hats. The migrants have left behind their

houses, farms, factories, shops, cars, insurance policies, gods, shrines, graves, precious sites of worship; by comparison my pitiful hoard of records, books and photos seems a negligible loss. As they swarmed to the airport, their jewellery was snatched from them at roadblocks manned by thieving soldiers with opaque eyes. This was happening long before Idi Amin's expulsion order legitimized such crimes.

Some of the women compare the scratches and cuts on their ears, necks and forearms. 'Bastards, *badmash*, *sala junglee* crooks, never worked a day, took every-thing, even my new wedding ring,' wails the youngish bride of startling beauty who needs no adornment. 'They will be shown no mercy by Allah, you will see, go to hell. Pulled my bangles so hard I cried. From England I will put a black curse on them. Their country will never be happy,' warns an old woman with crippling arthritis. She has a wicked look in her eyes; she smiles. From a large, hand-stitched bag embroidered with the map of India she takes out a tin containing several battered, fried snacks made of spicy mashed potatoes. She opens one carefully with her bent and brittle fingers. Inside are a couple of diamond rings. 'Many more in here, you have to be clever. Fifty-five diamonds and some gold – I fried the whole afternoon.' Some of the passengers look envious and ignore her for the rest of the journey.

Wise philosopher-housewives calm the most distressed ladies, tell them they are going to a much better place with polite soldiers and definitely the thickest, most nutritious, unadulterated milk in the world. They exchange recipes for milky sweets and drinks, bicker over whose methods are the best. Time and sorrow pass as they get engrossed in this game. Gujarati, Punjabi, English, Hindi bounce from seat to seat. In East Africa, religion gave each community its own heaven and earth without causing any serious rifts. Hindu, Muslim, Sikh and Christian Asians had to bind together, to survive as visible minorities whose skin never turned native under the stupendous African sun.

Passengers talk too loudly while the disapproving whites mutter, 'For God's sake!' and 'Sit down, will you?' All seat-belt signs are ignored. Bottles of sparkling Vimto are offered by strangers to strangers with the merest wipe of the neck; Tupperware boxes are passed round containing samosas, *dhal bhajias*, chilli *bhajias*, home-made *mithai*, fried *mogo*, bright chutneys that inevitably drip. They savour the last tastes of the tropical life they will never know again.

One English chap with a handlebar moustache smiles indulgently, takes a samosa, which he scoffs after plunging a corner into the green dip. The sauce lingers on his whiskers for many hours. That act of generous acceptance makes him into their best friend. So thrilled are they, the women cannot leave him alone. He pretends to fall asleep, winks an eye open to see if it is safe to wake up, only to be pounced on with further offerings. He farts a lot and looks miserable as the journey goes on and on. The old woman with arthritis smells him out and makes him eat a heap of *ajma*, bitter seeds to cure flatulence. He looks even more wretched as she stands over him, rocking unsteadily. He has no idea what the seeds are or of the protocol should she fall into his lap.

Fried Cassava

Frozen cassava or the real stuff – both can be bought in Asian shops.
Buy chunks if frozen, not the pre-sliced variety. About four pieces
or chunks the size of big potatoes feed six

Oil to fry – about 2 in. in a frying pan　　**A little lemon juice**
Water to cover the cassava　　**Salt and chilli powder to taste**

- Bring water, salt and lemon to the boil.
- Cook the large chunks of *mogo* – peeled or plopped out of a packet – until they look a bit like parboiled potatoes.
- Drain and leave for an hour to dry off.
- Slice into long, fat chips, taking out any stringy bits.
- Fry in oil that should be hot enough to cook steadily, not blazing hot. You need to turn the chips over frequently until they're crisp. They should look like a cross between chips and roast potatoes.
- Sprinkle with salt and chilli powder.
- Serve with Tamarind and Date Dip.

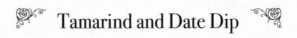

Tamarind and Date Dip

Equal quantities of dried tamarind　　**Boiling water**
and dried dates　　**Salt, sugar and chilli powder to taste**

- ⊙ Soak the dates and tamarind in boiling water so it comes up to 2 in. above the solids.

- ⊙ Leave overnight.

- ⊙ Rub the mixture through a sieve with a wooden spoon and add salt, chilli powder and sugar, tasting all the while so you end up with a well-balanced sweet/sour/hot sauce.

———

British milk turned out even more creamy, white and pure than imagined by the philosopher-housewives, who fed their toddlers melted Cadbury's milk chocolate back home. Evaporated and condensed milk too were cheaper and richer than in Uganda. *Khado*, my own favourite milky delight, was like, well, a wicked, nutty latte minus the coffee. In those early years after arriving in the UK, layers of compacted cream were laid down under the skin and remain there, impossible to shift.

Khado

Serves 8–10

1½ pints fresh full-cream milk

½ tin condensed milk

½ tsp grated nutmeg

½ cup finely chopped almonds and pistachios

1 large tin evaporated milk

½ tsp powdered cardamom

½ cup of water

- Heat the fresh milk and water and bring to a simmer. Sprinkle in the cardamom and nutmeg. Reduce the heat and simmer for six minutes, stirring from time to time to stop it sticking. Add the other milks and cook for another three minutes, stirring all the time. Add the nuts chopped roughly in a processor. Serve in espresso cups and drink warm to dispel winter blues or soothe heartache.

For children there was a cool option: hideous pink sherbet.

Sherbet

Same quantities as for *Khado* of fresh, evaporated
and condensed milks cooled in the fridge

Serves 6–8 kids

½ cup cold water

Takmaria – small black seeds you can buy in Asian shops (I have no anglicized name for them)

1 tsp vanilla extract or rose water

Cochineal colouring

- Rinse the *takmaria* in a sieve, then soak them for four hours until they resemble tiny, plump, glassy beads or caviar (kids love the texture).
- Whiz all but the *takmaria* in a liquidizer and serve with ice cubes and the *takmaria* in fat glasses with spoons to swoop it up.

Other than milk, almost all food in Britain disappointed. British ingredients were cleaner and cooked miraculously fast, but there was something special in Ugandan soil and water. Meat too never smelled as strong as it did in England, as if it had been wiped with a damp, dirty cloth.

Was that true? How can I tell? I remember retching in Kampala's meat market. A dense stench of congealing blood hovered in the hot air while a profusion of flies swept about audaciously, performing feats like air-display pilots. The dumbest among them sometimes wandered into your nostrils, and then you had to pull out black and shiny green bits, some still wriggling. Laid out on rusty trays were bones, offal, heads and maroon cuts, some turning black. The worst would be sold off to African shoppers who could afford to buy such luxuries. Scavenging dogs jumped on the bits of fat thrown to them. Fitter, thieving dogs jumped high enough to grab a tray, some of the real stuff. I was so frightened of them that to this day I can't stand to be near a dog or watch it eat.

Yet I also recall the beef, lamb and mutton in Kampala being more succulent and concentrated than anything I eat here. And the bones were full of rich marrow. Kids used to fight over these, the winner sometimes taking the prized tubes to the kitchen to be briefly reboiled in broth flavoured with cloves to release the marrow more easily. You sucked hard and noisily on them until there was only whistling air.

Back on the plane, the Tupperware ladies circulate. Their saris are tied tight, pushing out soft stomachs and smiling belly buttons. Useless bunches of house keys jangle from huge safety pins on their blouses. They stick boxes into my face, one after another. 'Have this *bhajia*, *beti*, better than your mother, better than your granny also, I am telling you, believe me, here, *beti*, take small one, want chutney? Tomato sauce?'

'No, don't take hers, here mine, first class mine, will eat your own fingers this *ondhwo* is too tasty.' The weepy new bride thinks she can persuade me. She reaches over holding a large chilli *bhajia*. Her hand, glistening with oil and enticing, is covered in vines, roses, curls, teardrops and crescent moons hennaed by a delicate romantic artist, I imagine. She lovingly coaxes, 'Don't be shy, no matter you haven't brought any food. Tell me your name, then you are my sister. Come, eat, open mouth, don't make me sad.' I smile stupidly, shake my head, then rudely turn away to the window.

Chilli *Bhajia*

Serves 3–6

6 long, large green chillies or long peppers (must have thick skins)

Stuffing

½ lb flat *gathias* (cooked Gujarati snacks made of gram flour). These are soft, unlike the noodle-shaped, crispier *gathias* described earlier. Both can be found in vegetarian snack houses or Indian grocery stores.

1 tsp crushed garlic

½ tsp chilli powder

¾ tsp sugar or a little jaggery

1 tbsp sunflower oil

2 tsp sesame seeds

A little salt, not too much as the
gathias are salted already

1 tbsp fresh lime juice

Batter

¾ cup gram flour

A pinch of bicarbonate of soda

Sunflower oil to deep-fry *bhajias*

Salt, chilli and a little lemon juice

4–5 tbsp cold water

- Half slit open the chillies with the top still holding on firmly.

- Gently scrape out the seeds, as many as you can.

- Pound together or process the stuffing ingredients until they bind and feel like soft marzipan.

- Stuff the mixture into the open chillies and press them back together.

- In a small bowl, mix the gram flour with the seasonings and bicarbonate of soda, then slowly add in water until you have a batter thick enough to completely coat the chillies. The texture should be like heavy wall paint.

- Heat the oil until a small bit of bread dropped in rises fast to the top.

- Dip and coat the chillies and carefully place them in the oil. I tend to do this with a tablespoon, but my mum used her hand. The oil may spit. Step back and let it; it will soon settle. Don't panic. Small oil burns are badges of honour.

- Wait a couple of minutes and turn the chillies over. Keep frying and turning until the *bhajias* look firm and slightly brown.

- Check one to see the batter is cooked through completely.

The plane wings on, unaware of the fissures and flavours within. I am already a snob, repelled by this crowd of *desis* who speak Indian English and behave like villagers on a bus. I have received pronunciation and can say 'p' and 't' with proper little explosions; I am a scholar of Dickens and Shakespeare, and make pretty apple pies and Victoria sponges light as kites. I am not quite one of them, or so I pretend, even though my mum makes the same snacks at home. She would be appalled to see how I am behaving. Saying no repeatedly works but is considered profane. A young woman is expected to respect her elders and happily accept all offers of kindness. They leave me alone, and I get hurt looks from some and furious glances from others.

There are other reasons for refusing to eat the delicacies waved in front of me, reasons they cannot be told. I fear I will smell of garlic and ginger and strong *masalas* when my TL kisses me on the mouth, crushing my lips the way he did at Entebbe Airport the previous year, a shocking moment for his clan all there to wave him off and for the watching crowds of other Asians too, whose stares burned into our faces. The most torrid lovers in Hindi films back then only held hands and danced. I am desperate for another such kiss at another airport. My mouth must be peppermint-sweet when it meets his. I am chewing a lot of gum on this flight. (TL always recoiled from strong smells and hated eating with his fingers. By the time I caught up with him in England, he was eating *roti* and *paratha*, chicken legs too, elegantly with a knife and fork.)

I accept the tray of aeroplane food, grey cubes of indeterminate meat in grey gravy, with greying potatoes and a sort of custard which isn't grey but tastes like it could be. The passenger next to me, who has, like the others, tried to be sweet, now prepares to move from her window seat, nauseous at the sight of my tray. She is enormous, and it is a struggle to get her over to the aisle, where she takes a deep breath and throws me a pitying look. In loud Hindi she curses me: 'Huh, thinks she is better than us, let her eat that plane horrible food. Smells like boiling towels. Even a dog would not be eating it.' What they don't know is that in my own hand luggage are two boxes of snacks for the plane ride, shoved into my hands at the airport by my friend's mum who ran a tea shop in Kampala. She is modern, didn't include stinky items. One contains hot cashews picked then roasted at a farm in Mombasa and the other *cocothende*, a fabulous biscuit that is also a coastal invention. It is covered in a layer of sugary crust you first suck off slowly. Our very own Danish pastry. And in a large bag are five boxes of mangoes, tied up with ropes, heavier than I am.

Cocothende

4 cups plain flour
1 tsp baking powder
¾ cups hot water
1 tbsp hot oil

1 cup semolina
¼ tsp ground cardamom (optional)
1 cup desiccated coconut
Oil for deep frying

For the syrup
2 cups granulated sugar

1½ cups water

- Mix the dry ingredients and then rub in the tablespoon of oil.

- Add the water (as hot as you can bear it) and knead into a pliable dough.

- Shape into a large rope and break off bits the size of small satsumas. These need to be shaped by hand into small sausages, then indented with three fingers to split and run over a ridged surface – the wooden part of a mandolin is good, or find something that will give you striped indentations.

- Place on a clean cloth and leave for an hour covered with another cloth.

- Heat oil in a fryer and cook until a lovely golden brown.

- Return to cloths to soak up oil.

Syrup

- Boil the water and sugar and simmer for between fifteen and twenty-five minutes until the syrup is stringy or forms threads when you handle a small amount. Careful, it is hot.

- Remove from heat and quickly dip the pastries in the sugar. Whip them out, then leave them to cool (tricky but well worth it).

Your kids will love these, and you for making the effort.

Hot Nuts

2 cups raw cashews, peanuts or blanched whole almonds, or all mixed together

½ tsp salt

2 tbsp sunflower oil

½ tsp chilli powder

¼ tsp citric acid

- Rub the oil into the nuts and roast in the oven (at medium temperature – 325 °F, 170 °C, gas mark 3) until light brown – about six to eight minutes.

- Remove and drain on thick sheets of kitchen paper.

- While the nuts are still hot, mix in the chilli powder and other flavourings.

- Cool and store in airtight containers.

The walking snack machines tire and find their seats. I conspicuously open my hard-back copy of *Sense and Sensibility* and pretend to read. The fat lady comes back, demands that I stand to let her in when the seat-belt signs are on, sits in her creaking seat and now makes no effort to allow me elbow room. Can't blame her really. She knocks the book to the floor. Not deliberately, I am sure. There is no way of getting it back. She burps, shuffles, blows snot back up into her flared nose. She curses me quietly through the whole journey. I am filling up with bile (both sorts), so I distract myself, rummaging through my bag to make sure yet again that I have what I need for entry into England, my England.

The papers confirming a postgraduate place at Oxford are there in triplicate: my degree certificate, First Class Honours in English no less, is in a plastic folder, ten copies in all so my mother can post them to rich relatives with stupid children. She had, with much pleasure and pride, sent them my O-level and A-level results too. Margaret McPherson, a doughty Scots lecturer in the Eng Lit department at Makerere University, has given me a fulsome testimonial to use in emergencies and help persuade an Eastern prince to grant me a scholarship. I have no money yet to pay for tuition fees or living expenses. I am very optimistic, though, as the minders around the secretive prince have sent enigmatic messages through clandestine networks which suggest that support will be forthcoming. Our mosque leader has given me a letter confirming that I am solemnly engaged to be married to my TL. It is all very grown-up.

My night-blue passport has a gold lion and unicorn, tails up both. The lion wears a crown and flanks a bigger crown, topping the insignia. '*Dieu et Mon Droit*' is stamped at the bottom, and other incomprehensible words glow in gold, making a solemn circle. The most jingoistic of European nations has foreign-language flourishes on its passport. I have been given the status of British Subject, Citizen of the United Kingdom and colonies – but not quite. The number of the passport is D 86092. That 'D' marks me as inferior to white settlers from Zimbabwe and Kenya. I am 'subject to control under the Commonwealth Immigrants Act'; they are not. Until I finally get myself an EU passport in 2000, I will have to go through suspicious interviews at our airports and prove that I do know my place, understand that I should never let myself believe I can ever be a pukka British national.

We land. The passengers clap and cheer. I rush to get away first, hand in my passport and am informed that a special interview needs to be conducted. 'You do speak English, do you?' 'Yes, of course, very well, I have a degree in English.' I am escorted through a long corridor to a small side room, an airless cell, painted cream with a glossy black picture rail. A photo of the Queen in a tiara gazes down at us. The same picture I remember as a child, on calendars, in post offices and at school. The royal lady means nothing and everything to me. Her picture was on a small tin I had as a child, gifted to all schoolchildren in Uganda on Coronation Day. Inside were milk chocolates which melted down just as we did in the heat, little ones in uniform, line after line, waving flags on the streets of Kampala.

I have to answer a long set of impossible questions posed by a young man with thick glasses. He has picked up on things I said, bits dropped carelessly as I walked towards the interview room. Received pronunciation is no damned use. How will the plane *desis* cope if I, Jane Austen fan, First Class Honours, feel this frightened and substandard? I had told him that all my family lived in London except for a distant relation in a place called Stokenchurch. He suddenly lunges. 'What is the address in Stokenchurch?' 'How do I know? Can't stand the woman, a vulgarian bitch who tears into mutton legs and people. She is so distant I hope never to be invited for a cup of chai to that place, Stokenchurch.' He goes silent for the longest time. I tremble. A woman comes in and takes him out.

He asks to look into my hand luggage. 'Why are you carrying so many mangoes?' That I can answer – for all the cousins, aunts and uncles, brother and his children; they miss Ugandan mangoes. If I leave any one of them out, I will not be forgiven. 'You see, sir, we have to take care of each other.' He barks back, 'Write out the names and addresses of all those you intend to present with mangoes. Here is some paper and a pad. I'll be back.'

He takes the list, ignores it and thumps his hands on the small Formica table between us. It is pale yellow and obviously much abused. 'You have a place at university but no evidence of financial support. Who'll be paying your costs? Have you any bank statements to show you can afford to go to Oxford?' He curls the word

Oxford round his furry tongue, spits it out and turns more hostile. I cannot tell him about the enigmatic prince who holds my future in his loaded hands. So I come up with a plausible alibi: my cousins own a string of run-down properties (true), and they have agreed to support my studies (a lie). 'You see, sir, we have to take care of each other.' He starts questioning me about their earnings, addresses, bank details. He is displeased and impatient with my hopeless answers and evasions.

After that we are both tired, and there are questions about this imminent wedding. How can I confirm that it will happen? I show him the engagement pictures and the good mosque leader's letter, stamped with an official emblem, a crescent and star in red and green. At least my tormentor says 'please' and 'thank you', slowly though, as if the words stick in his throat. Back at the British High Commission in Uganda, they never bothered with such niceties. To those mean men and skinny women we were not black savages but still only coolies, objects of contempt. One family friend who suffered from hypertension threw a chair through the British embassy's plate-glass window after trying in vain to get a visitor's visa. He couldn't stand the humiliation. What a hero. I think of him fondly as my interview proceeds slowly.

It takes an hour and forty minutes. The interviewer firmly refuses my gift of two mangoes, slaps shut his file and gives me a visitor's visa for three months. I see that he has no chin, not like a real man, and he most definitely doesn't wash his bottom. For years after that I have to go through yet more interviews every three months.

I fear that all my anticipation, the joy of the reunion, the planned embraces with my TL will have dissipated. Some of my *desi* companions have got out ahead of me and are making fools of themselves in the arrivals lounge, talking too much and too loudly to their relatives who have gathered to meet them. One of them spies me and starts to tell the story about my rudeness.

My TL is waiting as I emerge, leaning over the barrier, looking vaguely disturbed. I am wearing a black velvet dress with pearl buttons, short enough to show 6 inches of thigh. He is still gorgeous – that manly jaw, that aristocratic nose, those liquid brown eyes. He appears thinner in his tight jeans, now has a fetching moustache and long hair. Looks like Carlos Santana. I am not at all pretty, or so they always said, the kind worshippers in our mosque. But I am smart and funny. When I was young, parents liked their children to befriend me, especially the dopes who languished with bad grades (I look back with shame at my youthful vanity). My TL had managed to scrape through with one A-level when I met him. Brainy but a Narcissus, he was distracted by his own beauty and bewitched girls. At seventeen, I nabbed the best-looking guy in town. He has written to me every day since he left Uganda. He has endured national discontent and the misery of strikes, unknown back home, where workers know their place. He has survived on baked beans (warmed in the communal washbasin) and custard creams.

My TL has, I know, missed his mum's legendary cooking as much as our furtive lovemaking. At twenty-three I can only make *roti*, *puri* and rice, also English food learned in domestic-science classes. Mum believed that hands had to be trained early to make the delicate movements needed to roll perfect rounds of dough. Rice I observed her cooking until she shooed me off to do my homework: 'Plenty time in life to learn to cook. You girls have bigger future than us ladies, so innocent and ignorant we are. You must be somebody. Men are no good, have to stand on own feet. Make your own money, don't ask a man for anything. Yassi, you do that, *then* I will teach you rice and everything.'

Perfect Boiled Rice

Basmati rice   **Salted water**

- Boil lots of salty water as you would to make pasta.
- Wash the rice in a sieve, running water through it.
- Throw the rice into boiling water and cook for five to six minutes – it should be just softer than al dente. Don't let it cook to soggy.
- Pour all the water out through the sieve.
- Return rice to the pot.
- Cover and turn heat down to the lowest setting for five minutes. Take off the heat and leave for a further five.
- Quantities depend on how many you want to feed. One cup of rice feeds about three people.

Puris

3 mugs *chapatti* flour (I prefer a mixture of   **2 tbsp sunflower oil for the dough**
two-thirds white and one-third brown)   **Warm water**

½ tsp salt

Extra flour for dusting while rolling

2 tbsp finely chopped coriander
   leaves (optional)

Sunflower or vegetable oil to deep-fry

½ tsp turmeric (optional)

½ tsp chilli powder (optional)

◉ You can make plain *puris* and eat them with curries or with jam for breakfast. Or you can make them spiced up with the last three ingredients and eat them with plain yoghourt or *raitha*.

◉ For the spicy version add the turmeric, salt, chilli and coriander to the flour. For plain *puris* add only salt.

◉ Mix oil into the flour and then add water a little at a time until the dough binds but is quite stiff.

◉ Knead well, adding water if too stiff.

◉ Cover and leave for an hour.

◉ Break off bits the size of walnuts and roll them in the palm of your hand to make a ball, then flatten these.

◉ Roll them out with a thin rolling pin (bought from Indian shops). You need to try to make them as round as you can and as thin as a 5-pence coin. Try rolling round the left-hand corner, then turning the *puri* a little to the right after each roll.

◉ Heat the frying oil until a bit of bread dropped in rises fast.

◉ Carefully place two puris into the oil and press each one down with a slotted spoon gently as it starts to cook.

◉ Turn over and press down again. It should rise like a balloon.

◉ After a minute or two, turn over one more time and lift off to a platter spread with kitchen paper.

◉ Eat hot as soon as the oil has drained off. They are pretty good cold too.

I can't remember the first embraces, kisses, tears and laughter as I rush to my TL and lose myself in vaporous joy. Drat it – the excitement has opened all my sweat valves. He asks if I have a fever. 'No, I am only sizzling with excitement,' I reply, arching my eyebrows and twinkling my eyes at him immodestly. I have missed him so much, his beauty most of all. (When I am older I realize that it was the best, perhaps the only, thing he had to offer me. Our son has some of his father's face, memory in flesh. Sometimes, looking at my boy, I feel that same surge of pleasure as all those years back when I couldn't believe my luck.)

I have been transported to London, the capital of the world, to my future husband, with whom I will discover Oxford, the heart of greatness. Kampala hardly matters. That small-town life under the hot sun recedes, will not be missed all that much in those first years.

2 *Paradise Found, AD 68–1920*

As TIME PADDLES ON and the cavernous past slowly opens up behind me, I sometimes feel marooned on these isles. An irrepressible yearning takes over, and a quest begins to discover where and when it all began for my roaming tribe, the long search for what Simon Schama has evocatively named the 'loam of memory'.[1] Older exiles I know from Uganda also find that the old country loiters and calls out to them. They fear that these memories of African days and nights will end up in unremarkable graves or on funeral pyres. I sought out some of them, asked them questions they struggled to answer. It had been too long, many said. Some cried softly; their chests, weakened by the long winters, rattled and whistled. Mr Ravinder Singh thought he was ninety-two though he wasn't too sure. A civil engineer, he vividly recalled his journey from India to Mombasa when he was just fourteen and the golden years in Uganda: 'Dear girl, nobody knows about us. Nobody wants to. Blacks have been completely ungrateful. These British would have been nothing without us in East Africa. Always the same with these whites, they rule countries and walk away, never caring. We were over there long before them, that much I know and you must be sure to say in your book.' I promised that I would. He has since died.

My immediate forebears arrived with the British, survived and stayed, captivated with equatorial Africa. Its alluring coastline was irresistible, and the silent interior beckoned them. The arrival of Indian émigrés was fashioned into a parable of divine reward. Their gods had gifted them a piece of earthly paradise in recognition of noble deeds in previous lives. (Interestingly, in Milton's *Paradise Lost*, Adam is shown Mombasa by the archangel Michael.) I remember Uganda as improbably lush, fecund and green, a green I have never seen since, the colour of life itself. Plants and bushes grew quickly as if the seeds were magic, eager to plunge roots into the deep earth and rise to offer exuberant flowers, sweet-smelling fruits, a host of plump vegetables. Trees grew tall, reached out to stroke the clouds. When visiting Uganda as a young man, Winston Churchill wrote about the 'pearl of Africa', which astonished him 'for the variety of form and colour, for profusion of brilliant life, plant, bird, insect, reptile and beast'.[2] People claimed that Churchill had stuck his walking stick into moist soil and it had sprouted within hours, his cigars too after he had hurled them down impatiently.

The exiles spin heroic yarns to salvage pride from the humiliation of forced exile: 'Indians were first in everything, you know, we made the maps, and counting and ships, and brought everything to this place, balls, skipping ropes, chess, spices, writing, everything made in India. We were here in the first century, be always proud of that, children. We taught them how to live, how to grow vegetables, how to eat,' intoned one Sikh primary-school teacher during PE classes as he jumped and clapped his hands high above his swishing ponytail. 'Yes, sir, yes, sir' we were meant to chant back as we tried to copy his perfect movements. The children who pleased him were given small canvas bags of jaggery, so sweet it penetrated down through the layers of the tongue. His family exported jaggery to South Africa.

 Jaggery Spread

We used to have this on toast or cold *chapattis* after
school when we were ravenous and tired.

2 oz jaggery broken off and grated   2 oz butter
(you can buy the blocks shaped like
pudding basins in Indian food stores)

- Melt the butter on low heat and add the jaggery, stirring gently until it dissolves and starts to shine.

- Spread on toasted bread or *chapatti* and eat fast before it gets cold.

- If you cook it for too long, it turns into brittle toffee – '*gubit*' we used to call it. It had a slightly alcoholic taste, don't ask me why.

Early Indian sailors had come to the shores of East Africa in fragile boats, catching fair winds. Archaeological discoveries continue to reveal that the territory drew others from far and wide. Greeks, Romans, Egyptians, Sumerians, Chinese and Assyrians dropped in and departed. Arabs, Portuguese, Persians and Asians stayed longer and left their mark.

Coconut palms were introduced to the area by Hindus in the first century AD.

An ancient Greek travel and trade guide records ships from western India bringing glass beads and cloth, grains, oil, ghee, jaggery and wicker baskets for catching fish, still used around Mombasa. They took back cinnamon, frankincense, hides and gum copal.[3] Travelling from Brazil, the Portuguese transplanted cashew-nut and avocado trees and introduced guavas and cucumbers.

Arab Muslims arrived after the death of the Prophet in AD 632, some fleeing the conflicts that arose over doctrine and leadership. They brought dried shark meat and planted date palms and coffee. It was either Indians or Arabs who introduced sugar cane and betel nuts, woody chewing gums both, masticated after meals. In the eighth century, Chinese figurines, musk, myrrh, pearls, bright gold, rubies and intricate prayer mats were bought and sold by Arab immigrants and traders along the coast. By the eleventh century, Islam was widespread, as was slavery. Two hundred years later, the East African seaboard was replete with settlements, trade and perpetual mix and motion – a cosmopolitan marketplace.

Ibn Batuta, an Arab traveller, wrote about the area where he had lingered awhile for a hugely pleasurable sojourn in 1324: 'Rice roasted with oil is placed on a large wooden dish. Over this they place a large dish of roasted meat, fish, flesh, fowl and vegetables... they also cook unripe bananas in new milk.'[4] This rice dish, known as *akni*, has passed down the centuries and is, in an adapted form, a perennial favourite of East African Muslims. I love it more than any other cooked food on earth. It isn't easy to get right, but with modern techniques (an oven), I cracked it.

Akni

2 lb leg of lamb cut into bite-sized pieces – a butcher will have to do this for you. Make sure all the fat is taken off the meat or use a 5-lb chicken, skinned and cut into pieces, not too small otherwise it will overcook and break up

3 cups basmati rice, washed in a sieve

1 medium-sized tin of chopped tomatoes or 5 fresh tomatoes, chopped up

2 tsp crushed ginger or 1 tbsp ginger/ garlic paste (you can buy it in Indian food stores)

1 cup sunflower oil

4 tsp whole cumin seeds

4 cinnamon sticks

6 peppercorns

1 large pot plain low-fat yoghourt

3 onions, sliced

4 green chillies

2 tsp crushed garlic

2 tsp salt

5 cups water

4 potatoes, peeled and cut into largish chunks

5 cloves

5 cardamom pods

- Cook the meat or chicken over a low heat in yoghourt mixed with ginger, garlic and fresh chillies in an ovenproof saucepan with a lid. When almost cooked, remove from heat.

- Add the cinnamon sticks, cloves, peppercorns and cardamom pods to a mug of water.

- Parboil the potatoes.

- In another pan (yes, this is a problem with the dish – a pile to wash up afterwards), heat the oil gently and fry the cumin seeds and onions slowly until the onions are soft and slightly brown.

- Add the water with whole spices and the tomatoes. Cook for six minutes, again over low heat.

- Add the potatoes, meat, cooking juices and extra water, and let that come to the boil.

- Add the rice and salt and stir very carefully.

- Let that come to a boil, turn down heat and cover. Cook for six minutes.

- Place the pan in the oven at a medium temperature (350°F, 180°C, gas mark 4) for about fifteen minutes. The traditional way was to surround the pot with hot coals at this stage for a while, then wrap the pot in a thick sheet or with a seal of soft dough.

- Check that the rice is cooked and the potatoes too. If not, sprinkle over a little more water and return to the oven.

- Remove and let the dish rest for ten minutes.

- Serve with yoghourt, whole spring onions and radishes or tomato salad.

By the fifteenth century, Mombasa and Zanzibar were places of ever greater consumer indulgence. In 1415 a giraffe was sent all the way to Beijing, a present from increasingly prosperous seaside metropolises. Food was plentiful and included rice, wheat, butter, ghee, oils, millet, beans, groundnuts and cassava, myriad fruits, also wild fowl, fish, beef and seafood, pulses, chickpeas, kidney beans, basil and honey. Turks transported aubergines and sesame seeds in the sixteenth century. Market gardening spread as docking ships dislodged famished sailors. A fleet of marauding Portuguese in 1505 were amazed by the cornucopia. One eyewitness wrote: 'The sailors carried away rice, honey, butter, maize, cattle... the island of Zanzibar is very fertile and produces a large quantity of sweet oranges, pomegranates, lemons and sugar cane.'[5]

From 1698 to 1826, when the British laid claim to the coastal territories, Arab sultans ruled, except for periods when the Portuguese took over. In 1594 they had built Fort Jesus and established tight control. Indian artisans had been brought over for this job. The Portuguese initiated the large-scale cultivation of maize, food they thought fit for swine, slaves and their Indian workers. In 1728 they were finally forced to leave by the Arabs, though one redemptive memory of the Portuguese remains: chillies.

Arab rulers introduced large-scale clove production in Zanzibar in 1810. By the 1850s the island had nearly sixty thousand slaves working on these vast plantations. Between 1822 and 1873, various futile attempts were made by Britain to ban the slave trade. Finally they threatened naval bombardment, and that closed down the appalling business.

Through the nineteenth century, diligent Indian men were appointed by the Arab ruling classes to do their books and keep finances under control. These back-room men saw slavery mainly as a means to keep profits high. It was collusive amorality, known and duly noted. Sir Tharia Topan, the richest and most powerful Indian in Zanzibar in the mid-1800s and, like me, an Ismaili, was undoubtedly involved with the lucrative buying and selling of humans. This role of the Indians is still vehemently denied by East African Asians.

Arabs brought with them their traditional foods, which were never too hot or spicy. However, due to long contact with the Portuguese, one of their 'brand' foods became *mishkaki*, chilli lamb and beef cooked on small *sigris*, basic coal braziers. In Asian general stores in Britain you can buy a Mombasa *sigri* and metal skewers crudely made and impossibly rusty, but they work better than the most expensive barbecues.

 *Mishkaki*

2–3 lb leg of lamb or sirloin beef cut into very small pieces – the size of tiny new potatoes
Ask the butcher to give you some pieces of lamb or beef fat too.
Thin metal skewers rubbed with oil

Marinade

½ **cup fresh lime juice**   **2 tsp chilli powder**

Salt to taste   **A little sugar**

2 tbsp oil   **A sprinkling of crushed cloves**

- Prepare the marinade by mixing all the ingredients together in a large bowl.

- Marinate the meat for 24 hours.

- Heat up the coal barbecue until it is past the very hot stage and glowing.

- Thread the meat and fat on to skewers, alternating them, no more than four to five pieces and spread out.

- Cook slowly for at least fifteen minutes, turning frequently. Splash on marinade from time to time to deepen the taste and stop the meat drying out or burning.

- When it is well done, remove it and serve on plates with thinly sliced cucumbers, oranges and a dollop of thick yoghourt, also pita bread if you like, but that would be a modern addition. You dip the hot (in both senses) meat into the cold yoghourt with your fingers and follow each bite of meat with a bite of cool cucumber or sweet/sour orange. Sometimes *mishkaki* makers would wrap the meat in thin, long slices of cucumber.

Along the seafront in Mombasa, every evening for centuries, *sigris* burned brightly, selling *mishkaki* to Arabs, Africans and Indians, who drank sweet *madaf* water and ate *malai*, meaning 'cream', which is what the white, smooth, slippery flesh of these *madaf* coconuts tastes like. The *madaf* is large and green, shaped a bit like a pointy gourd, not at all similar to the brown coconut. At the end came *kahava*, strong, sweet black coffee carried by stooped vendors in *deles*, cone-shaped brass containers hanging off long rods. Mobile cafés, *madaf* sellers and meat cooks can still be found at the seaside in Kenya and Tanzania. Today you also see vats of hot oil frying cassava crisps, a snack Indians invented in East Africa.

Cassava Crisps

Fresh cassava, peeled **Oil to deep-fry**
Salt and chilli powder to taste

- Slice the cassava into thin rounds on a mandolin (slicer).
- Lay them out on clean dishcloths for an hour to slightly dry out.
- Heat the oil until very hot but not smoking.
- Fry batches of crisps until they are a lovely pale yellow, edged with light brown.
- Return them to the dishcloths to drain all excess oil.
- Sprinkle with salt and chilli powder.

Records of Arab/Indian ventures both before and after the abolition of the East African slave trade show that some Indian entrepreneurs were masters of commerce and niche supply. Long-established Arab merchants and rulers became their mentors and trading partners, brothers in arms, chasing lucre in the harsh interior. By the time British 'discoverers' arrived (innocents in many ways), these men had seen and done it all.

My maiden surname was Damji. One Ludha Damji, an early pioneer trader, provided essential goods and 'mutually advantageous' (you understand) banking for Speke and Livingstone. There is no evidence of family ties here, but I do feel a frisson that this unknown chap made himself indispensable to heroes of the impe- rial imagination. Speke was appreciative, understood the hardships of such lone merchants in the jungle, their 'utter banishment, worse than that of hermits'. Livingstone, on the other hand, complained that Indians were 'local Jews' who were sabotaging his explorations.[6] These explorers used knowledge gained by the Indians who had preceded them into the interior. Speke and Richard Burton were among those who were given information and advice. No credit was ever given to the brown pioneers.

In the jungle, a number of British explorers and early administrators found dark terrors within their hearts, deeper than any fear previously experienced, primeval. M. G. Vassanji captured the internal chaos of one colonial master in his novel *The Book of Secrets* (1994): '...bouts of sleeplessness, depression, doubt, taking to his diary to kill time and tire the brain, taking local women to kill loneliness'. One distant relative of mine who was a big-game hunter admitted to the same feelings and once pulped a young servant to near-death in the middle of the night in a camp close to the lions of Tsavo national park: 'You are going mad sometimes, because nothing you could trust, the eyes of the animals in the night all around, the eyes of the blacks looking at you, thinking maybe of killing you, just like the animals, something happening inside which you can't stop. The boy stayed with me but was blind in one eye and afraid to speak after that. But I took care of the family.'

Explorations by Europeans were driven by personal ambition and frontier adventurism. However, around 1850 the pressure for greater national influence became an imperative. British Abolitionists grew more determined to stop Arab slave traders, Christian evangelicals clamoured to take the Bible into 'the heart of darkness', and Britain's continental adversaries were establishing spheres of influence.

As the nineteenth century drifted into the unsettling fin-de-siècle, European colonial powers muscled up for yet more savage intra-continental competition, and the Scramble for Africa gathered pace. Explorations into parts unknown to the west had already begun. The formal carve-up of the continent took place from the 1880s through to World War I. In 1888 a royal charter was granted to set up a British trading company in East Africa. Political control soon followed.[7] The British establishment believed it was meant to rule over 'savage' Africans, who were expected to be grateful in return, a wholly new doctrine at this time.

Indian indentured labourers were transported over in the 1880s to build a railway line from the coast to Lake Victoria, a lunatic Victorian idea which in the end entirely justified its lunacy. The line finally reached its destination, Uganda, in 1901. Some of the Indian workers were skilled craftsmen, others were humble folk lured by wily agents who got illiterates to place their thumb marks on papers which bound them for years. The illiterates were from the poorest, landless classes, whose lives had got more wretched under British rule. In East Africa, they suffered further, living in unprotected encampments along the lengthening railway line. Death due to attacks by lions, disease and depression saw off many of the workers. Half returned as invalids.

This system also provided labour in plantations around the world. More than two million men and women were taken from India; most never knew where they were headed. They were dehumanized too. The merchants Gillanders, Arbuthnot and Co. officially described indentured labourers as 'more akin to monkeys than man. They have no religion, no education... no wants beyond eating, drinking and sleeping.' The same firm reassured a West Indian plantation owner: 'We are not aware that any great difficulty would present itself in sending men to the West Indies, the natives being perfectly ignorant of the place they go to or the length of the voyage they are undertaking.'[8] By 1910, concern was growing about this exploitation. The viceroy of India, Lord Hardinge, objected to the system 'of forced labour entailing much misery and degradation, different but a little from slavery. It is not the responsibility of the government of India to provide coolies for the colonies.'[9]

Just before he died, an elderly survivor, Lalli, described his enslavement to an oral historian:

I was jobless and heard that in Lahore some people were recruiting boys. I must have been fourteen at the time. I went there. They didn't say anything about Africa at all... The recruiter gave me a few rupees and I was damn happy. I went off without informing my parents even. Me and the other boys were put on boats to Karachi. I though we were maybe going to India, but we ended up in Mombasa. I was in the first lot of labourers to start building the railway.[10]

Mr Ravinder Singh told me:

My uncle was one of these kidnapped railway slaves. He used to tell us they were beaten on the boat and some were thrown over if they argued with the British captains. If they asked where they were going, they got no answers – they couldn't speak or understand English. So grown men cried like children. Some killed themselves. Sometimes these were younger boys who were forced to accept sex, the bad way, the sinful way, forbidden by God. My uncle worked making the line until one of his legs had to be cut off after an accident. Every time I travelled on that train from Kampala to Mombasa, I remembered the men who had made that line and how they were treated by the British.

No written accounts exist to tell us about these men, their last impressions of India and their responses when they came off the boats.

They docked in Mombasa. Some must have been overawed by the black men who rowed out to greet them, singing in strange tongues. But they must have felt a surge of pleasure and relief too after their hellish journey. The port shimmered and breeze cooled the skin on the hottest day. Mombasa smelled of the best things in life – food, flowers and salty sensuality. The men had left behind poverty, dry unyielding land and bad governance. How greedily they must have lunged or longed for pleasures to satisfy their desires. The town was described by an engineer, Lt. Col. J. H. Patterson, who arrived there in March 1898 to design bridges for the railway line:

> Everything looked fresh and green, and an oriental glamour of enchantment seemed to hang over the island. The old town was bathed in brilliant sunshine and reflected itself lazily in the motionless sea; its flat roofs and dazzlingly white walls peeped out dreamily between waving palms and lofty coconuts, huge baobabs and spreading mango trees.[11]

From September to May, the trade winds brought in boats and the town filled up. Sailors roamed, streets sparkled with lanterns and lights, boarding houses livened up, ladies of the night came into their own. Beautiful carved wooden doors – the designs amalgamations of Indian, African and Arab motifs – guarded the clandestine life within. Intense perfumes slipped into the lanes, the lure of femininity. Hidden in claustrophobic streets were darkened shops where these scents were made. Fathers and theirs before passed down these secrets to sons just as they had done since the seventeenth century. They were still there when we departed for the West.

Female customers waited shyly while one of these olfactory magicians touched their wrists to check their body temperatures, and sniffed hands and backs of necks politely to pick up individual body smells. He made them walk across the room and watched their moves. Then, patiently, he created small vials of bespoke yellow liquid, unique and exact, he claimed. Fully veiled women had only fragrance to entice attention. Many a man stalked and married the object of his infatuation only to be savagely disappointed when the black silk came off. The fragrance had made false promises. Wedding *oudh* was kept in a jewelled casket. During special ceremonies (ladies only), a bride-to-be would squat over a smoky clay pot with dying embers of *oudh* which was first flamed to slowly give up its sticky, musky scent. Small plates of orange-coloured *halva*, *karanga pak* (peanut brittle) and salted almonds were always on the perfumery counters and tables, and a *kahava* maker sat in the corner offering coffee.

Halva

1¼ cup tapioca starch	2½ cups water
½ cup slivered almonds and pistachios	2 cups granulated sugar
10 strands saffron or 2 tsp rose water	½ tsp yellow food colouring (optional)
½ cup clarified butter	½ tsp slightly crushed cardamom seeds
¼ tsp lemon juice	

◉ Mix the water with the starch, then add all the ingredients in a heavy saucepan and cook on high heat until it comes to the boil. Turn down the heat, stirring often until the mixture is transparent and smooth (not sticky), and easily leaves the sides of the pan, a bit like pre-baked choux pastry.

- Grease a glass ovenproof dish.

- Transfer the mix and smooth it down.

- Cook at a medium temperature (350°F, 180°C, gas mark 4) in the oven for fifteen minutes, then stir a couple of times.

- Cut into squares and serve hot or cold.

Later British visitors were entranced by this coastal town, but by then they had become the ruling, privileged upper class: 'Mombasa in those days was a lovely tranquil island... The sandy road had narrow-gauge metal lines besides them on which open-sided trolleys, with a fringe on top, were pushed along by natives of all sorts for the ease and comfort of the European.'[12] And here's a diary entry: 'Here we are, three white men in the heart of Africa, with 20 nigger soldiers and 50 nigger police, 68 miles from doctors or reinforcements, administering and policing a district inhabited by half a million well armed savages who have only recently come into touch with white men... the position is most humorous to my mind.'[13]

As their cramped legs walked on land, the indentured labourers from India must have been full of anticipation and trepidation, then dejection, perhaps protests and punishments, as they were pulled to their tasks. Had Mombasa been a mirage? Soon they were in the thick interior, hot and damp in the day, cold at night, black desolation, monstrous trees making eerie shapes, the cries of beasts near and far piercing their nights and making their hearts beat loud. Hyenas came audaciously close; some seized men with bleeding wounds to rip up an arm or leg; snakes hissed and injected poisons, silent scorpions bit, and plump leeches sucked greedily on injured ankles. Alarmed tribal groups appeared suddenly to pelt the unwanted troops with stones, sticks and arrows. The Indians killed en route were envied by some survivors, who dreaded what lay ahead – years of toil, perhaps sudden disability. For these men Africa was purgatory, not paradise, not yet.

Lt. Col. Patterson shot man-eating lions, a nightly peril for the unarmed men. Malaria, dysentery and black-water fever were stealthier and took many more. Five hundred and eighty-two miles of railway were laid; a bridge more than 1,200 feet long was built, plus 1,280 smaller bridges and culverts. Four workers died for each mile of railway laid, and many more were injured. Growing up in Voi, through which the railway had to pass, the writer M. G. Visram heard stories about these workers: 'A long travelled note from a friend or sympathiser would reach a remote village in India. The bereaved family would then submit to God's will and pray for his soul. At night the widow and her children would cry silently. No rupees would be coming from across the ocean either, they understood.'[14]

The staples were dried beans, pulses and rice. This old recipe given to me by a man I interviewed had been cooked by his father, once a 'coolie' railway builder. They had to be inventive. By placing an aluminium pan in a thick turban, they could cook rice and lentils – *khichri* – in a hole covered with leaves and soil. A fire was lit on top and the grains cooked slowly.

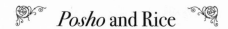

Posho and Rice

1 cup basmati rice	Chilli and salt to taste
1 cup dried beans – kidney or speckled pink	2 tbsp groundnut oil
beans commonly found in East Africa	1 large red onion, sliced

- Soak the beans overnight, then drain them, cover with fresh water and boil for about three hours on a low heat until they are very soft.

- Heat the oil in a pan and fry the onion and beans on a low heat for ten minutes. Add chilli and salt.

- Cook the rice (using the recipe on page 38).

- Layer rice with bean mix, and eat with plain yoghourt.

The cultivation of various vegetables and fruit away from the coast was yet to come. Decades later, children who were fussy eaters were asked to remember those men who built the railways, who gave their lives so we could get to the beach on the train. *Khichri* was what kept them strong and unbeaten. All kinds of properties were attributed to this simple dish. We still cook it on the first day of our new year, 21 March. It is best for baby, the old ladies say to nervous new mums eager to buy infant food in pretty glass jars. Dying folk ask for the soft mush as they prepare to depart, and sometimes this super-food revives them. Friends visiting my terminally ill mother brought *khichri*; some softened it with milk, others drenched it in butter. The day she died we found sixteen such boxes of love all piled up neatly on her bedside table by the nurses.

Khichri

1 cup split, unhulled *moong dhal*	¾ cup pudding rice
Salt to taste	2 oz butter
2½ cups water – add more if you need to	

- Boil the water and salt, and cook the rice and lentils on a low heat until the grains are very soft, almost melded together.

- Add the butter and mix it in furiously.

- Children love *khichri* with cold milk and a little sugar for breakfast. On a cold night, it is great with warm milk. Try it with sliced fiery raw onions, spiced vegetables, pickles or yoghourt.

———

The railway men also ate millet bread. With their sore and tired hands, bleeding and torn, they skilfully tapped and slapped the deep grey, wet, cement-textured dough into flat discs, then cooked them for a long time on clay griddles balanced on wood fires. My mum turned a single *rotlo* eleven times before it was crisp and cooked. I remember how we both loved to finish off a big bowl of crumbled *rotlo* with chilli yoghourt: 'Don't eat with a spoon, spoils the taste, eat carefully with the fingers so you can feel the hot and cold together. This is better than the most expensive king's dish. Without it all those brave Indians who came to build the railway would have died even faster than they did, poor things.'

 *Rotlo*

1 cup millet flour	**Butter for spreading**
1 tsp butter to rub in	**½ cup water**
½ tsp salt	

- Mix the flour and salt.

- Rub in the butter.

- Slowly add water and knead continuously until it binds into a soft, wet dough.

- Divide into three potions.

- Take each piece and flatten gently on a small piece of oiled tin foil using your palms.

- Shape into a circle as best you can. Mine end up looking like strange maps, but it doesn't matter.

- Keep dipping your hands in a bowl of warm water – it helps.

- Be warned: this is as messy as clay work in a toddler's nursery and as satisfying.

- Turn over and flatten a round until it is the thickness of a pound coin. You can put another sheet of oiled foil over the flat dough and press down gently that way.

- Heat a flat griddle until it is hot enough to sear, then slap on the *rotlo*.

- Turn over quickly and reduce the heat a little.

- Using a clean cloth, gently rotate the bread before turning it over several times.

- Take off the heat and smear it with good, slightly salted butter.

As the years passed and they got acclimatized, a small number of railway Indians deliberately 'disappeared' and cut off contact with their home villages to start new families with African women in remote places. The community went into denial about these mavericks who couldn't resist interracial copulation. Look at this letter published in the *Uganda Mail* in December 1902: 'Sir, with reference to your advertisement headed "Indian Marriage" I would first protest that it was not an Indian Marriage as both the bride and groom are natives of East Africa and the latter was born to an Indian but his mother was pure Swahili.'

In 1996, back in Uganda to make a Radio 4 programme, I met Bano, an old man who had lived most of his life near the Ruwenzori Mountains. He had a flat African nose and a light brown Afro. He told me that his father, married to a child bride in Jamnagar, had been one of the men who had broken ties with his Indian past and been presumed dead. His Indian wife had spent the rest of her time on earth a miserable virgin widow, ostracized by his family, who had accused her of bringing evil into their home. Meanwhile seven boys had been born to his African wife. When he was twenty-three, Bano went back to Jamnagar and was shunned by his father's family. He got himself a young Indian bride and tried to reclassify himself back in Uganda: 'Not possible, my dear, my nose came in the way, and this hair like wire. The Indians could not take to me. My wife they liked very much, beautiful girl, light skin, you know? But not me. So we kept to ourselves. Our children had her pretty nose, thank God. But when Amin threw you people out, I became a very rich man, never left. Then I became an African. So you see, nose not all bad. Now these Indians want to be my friend, but I cannot forget.'

Men like Bano ate African food, sometimes adding spices from the subcontinent. They melted into the local population, spoke local languages. The earliest arrivals were capable of overcoming prejudices, but such crossovers became rarer when class and race hierarchies were codified under colonialism and when Indian women began to come over. (Indian history followed exactly the pattern of integration and separation between whites and 'natives'.) *Matoke* with groundnuts is the first dish known to have come of this intimate encounter between black Ugandans and Indian settlers.

Matoke with Peanut Curry

10 small green African plantains

Butter

Greaseproof paper or, better still, banana leaves

½ lb unhulled groundnuts zapped in a food processor, with a little oil and water, sugar and salt to taste. The nuts should be broken not pulverized. A jar of coarse peanut butter of good quality can be used instead.

2 tbsp vegetable oil

½ tsp chilli powder or more to taste. I love this really hot to pep up the starchy bananas.

1 small onion

½ tsp crushed garlic

3 fresh tomatoes

1 tsp mixture of *dhania* and *jeera* powder, a spice mixture frequently used in Asian cooking

⊚ Butter a large piece of greaseproof paper or some banana leaves to wrap round the plantains (unpeeled). Don't pack them in too tight.

⊚ Place parcel/parcels on a baking tray.

- Bake in the oven at a medium temperature (325 °F, 170 °C, gas mark 3) for twenty-five minutes.

- Open carefully and check; the plantains should be cooked but not mushy.

- Meanwhile chop the onion and fry slowly in the oil in a pan.

- Add the garlic and tomatoes, and fry on for a couple of minutes.

- Add the spices and stir until the tomatoes break down and merge into the mixture.

- Then add the peanut butter or groundnut paste and a little hot water, and let it simmer.

- Serve a couple of plantains with the sauce poured over – quite a lot so each mouthful is more sauce than plantain.

Chilli *Matoke*

Serves 4

5 green *matoke*

2 tbsp vegetable oil

3 hot green chillies, finely chopped

½ tsp turmeric

1 small onion, chopped

4 fresh tomatoes, finely chopped

1 tsp crushed garlic

Salt, sugar and lime juice to taste

- You can cook the *matoke* as above or boil it, unpeeled and cut into chunks.

- Fry the onion until it starts to turn light brown.

- Add all other ingredients except the salt, sugar and lime.

- Cook over a low heat for ten minutes.

- Mash the *matoke*, stir into the onion mix and cook for five minutes.
- Add salt and other seasonings to suit your taste.

When I was pregnant with my son in 1977, I longed to eat spicy *matoke* more than anything. I tried to use unripe, ordinary bananas, but they didn't work. Didn't have the starch of real *matoke* and had too much sugar. A wealthy friend smuggled some *matoke* in when she was over from Nairobi, hidden in her neatly folded fine clothes. She cooked it as best she could using peanut butter. After six long years in exile, memory filled in the missing taste, and I was content after weeks of demented cravings.

Another old recipe is a dessert made with a different species of Ugandan banana, *ngonja*, yellow with black markings but rigid and pinky-white inside until cooked, when the flesh dissolves into liquid sugar. Cut lengthways then fried in butter, they turn a deep brown colour. Sprinkled with ground cinnamon and with a dollop of cream, they make a self-indulgent Sunday breakfast. Ibn Batuta wrote about eating something similar when he was in Zanzibar.

Ngonja in Coconut Cream

6 ripe *ngonjas* (Ugandan bananas)	1 tin top-quality coconut cream
¾ cup caster sugar	A few cardamom seeds

A little nutmeg   **2 cups water**

- Peel and slice the bananas lengthways.

- Boil the sugar and water in a wide, shallow pan for three minutes, then add the bananas, which must cook without being disturbed. They should be soft.

- Move the bananas into a glass dish.

- Add the coconut cream to the remaining syrup and a little water if the mixture is too thick.

- Bring to the boil and add cardamom and nutmeg. Taste and adjust for sweetness.

- Simmer for ten minutes on a low heat.

- Pour the cream over the bananas and cool a little before serving.

———————

The frightful experiences of indentured returnees to India didn't put off intrepid men who were excited by their tales and decided to go across and take their chances. As an English official in Bombay noted in 1896, 'Artisans go by every steamer to the various ports on East Africa, tailors, shoemakers, dhobis, cooks, shopkeepers and others all on their own responsibility.'[15] Some were troublesome boys and men, loafers banished by unforgiving families to die or grow up. Doting mothers had to turn into stoics. One of my interviewees, Zul, who was thus banished in 1918, remembers his mother's last words to him: 'See how Rehmet's son went and became proper son, sending mother so many rupees. Go, go, I will close down my heart until you come back and show us you can be something. Even that *daku* Saleem has changed in Africa, now working with English people, so go, go now, dhow arriving this week.'

After some research I finally discovered that my mother's grandparents had converted from Hinduism to Shia Islam. Hundreds of thousands of these conversions took place between the twelfth and the nineteenth centuries, some because people could no longer accept the pernicious caste system, some because people had their faith turned by charismatic missionaries. We Ismailis commit absolutely to the fundamentals of Islam – submission to one Allah and his Prophet Messenger, Mohammed, daily prayers and charity. However, we also believe that the line of the Prophet has continued, leaving us leaders born with the light of knowledge to guide us. The Aga Khans are these enlightened descendants, imams who are not worshipped but respected and trusted by the truly faithful. To millions of Sunni Muslims we are damned sinners because we revere a living being. But our prayers call to Allah just like theirs and are drawn from the Koran.

My mother's family came from Porbandar and Jamnagar in Gujarat. Mahatma Gandhi had been born in Porbandar in 1869 to an upper middle-class family; my ex-husband's maternal grandfather went to the same school as Gandhi. The Mahatma sailed over to London in 1888, to study law, and the rest is history. From the same town in the same year, my impoverished maternal grandfather, Ramji Mohammed, only ten, was sent off to East Africa as a child labourer with a merchant who paid for the journey. Was the boy that unforgivably naughty? Or were his family so unimaginably poor that they threw their young son to the winds? My grandfather made a small fortune, then died prematurely. My grandmother Puribai had passed away earlier, soon after the birth of her youngest child, Pyarali, who came after my mother.[16]

In her final years, my mother recalled some of her childhood and stories told to her by her older brother Popat. When only eleven, their father was left in a *dukan* (a small Asian shop) in an East African village by his 'master', a rich Indian. An older man, another indentured worker, Sherali, was left in charge. Sherali had one swivelling, marbly eye and a constantly dripping nose he wiped with his shirt sleeves, soon stiffened with dried snot. The boy was treated abominably by this sadistic boss man, who starved and beat him, left him outside in the dark when the animals stirred, and told him his parents never wanted to see him again. Sherali was much worse to the African servants, so they grabbed him one night when he was peeing and tied him to a tree near an anthill. They stripped him. Then they broke the hill up bit by bit and laid the chunks on his shoulders to send the vicious insects demented and vengeful. My grandfather was caught between pity and pleasure as he watched this punishment. Sherali was never the same again, said my grandfather, who learned a lesson himself about how to behave well towards natives.

A legend in his own time was Allidina Visram, another Ismaili. Born in the Kutch village of Kera, he had arrived in Zanzibar, a dreamy young pauper, in 1877 after a thirty-five-day sail. Twenty-five years on, he owned more than two hundred general stores from the coast to the interior, and also profitable sugar and cotton businesses. He lived and died simply, opened schools and clinics, set up small banks to lend people cash at low interest. We lived on a road named after him. When I went back to Uganda in the late 1990s, Idi Amin's henchmen had removed the road name and erased the man from history, a reminder of how we were destined to be a people who leave no trace.

After 1910, the flow of émigrés from India grew, as did the variety of goods exchanged. They brought rice, grains, ghee and jaggery, beads, cloth, cooking pots, black peppercorns, cinnamon and other spices and flavourings, and took back African ivory, wax and cloves. One traveller never forgot the hard sailings, even though his own personal investment paid off magnificently: 'Water was rationed on the dhows. There was rice, onions and *atta*. We cooked small amounts of food with seawater and a little oil. So many people got burned on the dhows. My father brought saffron and soon he was rich.'[17]

Most of the early arrivals built up wealth slowly and through thrift. Like Chinese takeaways in the UK, they opened small *dukans* in mostly inaccessible places where there were profits waiting to be made and no competition. In these tiny hovels you could find dried fruits, matches, cigarettes, oil, salt, black pepper, dried fish, dried coconuts, sugar and candles. By 1900 a small number of books could be purchased at these stores, and in 1908 bicycles as well. Money transactions were introduced by the Indians into the bartering system, the beginnings of a capitalist economy. The rupee was the first currency of East Africa under the British. That tells us something about the nature of political power and the unseen yet more potent influence of commerce in empires.

By the beginning of the twentieth century, white South Africans and Britons were taking over the most fertile lands, mostly in Kenya. In her dainty little book of observations on the growing railway, Olive Grey, a memsahib, excitedly noted vanilla, coffee, cloves, limes, lemons and guinea fowl in abundance. One station she found 'very healthy and the climate delicious. This would be an ideal country seat for a gentleman with a stud farm as sheep, cattle or horses would thrive here. Any capitalist wanting to make a good bargain should be early on the field and get a slice of this very beautiful and fertile spot.'[18]

The life coveted by whites was built on the labour of the black serving classes and the work ethic of brown middlemen. Financial services and goods provided by Indians were in demand and used by both privileged whites and poor blacks. Furthermore, the rapid development of the economy and infrastructure would not have been possible without these migrants. A missive to the Foreign Office by the explorer Sir Harry Johnston raised the implications of planting another culture into East Africa:

I wonder if in England the importance of the railway connection has been realized. It means the driving of a wedge of India two miles broad right across East Africa... Fifteen thousand coolies, hundreds of clerks, mechanics, surveyors and policemen are carrying the Indian penal code, the Indian postal system, Indian coinage, clothing right across these wastes, deserts and swamps.[19]

However, as is so often the case, although they were indispensable, being in the middle made Indians vulnerable to perpetual spite, resentment and contempt from above and below. Indigenous Africans were getting suspicious of what they saw as preying, grasping, funny-looking interlopers who assumed they had the right to set down wherever they chose. Sometimes violent opposition stopped further inroads.

Dukans were burned down, stock stolen, Indians murdered – all crimes never expected to be solved. The traders had no spears, only goods and wile. Free gifts of trinkets and rice (plus lessons in cooking it) calmed fearful, fearsome tribes.

It must have been unspeakably harsh for Indians, this life of big dangers and small pickings. They had to live with the terror of being in an alien place, pressed in by people they did not understand (black too, the colour of the devil in their myths), speaking their languages only in their own heads until family members joined them.

What grim determination they had, these bourgeois forebears whose pluck and spirit pass on down the line. Starting afresh in Britain in the 1970s, East African Indians opened corner stores in quiet, boring suburbs, working day and night for small profits, surrounded by mean and suspicious natives, once again needed yet resented, some eventually becoming Thatcherite model citizens. The dead codgers up there must have laughed: 'Call these hardships? Opening shops in small, safe streets, no hyenas or witch doctors with nose bones making fires at the door? Nothing to it. In the jungle, we never slept for twenty-two years, too many dangers. But we could not be stopped.'

Indian *dukanwallahs* were kind to their own. In her book – more a hagiography – the Gujarati writer Bhanuben Kotecha describes their bonds:

Whenever Indians came across an Indian shop along the forest tracks, they immediately felt at home... The owners of the shop would even get up in the middle of the night to provide them with a hot meal of moong dhal and rotli or puri with vegetables. When they had finished exchanging news they would take the rolls of American cloth which they had on sale and spread them along the counter. The visitors then lay on the counter, covered themselves with blankets (also on sale!) and fell asleep… mutual warmth and understanding in a foreign land bound them together.[20]

My mum, uncle and I were welcomed in exactly this way, only after the *puris* and sprouted moong we slept in the car. I remember the back of the shop where we sat on sheets and ate, hurricane lamps casting a gloomy light, and the women sitting next to us cooking *puris* on Primus stoves. They did have electricity, used only on special occasions, they said, like nice clothes and one covered-up sofa.

 Sprouted Moong

Serves 6

2 mugs moong beans
¾ tsp each mustard and cumin seeds
   mix
¾ tsp turmeric
6 fresh tomatoes, chopped small
½ tsp sugar
Lime juice

3 tbsp sunflower oil
1 tsp crushed garlic and green chilli
1 dried red chilli
A pinch of asafoetida
2 tsp mix of powdered cumin and
   coriander (*dhania jeera*)
Salt to taste

- Two nights before you want to cook this dish wash, then soak the moong beans.
- The next day, drain and wrap the beans in two clean cloths and leave in a warm place.

- Check that night to see if they are sprouting.

- The next morning they should have pretty little shoots.

- Warm the oil, and chuck in the seeds and red chilli.

- When they splutter, add tomatoes, spices, garlic and asafoetida, and stir as they cook for a good seven minutes. You may need to add a little water if they stick.

- Add two mugs of water and when that comes to the boil put in the beans.

- Cover and cook for five minutes, then remove the lid and simmer slowly until the mixture is quite dry.

- Add sugar, lime juice and salt.

Firoz, one of the old folk whose parents ran the *dukans*, told me, 'The profit was so small, maybe we made two shillings a day. We were never unfair to Africans. That is not true at all. Our home in up country was like a shed for goats, nothing at all. Pit dug for the toilet. Flies always flying around the smelling hole. The floor was mud. Some hard beds and mattresses which we slept on, ate on, sat on and prayed on. And everyday same food, *khichri*, or *rotli* and watery dhal.' Fatma, nearly ninety, remembered her deprivation and struggle: 'Mosquitoes used to bite us everywhere and make us sick. My parents, you know making more children on the gunny sacks in the shop and it was not very good behaviour. My father made a lot of noise and my mother's voice was like a lost kitten. She died when baby number fourteen got stuck. Good, she was free after that. Everything was in this small shop, tinned fish, Aspro, soda, biscuits, flour, rice, dhals, sugar, tea. But my father was stingy so we children only given small plate of rice and watery dhal.'[21]

Many families survived on rice served with a dollop of home made-yoghourt and watery dhal sipped piping hot from small cups. This is Fatma's recipe.

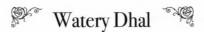 ## Watery Dhal

Serves 4–5

1 cup *toor dhal*, a kind of lentil

2 tbsp vegetable oil

½ tsp black mustard seeds

1 green chilli, cut half open, seeds left in

½ 400g tin chopped tomatoes

¼ tsp asafoetida

Juice of a lime

2½ pts water

2 cloves garlic, sliced thinly

½ tsp fenugreek seeds

1 dried red chilli

Handful of curry leaves

2 tsp combined powdered cumin
    and coriander seeds

½ tsp turmeric

3 tsp sugar

Salt to taste

⊙ Wash the dhal thoroughly and pick out any grit or foreign particles. *Toor dhal*, in particular, needs assiduous attention.

⊙ Boil the dhal, then simmer slowly in salted water in a saucepan over low heat for up to an hour, perhaps longer. It is ready when you can mash a grain easily with your fingers and thumb. When cooked, there should still be plenty of water in the pot. If there isn't, add some from a just-boiled kettle.

⊙ Whisk the mixture with a hand whisk or, better still, an electric one.

⊙ Heat the oil and add red chilli, garlic, fenugreek and mustard seeds.

⊙ When they sizzle and pop, add the tomatoes and cook for a minute.

⊙ Then add the rest of the ingredients except the sugar and lime.

- Cook slowly, stirring until the mixture thickens.

- Add this to the dhal – be careful as there is some spluttering at this stage.

- Chuck in the sugar and cook the dhal for another ten minutes.

- Let it rest for ten minutes, then add the lime juice and serve in teacups.

- You have a little rice on a plate which you eat while you sip the dhal.

My mum was born, we think, around 1919. Her early childhood memories were simply imaginings, wishes, longings, empty cases without remembered faces or voices. Both her parents died young, and her older siblings took care of the younger ones. Death in the tropics took so many away that it would have been indulgent to mourn them too long or fight against it. In London she befriended Fatma, and the two of them spent hours speaking histories, disagreeing, correcting each other and trying to recall what was too far away. Jena always said she was luckier than Fatma, who had had to live in the jungle with her mean father, who collected loot and buried it under the only bed in the back of the shop – his bed. At least, said Jena, she lived in a big place with schools and a consoling sea from which she thought she often heard the songs of plaintive maidens. Fatma was prepared to agree.

As the years went on, while their own families were made to survive on rations (profits were not made to be squandered on wife and children), the canny *dukan-wallahs* packed their shops with goods from England, Arabia and India. A white travel writer described a typical *dukan* this way:

The miserable hovels, dignified by the name of shops, kept chiefly by Her Majesty's East Indian subjects were packed with coils of brass and iron wire varying in thickness, strings of beads of many colours and sizes, white hip cloths of the ordinary make from Manchester... There were breast and shoulder cloths for women flaming with designs, garlic and onions in small quantities, betel nuts, grain, salt, knives, looking glasses, skeins of Berlin wool and a thousand trashy items of small value, manufactured expressly to captivate the eye of the unsophisticated nigger.[22]

Another white traveller who went to East Africa in 1908 found a cornucopia of goods in such places:

The low ceiling of the shop was strung with wire lines from which were suspended a multitude of jangling and clattering wares – tools, boots, saris, pots, gewgaw ornaments from Birmingham, packets of Post Toasties bundled into a fishing net, walking sticks, canned salmon stacked in bird-cages, rakes, rolls of muslin, books, patent medicines, potatoes, flour, razor blades, stacks of soda water... Rammal [the shopkeeper] contemplated the disorder with complete equanimity.[23]

The *dukanwallahs* did not allow themselves any indulgences. The pretty things were for other people, white and black, too stupid to understand thrift.

By the end of the 1920s, indigenous East Africans had no choice but to accept their third-class status and adjust to a bewildering market economy. They were beaten by those who controlled their lives and their own awakening consumerism. Their desires were stirred for objects hitherto unknown and unneeded – beads, blankets, bright-coloured cloth, sparkling boiled sweets, booze, sugary drinks. Diets and lives changed. Soon they had their own 'native' recipes, inexpensive versions of what they smelled and saw serving food to the *mzungu* (whites) and *wahindi* (Indians).

In her novel *The Feast of the Nine Virgins*, Jameela Siddiqi described a jungle shopkeeper, hard-nosed, perpetually insecure and up to many tricks:

...he knew how to extract the largest possible amount money from any customer... Useless African fellows, they couldn't be trusted. Lazy as hell. They just sat around in the sun laughing and talking and eating bananas... [They] could not afford Soda Baridi (cold soda) at one shilling a bottle, so he cheated and sneaked in a few bottles of tap-water to become ice cold in a special chest. He then charged black Africans ten cents to be able to drink an ice-cold version of the sweet water of their own land... But if an Indian stopped by for a cold drink, there was no charge. And on the rare occasion that a European happened to get thirsty in the area, forget water! Shopkeepers vied with each other to be the first to offer him a free bottle of Soda Baridi or beer.[24]

Africans understood the injustices meted out to them. Many were astute and imaginative, and bit by bit they acquired impressive skills by watching their masters and inventing dishes we should have appreciated more. They dug holes in the ground and lined them with stones. A wood fire burned at the top, and a well was made to catch hot ashes on which they placed washed old paraffin tins to bake bread dough, sometimes cakes and biscuits. These were sold on the streets. Dingo, a gardener in my primary school, showed us how to make an oven out of an anthill, a trick he said he had learned from his grandfather, who had worked for an Englishman and had grown to love the smell and taste of bread. We watched as he scooped out livid ants, which stung him as they rushed up his long arms. He didn't even flinch, just brushed or shook them off. At the top of the fragile hill, Dingo made a small escape hole for smoke, then lit a fire in the curve he had dug out. Once the flames had subsided – his eyes ran like taps – he placed a covered tin over the coals. It contained his bread dough raised with banana yeast. As it cooked, the smell wafted across the school garden.

Bread with Banana Yeast

Yeast

2 ripe bananas or, better still, plantains	1 large tbsp sugar
1 large tbsp plain flour	½ cup warm water

⊙ Mash the skinned bananas, add the other ingredients, then seal in a container (a plastic box wrapped in foil works).

⊚ Leave for two days while it ferments and gets frothy.

Bread

8 cups white flour   **½ tsp salt**
1 tsp sugar   **½ cup banana yeast**
Warm water to make a softish dough

⊚ Mix everything and knead for five to six minutes.

⊚ Grease a loaf tin and stuff dough into it.

⊚ Let it rise for two hours.

⊚ Bake in the oven for forty minutes at 350°F, 180°C, gas mark 4.

⊚ Or find and break up an anthill.

By the 1930s, some impertinent Indians were starting to expand into large-scale cultivation and tin and gold mining. They were overreaching themselves and threatening the social order. As this buffer class grew more prosperous and ambitious, British racism rose up to cut it down. Indians found ways to fight back with guile and a cheery smile. They always overcharged whitie and gave him less than his due by cheating with the scales. These consumers were even then gluttons for Indian food, ordering it to be cooked by the *dukanwallahs'* wives. The tricksy cooks made the chicken curries inhumanely hot to make the bwanas weep.

Gora Chicken

Serves 4

1 skinned chicken, cut into smallish pieces	1 tbsp hot chilli powder
5 bulbs garlic, crushed, or 2 tbsp crushed garlic	2 tsp sugar
	2 tsp ground black pepper
Lemon or lime juice	2 tsp *garam masala*
3 tbsp vegetable or sunflower oil	½ cup water

- Whiz all ingredients except the chicken, water and oil and beat them to make a paste. It should have the consistency of tomato purée. Add extra garlic and lemon or lime if too dry.

- Heat oil in a *karai* until it is just hot enough to sear food but not flaming hot.

- Stir-fry the chicken in oil for eight minutes.

- Add the paste and water, and continue cooking for a couple more minutes.

- Stick in an oven at 350°F, 180°C, gas mark 4, covered with foil, for twenty-five minutes. Check the chicken twice and turn the pieces over.

- Serve with fresh baguettes (at home it was white bread).

In Entebbe on the edge of Lake Victoria lived a witchy Indian woman who claimed her potions could cure malaria. She spoke some English so white customers went to her when nothing else worked. Most especially for them she added her own urine to the pastes and concoctions she handed them with strict instructions on how and when they were to be imbibed. The extra ingredient, she said, was revenge for their supercilious behaviour towards her people.

Asians were in a pernicious trap with no escape. If they did well, poisonous envy was raised against them; if they were poor, they were accused of being a drain on a poor country. Some white colonials periodically argued for strict controls on immigration from India, yet these immigrants were told by other colonial masters that East Africa was to be their America. The white ruling classes knew they were entirely dependent on the services of the coolies, that their settlement would be doomed without the middle brown men. Examples abound of the deals struck between the two races and classes in spite of hostile feelings between them. There was always dishonesty on both sides as they tried to hike up profits. Churchill's was a rare voice that recognized how the pioneering Indians were indispensable for the growing Empire:

It was the Sikh and Punjabi Muslim who bore an honourable part in the conquest and pacification of the East African territories. It is the Indian trader who, penetrating and maintaining himself in all sorts of places to which no white man would go and in which no white man could earn a living, has, more than anyone else, developed the early beginnings of trade and opened up the first slender means of communication.[25]

And they kept coming, venturing into the countryside or setting up in the towns, creating their own oriental localities which fascinated and repelled Europeans: '[Nairobi] is a town that exudes ghee and the colours of Asia and with its bazaar and bungalows, and helmets and puttees has more of an appearance of India than Africa.'[26] A. M Jeevanjee, one of the earliest Asian pioneers to chase the African dream and make a fortune, built a statue to Queen Victoria in Nairobi town centre.

In 1910, Indian banks were starting up. By 1920, 145 ginneries were owned by Indians, and Indian-owned sugar plantations were doing exceptionally well. Africans had to accept controlled prices, and resentment grew. The first boycotts against Asian traders were organized by the biggest tribe, the proud Bagandans. Meanwhile other Indians were building middle-class lives and occasionally became victims of crime or very rough British justice. In 1916, for example, there was a skirmish in the streets of Mombasa between some Indians over one rupee. One man stabbed another. An innocent Indian, Hasan Kana, was arrested and tried, unfairly it was believed by most witnesses. The Ismaili Allidina Visram hired lawyers, but Kana was found guilty and sentenced to be hanged. Outraged, his four brothers asked to die too, so they were all hanged by the British, five brothers for one rupee.[27]

In 1920 there were 2001 Europeans in Uganda and 12,000 Asians. An official communiqué in that year paid the Asians tribute: 'The country owes much to the Indian trader and we consider that a broad policy of toleration should be adopted towards him. He has shown energy and enterprise and has assisted in the opening up of the more remote districts. He is also of value as an agriculturalist.'[28] But as R. C. Pratt noted, 'Little was done to facilitate the tranquil integration of the Indian minority into Ugandan life. Government, education, land, internal trade and medical policies accentuated their separateness.'[29] The scene was set for perpetual suspicion.

Indians continued to commercialize new areas and build the physical, social and economic infrastructure while on the whole sticking to their assigned place. Their territory grew bigger than was planned by their rulers, but the system was not challenged except by the very few who had been inspired by liberationist politicians. Of course they felt the humiliation and sometimes found ways to subvert white power and insolence. Subtly, however, Indians were induced to become the unobtrusive agents of Empire and to accept the status quo. Many East African Asians still cannot break free from that historical subservience. Witness this account written in 2001: 'The memsahibs in those days enjoyed almost the life of a queen. [They] were compassionate and cultured and always provided the *fundis* (carpenters) with a cup of coffee or tea with biscuits and sandwiches. They were all Mother Teresas.'[30] Not a speck of irony here. To be considered more worthy than Africans was reward enough.

3 Born in Elysium, 1920s–54

M̲Y MOTHER, JENA, WAS raised in the coastal town of Dar-es-Salaam, meaning 'Abode of Peace' in Arabic. Like Mombasa, it was a cliché of seaside gorgeousness but more languid. The lobsters and crabs, she said, were slow of movement, and birds slothfully hung around on trees most of the hot day. The sea was part of the music of her soul; her favourite Hindi song was about the sound of melancholy waves leaving traces of sadness on the sand.

Her father had made good, and was kind and generous, she was told by those who knew him, a man who valued humanity and God equally, a radical position for those times. Then disease took away both her parents. Jena and her younger brother Pilu were orphaned too young. Graveyards in the tropics are full of such premature deaths. There were no photographs or images to give shape to the sense of loss the siblings must have felt. Jena spent her whole life peering at family faces, seeking clues and signs so she could construct identikit images of her mother, Puribai, and father, Ramji. When her granddaughters were born, Jena always said, excitedly, 'I dreamt she is my own mother returned – her face must be my mother's face. Look at her, pretty nose, she doesn't look like any of us, must be my mother.'

Young Jena and the infant Pilu had to be taken away from the seaside to a lakeside port in Tanganyika called Mwanza, best known for its virulent malaria, fat, vicious hippos, flavoursome tilapia fish and swampy pong. They were cared for by their older brother Popat and his wife, my tender Maami. They loved Jena and Pilu as they did their own five children, but Popat was struggling to keep them all, and the anxiety led to chronic health problems. His gentle face is perfectly round in the pictures I have of him; his eyes seem to be looking warily beyond the camera at some approaching trouble.

The Great Depression of 1930 hit Africa like an unexpected typhoon, wrecking many, including some wealthy dynasties.[1] Jena could name at least five Asian men who committed suicide by throwing themselves under the trains coming in from Mombasa. She watched her beloved sibling guardian sink into hopeless debt and disquietude as his fragile business ventures crashed, his worst fears materialized.

Fish was cheap; they ate a lot of it. My mother cooked fish better than anyone in the whole world, even way back then: 'Popat loved my fish *masala*, and he ate it even when he was sick and paralysed. I gave him small bites.' Decades later the dish would bring forth tears as she remembered her surrogate father.

Fish *Masala*

Serves 6

You can buy frozen tilapia in Indian grocery stores, but they are skinless fillets which cook too fast and break up, unless you can get hold of the fatter variety. Back in Mwanza they used to cook the whole fish taken fresh from the lake. Good substitutes are cod, halibut or coley steaks, or any whole fish which has firm flesh.

Whole fish weighing 4 lb or 4 lb of fish steaks

Preparation

◉ If using a whole fish, get it scaled, then make three to four slashes on either side. You can take the head off, but I don't. My ex-mother-in-law liked no other part of a fish better, and in her memory I always keep the heads on.

◉ With fish steaks, wash and then sprinkle them with a little salt. Leave for an hour.

◉ I usually use 4 lb of fish for six people. Other ingredients are for this quantity. For less or more, you'll need to adjust accordingly.

2 lb medium-sized potatoes
½ cup oil

Masala *Paste*

¾ **cup tomato purée**	1 **tsp turmeric**
¾ **tsp chilli powder**	1½ **tsp *garam masala***
1 **tsp coriander powder**	1 **tsp cumin powder**
3 **tsp crushed mixture of ginger and garlic**	**Juice of a big lime**

◉ Mix together the ingredients for the paste.

◉ Peel, halve and parboil potatoes for six minutes.

◉ Cover fish with some *masala* and in a separate bowl mix a little *masala* into the potatoes. Leave for a couple of hours. Hang on to any leftover *masala*.

◉ Pour half the oil in a wok and, when hot (not sizzling), lay the potatoes down, cover and cook for fifteen minutes, stirring from time to time.

◉ Remove potatoes and spread in a pretty ovenproof dish.

◉ Add rest of the oil (except for 2 tbsp) to the wok and carefully place the fish in.

Cover and cook. Turn over after five minutes and cook for a further five. Lift the fish and lay it over the potatoes.

- Heat the remaining oil in the wok and cook the leftover *masala* on high heat, stirring so it thickens and browns but doesn't burn.

- Scrape this over fish and potatoes.

- Let it rest.

- Just before serving, zap the top under a hot grill if you wish (not really essential).

- You can garnish this with thin slices of ripe lime.

———— ⌣ ————

In 1936, a stranger rode into town, said he was from Karachi but had lived for years in London and had arrived in Kampala a *topiwallah* – a gent in a hat. He impressed the small-town people, some of whom had never even been on the steamers coming and going on Lake Victoria. This was my father, Kassim Damji, briefly in Mwanza for a business deal. Jena was only sixteen. She caught his eye as she swept the yard, contentedly singing songs of praise. He stopped, took off his trilby, stared and fidgeted until she noticed and ran in, leaving her flip-flops in the sun.

Compulsively impulsive, he proposed marriage. Popat accepted on Jena's behalf – one less mouth to feed, and the stranger was impressively decisive. There were no in-laws or dowries to worry about. Kassim was sixteen years older than Jena, an urbane international traveller, manager of an English car firm. What he thought he would do with this girl with a broom I don't know. By the time of Popat's death at forty-five, both men felt regret and guilt about the hasty nuptials.

Despite the Depression, Popat had sent Jena to school until she was fifteen. (In time her literacy would keep us from destitution.) Kassim, a tireless advocate of female education, was proud that his young wife loved books. When age wore out her eyes, she said she missed reading more than anything else. Extraordinarily, our Imam, Aga Khan III, grandfather of the present Aga Khan, had called for female emancipation and education as early as 1910, long before the sluggish, powerful men in the West, for whom the status quo seemed good enough to last forever. The Imam wrote, 'No progressive thinker today will challenge the claim that the social advancement and general well-being of communities are greater where women are least debarred, by artificial barriers and narrow prejudices, from taking their full part as citizens.' Throughout his imamate, Ismaili mosques were instructed to protect and educate girls and women.[2]

In his erudite book on the Ismailis, Farhad Daftary detailed other achievements of this Aga Khan, known in the West only for his love of girls and horses and the aristocratic lifestyle: 'He created a variety of institutions with their benefits accruing not only to his own followers but to non-Ismailis as well. He founded and maintained a large network of schools, vocational institutions, libraries, sports and recreational clubs, dispensaries and hospitals in East Africa and the Indo-Pakistan continent and elsewhere.'[3] I look back in awe at the audacity of this leader, his use of personal power to drive through progressive ideas, to free my people from superstition and oppressive values. Misogynists and misanthropist Muslim leaders of the twenty-first century want to use theirs to push Muslims into a new dark age. To them we Ismailis are wretched infidels. The present Aga Khan carries on the delicate task of balancing cultural evolution and inviolable tenets of faith. I am wary of the adulation given to a living being by our masses and the principle of inherited privilege – both inherent in our imamate – but in the emerging global clash between viciously Talibanized Muslims and reformists like the Ismailis, I know where I must stand.

My father had first migrated to England from undivided India in his youth for reasons he kept secret. There was a family row; he was angry about something and fled his family home in Karachi. He never saw his parents again. He had also been excommunicated for rages against religion, too much of a rebel even for our soft and usually relaxed congregations. Papa expressed no regrets, told us no stories of his childhood and family, and so my paternal grandparents disappeared into the ether, nameless, formless, unforgiven and denied a place in our lives. My mother made one visit to Karachi with my brother, only a baby. Her in-laws apparently adored her and couldn't understand why she had wasted herself on the bad boy of the family. She wrote to my father's brother, sisters and their children, sent gifts when she could afford it, as did my brother. Papa never gave a damn. During some of their most wounding rows, my mother would scream in Gujarati, the language they spoke to each other, 'I lost my parents and I still miss them and you killed yours while they lived. You are monstrously unfeeling, care about your shoe polish more than your own mother.'

In the years before he made his dramatic appearance in Africa, Papa had lived as a brown sahib in Britain at a time when the country was almost wholly white, class-ridden and puffed up with imperial pride. As a child enchanted by the two blondes Goldilocks and Cinderella, I pestered him to tell me more about that magical place

– England. He dismissed my entreaties – glass slippers and fairy rubbish made him contemptuous – reminiscing instead about the bracing beaches at Poole in Dorset, London's cold and copious libraries, and the palaces of Westminster. In 1932, he had witnessed the crowds cheering Mahatma Gandhi in London and couldn't understand why such a clever lawyer was dressed like 'an ignorant peasant'. Around this time he also had seen Paul Robeson as Othello at the Savoy Theatre and followed the furore caused by a black actor touching and kissing Peggy Ashcroft on stage. A *Times* reader (of course), Papa was unprepared for the exposure of middle-class racism in the Letters pages as provoked theatre patrons slammed the audacious production, Robeson and Ashcroft, and it shook him up. (In 1966, another such furore on another stage would blow back that memory and blast our lives.) These few fragments of information were all he shared. Yet England made him the man he was.

Kassim was the perfect Edwardian gent: disapproved of sentimentality, held in his emotions, wore good English tailored suit and hats, had a fine appreciation of wines and whiskies, was fond of books and classic English cars, liked to order delicate beef consommés, melba toast and perfectly coddled eggs. But he also had the restless, impatient soul of a free-wheeling bohemian and could never be placated or tamed or bent to follow rules. (I have his restive spirit, my son his fierce independence.) His new wife must have found him alarmingly inconsistent.

In 1937, fortunes were picking up again, and Kassim took his young bride to Kampala (such tears were shed as she left her brother's family). And so it began, this long marriage of misfits. Mum confronted tribulations, then immortalized them as achingly funny yarns. He carried on with his wayward ways. The world, he felt, never understood his brand of genius. There were grim times, some catastrophes, but like most other wedded couples of that era, habits, mores, familiarity and invisible ties kept them from separating. Our languages didn't have words for divorce until the 1950s. They used the English word, only mispronounced as 'die-worse' – perhaps subliminally describing what they thought of the act of marital severance. Jena said she sort of grew to understand her husband; certainly there was time enough to do so: 'He was not a bad man, just too careless. Poor Kassim, not able to be a good husband. But he never stopped me working, going out, having friends. I did what I wanted.' My mother had feminism thrust upon her.

In the very first month of their marriage, Kassim took Jena to the cinema, stepped out to buy cigarettes, forgot he had a bewildered girl-wife, wandered off home distractedly and went to bed. It was an omen of things to come. From that day on, she always went on her own to picture houses full of united clans and protective husbands. She took time to dress up and splashed on so much perfume, she smelled like a boudoir camellia. It helped to keep pity at bay. Incredibly hard-working, at one time she was doing three jobs – cooking, teaching and sewing – to keep the family from penury. After her second child, a daughter, was born in 1939, Jena banished Kassim from the marital bed, for both their sakes, she said.

I only have three photographs of them in the early years, each looking lonely as they jointly stare at the camera. She was beautiful, with intense dark eyes and a full, kissable, soft mouth. He was tall and lanky then, with an impatient, slightly arrogant demeanour and big ears which look like they could fan down his feverish brain.

The capital was growing fast, filling up with rural people who had had enough of the isolated *dukan* life. The most resilient refused to move. There was just too much money to be made in places where one shop had the monopoly, was the only supplier of goods and services. Some told me they believed a day would come when there would be no need to toil, but many rarely reached that point. Small shop-keepers rarely do. Baden-Powell told a good story about tiny *dukans* ready to supply anything and everything to white customers:

Our village shop belongs to an Indian and it would be hard to find anything he doesn't sell there. I tried to get a Wilkinson's razor blade, a rather rare article, but he had them all right. A lady came in for groceries and clothes she wanted. He had them all. This encouraged her to ask; 'Have you got such a thing as a parrot?' 'Certainly, madam. Grey or green?' And she took a green one home with her.[4]

They knew how to please customers and were even more skilful at entrapping their desires. Africans were commercial innocents, and the *dukanwallahs* were smooth operators who could lure the most resistant tribes. One witness described a memorable interaction:

During heavy rains the Masai were moving thousands of sheep from one pasture to another and were met on the banks of a drift by this enterprising pioneer with a wagon-load of umbrellas. He induced one or two of the leaders to use his umbrellas and soon sold the whole lot for a sheep – if not two – apiece. After this the incongruous sight could often be seen of a perfectly naked Masai herdsman holding up an umbrella in one hand and a spear in the other.[5]

Prejudices against this small commercial race and class, ever present, were stoked up by white colonialists in the inter-war years, which had the effect of making the shopkeepers even more determined to increase their numbers – ten, twelve children per family were common – and profits, which in turn made whites and blacks turn more hostile. Official publications and books by white settlers described Indians as 'unsanitary', a curse, economic parasites:

The Indian is prepared to live on next to nothing and make a small profit on small wares. Profits are sent straight back to Bombay. The Englishman endeavours to make money by developing the resources of the country but the Indian's wish is to drain it of whatever wealth exists... They are drawn from the most undesirable class in India. Their style of life is very low scale, which makes them unfair competition. In squalid conditions, ignoring sanitary precautions, they are often a danger to the community. Typhoid, smallpox, and the plague were unknown in East Africa before the Indian came.[6]

On the other hand, there were always some whites who chose not to join the clubs of racist imperialism.

World War II put both Asians and Africans in an unenviable position. The Germans were in Tanganyika, while Britons were never sure if their black and brown East African subjects were loyal to the Allies (most were). There were false accusations, punitive summary punishments and an atmosphere of fear, especially in the lakeside ports like Mwanza and in rural posts along the railway line. The Germans were even worse. Jena said they would hear such stories of frightened *dukanwallahs* who were beaten up and tortured because they were suspected of collaboration. Some were killed: 'They were small people, always afraid, trying to hide so everybody stamped on them as if they were ants.'

Back in Mother India, rumours had grown that her plucky children across the waters were losing touch. Without godly rules and the incomparable power of social disapproval, the fear was they would become '*junglees*' and spend all their money on worldly pleasures instead of on temples and mosques. So we got an influx of the bearded ones – pundits, gurus, mullahs. A handful had the sacred glint in their sympathetic eyes, but the rest were bogus. Anyone who claimed to know the right way 'thoroughly, through and through' was given free passage – super second class – on the SS *Karanja* or *Bombay* and invited to lodge in homes where there were no unmarried daughters. God's emissaries were necessary for a comfortable afterlife but not good enough for the children of steadily prospering merchants.

Society started to become mindful of the afterlife, careful and conformist in matters of religious practice. The voyager-moralists made up new rules to exert petty power; they had to show some returns on investments. 'Kalyug' arrived, a warning of another age of darkness and shamelessness that would presage the end of the cosmos. Some of the creeps got fattened and spoiled by families anxious for blessings to cover the many years they had lived without due respect for stricture or scripture. This was their last-chance saloon, really, the final phase of proxy attachment before they became hybrid creatures of no fixed address.

By the time I was a child in the early 1950s, the religious brigade was well settled in. I remember the *bhajans* sounding forth from temples, the early call of the muezzins before you could easily open sticky eyes, church bells all day on Sundays, radio stations badgering you about this and that religious duty. Dee Auntie, a Parsee family friend, had a holy hanger-on living in the house. She was a widow, and although she suspected he was ripping her off, she didn't dare eject him in case he wasn't. His fingernails were filthy, his teeth a greeny yellow. After initiation into the faith as children, all Parsees have to wear the *kushti* (sacred thread) and *sudra* (a muslin vest). This priest believed that to clean the vest was sacrilege; it was one of many bans he issued, written in red ink on half-pages torn from Dee Auntie's housekeeping-accounts book. He slurped hot, sweet *masala chai* with his meals and always lunged first at the food as it arrived. This lady was famous for her *dhansak*, a sweet, spicy mix of meat, vegetables and dhals. She always made it for us as this was one of the few dishes my mum couldn't ever make better than the original.

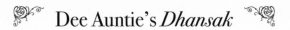 Dee Auntie's *Dhansak*

Serves 8

The list of ingredients is long, and the recipe appears daunting, but put aside half a day, turn on music and slowly cook this pot of myriad overlapping tastes. You and it are surely worth it. I classify the ingredients so they can be piled separately and used when needed. It is best made with meat from a leg of lamb.

2 lb leg of lamb, chopped by the butcher into small chunks	5 tbsp sunflower oil
	3 pints water
Salt to taste	

Dhals

A teacupful of the following dhals, all hulled:	2 tbsp *channa dhal*
masoor (red), *toor*, *moog* and *urd*	Salt

Vegetables

1 small butternut squash	1 small pumpkin or 3 courgettes
12 pickling onions	

Flavourings

3 tbsp tamarind paste. Buy tamarind in a block, tear off half and soak in water just boiled (the water should come ½ in. over the soaking tamarind). Leave for two hours while you get on with other stuff. Then crush the mixture with your hands and push through a sieve.

Bunch coriander	Bunch mint
2 tbsp grated jaggery	2 limes
3 finely chopped onions	1 400g tin chopped tomatoes

1 large tbsp crushed ginger, garlic and fresh green-chilli mix (you can buy these at Indian food outlets or make your own, whizzing with a little water, 2 chillies, 8 cloves of garlic and a large lump of peeled ginger cut into small pieces)

Spices

½ tsp fenugreek seeds	½ tsp black mustard seeds
½ tsp fennel seeds	2 star anise
2 tbsp cumin/coriander powder mixture	1 tsp red chilli powder
1 tsp turmeric	1 tbsp *garam masala*
½ tsp black pepper	8 curry leaves

- Grind together in a coffee grinder the fenugreek seeds, black mustard seeds, fennel seeds and star anise.

- Now, wash the meat and boil in half the water with salt and half of the garlic, chilli and ginger paste. You want it almost cooked.

- Meanwhile, rinse water through the dhals and boil in the rest of the water with salt until it has cooked to soft. You can add more water if needed. It should be a slop at the end. Add a glug of oil to stop the mix getting lumpy.

- Peel, cut and cover vegetables with a little oil and roast until nicely browned.

- Heat the oil in a largish flat pan and fry onions until red brown. Add tomatoes, remaining garlic/ginger/chilli, sliced green chillies and all the spices. Lower the heat and cook slowly, stirring once in a while for at least twelve minutes. Add the jaggery and let that melt.

- Take this cooked *masala* off the heat and add the tamarind.

- Whisk the dhal a little, and add the meat to it with 2 cups of meat stock. Then add the *masala* and simmer for thirty minutes. You will need a big pan. Add more stock if it gets too thick. Add the roasted vegetables and return to the boil for another five minutes.

- Add lime juice, chopped mint and coriander.

- Serve with rice or fresh crusty bread.

Even though they deferred to the religious police, hedging their bets like Dee Auntie, Indian émigrés receded culturally, then seceded from Mother India in all other matters, keeping their proclaimed eternal bonds for ceremonial and recreation purposes. God and films still had to be Indian to satisfy; other connections were floating away like driftwood. Strong links with Mother India made economic sense, said our leaders. Costs of shipping goods and spouses were rising too fast, and quality had gone down. Snaky Indian operators who knew Asians were getting wealthier had made the most of this distant good fortune. Cheap oil was added to the ghee, powder colours to the turmeric and chilli powder. Some high-charging matchmakers had sent over very dark-skinned girls even though families had made it clear that creamy pink to toffee was most necessary. To pay so much and get inky, sullen girls with scaly feet was intolerable. Someone invented the *channa* treatment to lighten skin, a tradition that settled and blighted lives of future generations. (It has followed us here.) Our mothers slapped it on our faces until it cracked and pulled the skin. It did make our faces glow, but alas nobody turned a light rose pink. With fewer girls coming, competition was cut off, but the best boys still went to wheaten-complexioned wives.

Somewhere along the line, we were relabelled, no longer called 'Indians' but 'Asians' (an illogical label), thus confirming a shifting identity and the seep of modernism. More Asians had moved on from hard lives in rural East Africa to settle in urban centres, soft like the vast sofas they could now afford with ease. Asians become conspicuously richer than the people left behind in India and the African populations. Kampala and Nairobi expanded. Many small *dukanwallahs* became owners of impressive large shops on main streets with huge, lit-up display windows. Although the Europeans continued to resent the upstarts, an increasing number of Asians acquired capital to move on to plantations and into factories. Vast fortunes were made dealing in gold, tin and other mined resources.

While some *dukanwallahs* in the countryside lived humbly, integrated into the villages they served, colour-coded class divisions between whites, blacks and browns became ever more embedded and unyielding. Asian schools opened in cities and towns, some with boarding facilities for families still in small outposts. Initially they were funded by fabulously rich philanthropists, but as education became a coveted commodity, communities started collective initiatives, some with a little help from their white masters, who knew this middle class was essential to shore up the colonial edifice. The first Aga Khan Schools for boys and girls in East Africa had appeared in 1919 and by the 1950s were superb academic institutions if a bit absurdly fixated on English school uniforms. Woollen blazers in the tropics drenched with sweat smelled like bad eggs.

Few Asian or white émigrés cared about the educational needs of the majority black population, though white missionaries did, but only for the chosen few. At the turn of the twentieth century, they had transplanted the public-school method and madness to Uganda to bring on an élite crop from the sophisticated Baganda – most by then devout Christians. Henry Walter Weatherhead, Cambridge graduate and fervent missionary, set up one of the most famous such schools, Kings College Budo. The alumni of these schools – prime ministers, bishops, surgeons, judges – proved that they did work. Asians were not accepted into the circle of privilege by the leader-makers, however. We were not thought of as East Africans, nor as people who could influence politics. The racism of blacks and whites excluded us from possibilities that might have given us a different future in Uganda. In time, missionaries also set up basic educational facilities for villagers and the urban poor.

More Asian patriarchs were beginning to agree that a little more education and freedom for the ladies was a very good idea; they could then help in the shops, do the books and save money. The first girls' schools appeared in the late 1920s. Pretty girls were always married young enough to have the time to breed and produce several sons to add to the family fortune. Now, in top Asian circles, brides were sought who were beautiful *and* educated, though not too educated, mind. Community schools were opened up to girls. Home tutors – chaperoned if men – were brought in. It was money well spent as dowries would be negotiated down for such girls as long as they were demonstrably homely. A skulk of unmarriageable women – too dark, too thin, too sullen, too poor, too sharp-tongued – went on to become midwives or teachers.

Ugandan Asians kept their heads down, built up more wealth and acquisitive, middle-class lives. Their eyes often looked westwards to England. They became gluttons for imported goods – crockery, toys, whips, musical instruments, saddles, canned foods and gadgets. Asians without much money were an embarrassment for an aspirational community, but oddly Papa was indulged and became a kind of local hero. Although he had no business sense, many saw in him a classy Englishman who could tell them of the world out there, take them beyond their shops and small concerns. He read newspapers and books, always listened to the new BBC Empire Service. After Friday prayers, folk would come over to our small flat to hear from Kassim about what was happening in England, India and Pakistan.

Some travellers and new settlers were rapturous when they encountered the multicultural mix of urban East Africa:

> Nairobi, the seat of government of this Protectorate, now has a total white population of eight hundred and fifty, including the military and police, while its highly variegated assortment of colours, ranging from pale saffron to ebony, numbers eleven thousand. Its streets are thronged with Orientals and native savages, the former as weirdly picturesque in the variety and styles of their costumes as are the latter in the scantiness or entire lack of any costume at all. Grave Sikh constables, bearded and turbaned; Parsee merchants and clerks in long black coats and flat-topped skull caps; Hindu mechanics, turbaned and often carrying water pipes half as big as a foot bath; coast Swahilis in long nightgown-like kanzus of thinnest muslin and embroidered white skull caps; flowing-robed Arabs with sashes stuck full of life-taking steel to arm a half-dozen men of any other race; tall, slender, graceful Somalis in khaki jackets, turbans and flowing waist cloths; Goanese merchants and clerks in white drill; Indian women and children wearing more brilliant colours than even a kaleidoscope can boast...[7]

This didn't mean there was growing equality. In 1931, Julian Huxley wrote, 'For all his ancient civilization the Indian is dirtier than the African. He is more unsanitary when left to himself and is bound by tradition and superstition that is more difficult to persuade into change.'[8]

East African Asians who were familiar with Gandhi's politics of resistance realized the vulnerable position they had been placed in. A few joined African liberationists and fought for independence. White prejudices grew as previously obsequious 'coolies' started standing up for their rights. One of them, the political activist Shamsud Deen, observed bitterly, 'I really see very gloomy prospects for those who choose to remain in a foreign land inhabited by millions of Africans, who, though not originally and naturally hostile to Indians, will not long remain unaffected by the propaganda which has persistently been put out by Europeans...'[9]

By this time official records noted that the country had thirty-five thousand Asians. Many more lived in Tanganyika and Kenya, and, as in the UK, the British started imposing quotas to limit numbers coming in. More white South Africans were encouraged to move into East Africa during this period. Asians by this time had mastered the arts of flattery (all minorities everywhere must learn this to survive) and of delicate influence. One old man, Topan, told me how 'every Christmas, we gave white customers whisky, brandy, chocolates, dried fruits and nuts, cigars for men, chocolates for the ladies. Our own children didn't get these delicious things. We would deliver them year after year. But did they give back? No. Not even invited into their houses. Looked down their noses.' Sometimes the disdain got too much to bear, and hot blood was raised against those white bwanas who behaved with condescension and boorishness. There were street fights, court cases and sometimes interventions by colonial officials, who did try to play fair. In *Out of Africa*, even Karen Blixen revealed her own suspicious relationship with brown-skinned traders: 'They were such grasping tradesmen.'[10] And yet these were the men she called on night and day to provide her with supplies and who put up with her ever more whimsical requests.

Kenyan Europeans were the most intolerant, living in fine enclaves where notices warned 'Strong Smells Not Permitted'. One wealthy relative managed to buy a home there and thought that made him a white bwana. On his walls were framed pictures of shire hunt parties and Constable reproductions. He started each day with porridge, using only 'Settler u-like-me' oats. The box had a picture of a white man in knee-length khaki shorts, safari shirt, wellies and topi, hand on heart and looking as if he owned the world. He did.

As they got hubristic, English, Welsh, Scots and Irish displayed more contempt for all things Asian, including our food (though they did have their own curries laced with jam and bananas and, of course, mulligatawny soup), but when it came to cricket they were more than willing to play with Asians, to beat them, of course, and reassert their master status. Only the results didn't always go the way of the rulers. When they were beaten they sulked, walked off, pushing aside post-match Asian snacks offered by grinning '*baboos*', turning instead to their own comfort foods – Victoria sponges and cucumber sandwiches with English tea, not that horrid Indian tea boiled to death and smelling of cardamom.

Urban Africans, meanwhile, loved our strong smells and tastes, adopted Asian food and relished it, another of our cultural legacies utterly unrecognized by the black élite. Shariffa Keshavjee, a Kenyan Asian, remembers how 'African servants working for Indians, picked up much of the cooking, so that ghee and mchuzi (curry) have become part of the vocabulary of East African cuisine. How common it is today to stop at a wayside kiosk and ask for chapattis or samosas, kebabs or bhajias? How many Kenyans realise the origins of these popular foods?'[11]

Meanwhile at home my brother and sister were growing up, and their needs were mounting too. The cost of living had shot up. Jena had to find regular money for school fees, doctors' services (she now had dangerously high blood pressure), food, rent, clothes, interest on debts, extended family duties and small luxuries. She taught young children at the mosque nursery school until lunchtime, catered for weddings and engagements in the afternoon, sewed sari blouses for customers late into the night, her radio on, soothing her with Hindi songs about broken dreams. By this time she had gathered around her a wide group of loyal friends who bailed her out when she was completely desperate, threw us a line when we were sinking. Some of them were very wealthy but had such respect for this tiny, determined woman. Kassim did his bit when he felt like it. He was still banished, forced to sleep in the living room. The last thing either of them wanted was another child. One fateful night in May 1949, however, lust overcame my father, and my mother went to his bed. I was conceived in folly and turmoil, passionately unwanted: 'Didn't like it, but what to do? He's my husband.' Soon after, he stepped out for a packet of cigarettes. Begged money from his wife, who as usual protested, then relented, fishing out wet notes from her bra and handing them over. It was more than eighteen months before he returned from the shop. (During my childhood

Kassim disappeared three more times, for months on end and returning amiably repentant.)

At birth I was tiny, barely 3 pounds, blue-purple like a small aubergine, apparently. Jena was weak and exhausted. Then she succumbed to meningitis. I have been told the story so many times, I think I watched my own bloody delivery and the agony that spoiled any chances of ecstasy. She wept at my birth, and who would blame her? There was no money to pay the hospital bill. My brother, only eleven, and our ten-year-old sister walked to hospital carrying tea in a pot for Mum, arriving weeping and drenched in the beverage. Our Hindu neighbour Raman Patel came to pick us up and settle the bill. He treated me like his own daughter, had to really as I clung to him, clamoured to sit on his lap, for years afterwards. By then, religious differences had lost their potency to divide. Mum fattened me up (with some financial assistance from Raman), fed me bottles of Cow and Gate baby milk, made in England.

Where did Papa go during all those lost years? He always ended up back in England, that much we knew. I used to imagine that he had a thrilling secret life – maybe was part of an underground freedom movement. Or was there a siren who beckoned him over to London or Poole? Perhaps a blonde landlady who fell for the quick-minded maverick? I cannot forgive him for these absences, not since I was told a few years ago that even when he came back after I was born, he first went to visit his glamorous female friend who wore stiff, pointy bras and saris tied right down around her sexy hips. Her belly button was a long slit punched with jewels; she knew all about sundowners and whisky mixes. She told him he had another daughter who looked just like him. Just as well. People in the mosque would have ostracized my mother and me too if there had been any suggestion of adultery. How do you do that much damage with so little malice?

And so it carried on, clever Kassim dipping in and out of fatherhood without warning.

The house grew damp with resentment.

When I was in nursery and primary school, Papa often forgot to pick me up. I am told I waited still with patience as the last of the children were collected. Sometimes an ayah of another child would walk me home. Once I was inadvertently locked in the nursery and the cleaners found me asleep, worn out after hours of sobbing and screaming. One of the few presents my careless father ever bought me was a book of severe morality tales by some stern chap called Uncle Arthur who made naughty or forgetful kids suffer the most terrible retribution – deaths of mothers, storms and lightning. I had a few precious toys, almost all home-made by Jena – tiny dress-up dolls with matchstick arms and legs and cigarette-box furniture.

It was an almost happy early childhood, though perilous. My photos taken at four in a studio show a wary girl, way too serious for her age. At ten, the foreboding appears stronger, but there is a new determination. At twelve, I look defiantly at the camera. I was going to make it.

In the year before she died, Jena told me such stories, a number of which I had never heard. She had kept them locked up till the end. They were strange, honest streams of conscience, dwelling on what she was, might have been, how many men fancied her, her loveless marriage, her many disappointments, the envy she felt of her friends. Her best mate had six sons: 'They all want her to live with them, love her so much, Yassi, she is already in heaven. What did I do wrong in my last life? So little love in our family. I tried my best, but not enough.' One suitor wanted her to leave my dad and become his second wife. He was a portly importer/exporter who daily ate hunks of meat off the bone. He thrashed children and servants with his thin silver-tipped stick. He had money, a cavernous house and a wife as coarse as he was. My mother taught him to eat vegetarian food he had always said was for puny, unreliable *banyanis* (Hindus). He became besotted. 'Fat, cruel man but he became so quiet when he was drinking my watery dhal you know, like a pussy cat with creamy milk. Best he liked my stuffed brinjals and thin chapattis.'

Stuffed Brinjals

Serves 4

5 small, round aubergines
4 tbsp sunflower oil
Large tin chopped tomatoes
1 tsp crushed garlic
½ pint water

8 medium-sized whole potatoes, peeled and parboiled
1 onion, chopped
1 whole green chilli, slashed open
Salt to taste

Stuffing

1 tbsp desiccated coconut
1 tsp *dhania* powder
1 tsp *jeera* powder
½ tsp each chilli powder and turmeric

1 tbsp broken roasted peanuts (you can whiz them in a food processor)
1 tbsp grated jaggery
Juice of 1 lemon

⊙ Heat the oil in a shallow pan with a lid.

- Fry the onion until slightly brown, add the tomatoes and garlic, and cook until it thickens.

- Add water and bring to the boil again, then take pan off the heat.

- Mix all the ingredients for the stuffing, wetting it with water if you need to.

- Cut open the aubergines two-thirds through, so they are attached at the stalk end.

- Half-cut the potatoes in the same way.

- Carefully push some stuffing on to one side of each vegetable and close it firmly.

- Heat the onion and tomato sauce to a gentle simmer, adding the chilli.

- Place the vegetables in the sauce and cover to cook for twenty minutes. If it looks too runny, take off the lid and finish cooking.

- You can pour a little yoghourt over just before serving.

When clearing her flat after she died, we found in one of my mother's many plastic shopping bags old recipes in Gujarati, letters and some photos of people she knew. One was a formal portrait of a woman she had told me was called Motibai. Jena was haunted by this family, our neighbours in the 1950s. On Motibai's head was draped a black chiffon *pacheli* with a wide border embroidered in the Parsee style, silk threads overlapped to raise vivid roses. She wore a five-diamond-and-ruby nose rose hanging off a pierced hole which had stretched precariously over the years – a loving gift from her devoted son, Bahadur (meaning 'brave', no name really for the dependent, spindly boy-man, said Jena). Her husband had died soon after Bahadur had been born, an act of benevolence, thought Motibai. The Almighty knew two males craving love and attention would have been too much for her. Khusa, her daughter-in-law, appeared stiff with resolution, her face melancholic. Khusa was in a white silk sari, her dowry necklace clasped around her long, thin neck as if to choke the life out of her. Unusual by then, she was an imported bride from a village in Gujarat. Mum said Motibai slapped Khusa's face with wet *chappals*, often dirty. If her daughter-in-law sang to herself the old songs by then barely alive in her memory, Motibai stared at her with such wintry eyes that they made the young women's teeth chatter, and the songs all flew away like disturbed butterflies.

Bahadur had felt some affection stirring for Khusa after she had given him two boys at once without complaining. For twenty-eight hours, she sank herself into ceaseless, pulverizing pain until two 6-pounders tore out of her too fast. Her wound looked like a bloody scream, said the midwife to my mum, but Khusa made hardly a sound, bit into a pillow instead.

The howls came later when she lost her twins, Amir and Amin, only eight weeks after birth, as they lay next to Motibai in her big bed. One smelled distinctly creamy, the other milky, Khusa confided to Jena. The grieving mother was convinced that the crone Motibai had added mercury to the smears of honey she liked to place on the small, pink, pointed tongues which were always moving and seeking.

Every year on the anniversary of the babies' deaths, Khusa made *shrikand* from cream for Amir; for Amin she made the milky-sweet *dudhpak*. Almost a whole teaspoon of *kesar*, Kashmiri saffron, went into the pure white delicacies to streak them with the colour of the sun. Dark red rose petals were scattered over the plates. (Khusa always cried at this point as she remembered the birth.) Then silently, she fed children in the neighbourhood the sweets from small bowls.

Shrikand

Serves 8

2 cups sour cream

4 tbsp caster sugar

Juice of half a lemon

½ tsp saffron

1 cup curd cheese or ricotta

¼ tsp ground cardamom

¼ cup chopped raw pistachios and
flaked almonds

- Mix all ingredients except for the nuts and refrigerate overnight, covered with cling film.

- Before serving beat the mixture. Add the nuts and serve.

Dudhpak

Serves 6

¼ cup pudding rice

1 tin evaporated milk

½ tsp grated nutmeg

½ tsp saffron

2 pints full-cream milk

1 tsp ground cardamom

¾ cup caster sugar

½ cup flaked almonds

- Soak the rice in cold water for two hours, then drain.

- Cook it in the two milks in a non-stick pan, stirring continuously. Your wrists will ache.

- When the rice is cooked, add the sugar and carry on cooking, still stirring madly.

- Add the saffron and spices, and cook for five more minutes, then add the nuts and take off the heat. Serve piping hot.

My memories of growing up in the early 1950s in East Africa are too vivid to be entirely accurate. The stories I heard and what I experienced are hard to disentangle. I do recall that I didn't fit in and was always confused about the country where I'd been born. Was it Africa? An extension of India? Or Little England, only sunny?

Jinja was where the two wealthiest Asian agro businessmen and industrialists had mansions with English-style arboreal and formal rose gardens. (The pukka sahibs spoiled the illusion by getting their gardeners to cut wacky topiary – trumpeting elephants and serene Buddha bushes.) Nile waters rush out through Jinja and head up to Sudan and Egypt. In 1947 a dam and hydropower station were installed there. We drove over on Sundays to gaze at the awesome construction, and as the water fell with colossal force, fishermen placed themselves on perilous rocks to catch bright silver fish that seemed to fly on invisible wings. I thought they were fairy mermaids and refused to eat any.

Other early memories wash in of those times. All those long vacations spent in Mombasa with a beautiful widowed friend of my mother, Mubinabai, and her daughters. The town was easy, wafted dulcet pleasures and made you shed caution. There were not many resident Europeans (though still plenty of fun sailors), which made it feel like our place. They told me that once upon a time there had been opulent white villas on the beautiful seafronts where the *mzungus* lived. They had since gone to Nairobi and other more clement climes, leaving the abodes to rich Asians, who never tired of telling you that their houses were made for a Mr Harris or a Sir Alfred, imperious gentlemen of standing.

I remember being taken by Mubinabai to a legendary Asian business family whose house was like a museum. Their grand living room had antique Persian rugs, Ali Baba pots and authentic ancient Egyptian artefacts, including pharaonic attire. There were gold crowns and jewels belonging to various kings and queens of yore and old Chinese pottery in sea blue and grass green, and ochre covered every wall. Two elephant tusks embedded in mahogany stood proudly at the door. Everything was beautifully clean and polished. Overwhelmed, I had to sit quietly as we were served *chai*, pomegranate juice and *vitumbua*, delicious rice-and-coconut dough-nuts. My greasy hand left marks on the furniture, wiped surreptitiously by my anxious escort. I was never taken there again.

Vitumbua

1 lb pudding rice	1 cup grated coconut cream
1 egg	1 tsp dried yeast (not fast-acting)
1 tsp sugar	1 tbsp warm water
½ cup boiling water	1 cup whole milk
A few crushed cardamom seeds	1 cup granulated sugar
(don't turn them to powder)	Sunflower oil for frying

- You need to buy a small *karai* for this – the tiniest one you can find, enough to hold a cup of water. A nice round shape helps.

- Soak the rice for five hours.

- Mix the teaspoon of sugar and tablespoon of warm water, add yeast and leave to foam.

- Add the coconut to the boiling water and dissolve.

- Drain the rice well.

- Liquidize with the diluted coconut cream and milk.

- Add the yeast and cardamom to this mixture, cover and leave in a warm spot until the next morning.

- Now mix in the rest of the sugar and the egg.

- Heat oil in the *karai* until a small bit of bread rises fast when you drop it in. Gently pour a ladle of the mixture into the *karai* and leave until you see bubbles at the top, like you do when cooking Scotch pancakes. You must not turn the doughnut too soon. Keep your nerve.

- Turn over and cook on the other side.

- Sprinkle with icing sugar if you want to really indulge.

The streets of the old town in Mombasa were narrow and mysterious with human traffic, animals and bicycles. The long Arab presence still pervaded everything. Pavements were extensions of small shops selling general goods. A glance upwards revealed jutting balconies – some alive with songbirds trapped in rusty cages and coiled sweet jasmine plants, others with quiet old men and women who sat chewing *paan*, throwing nut shells on passing heads, smoking hookahs and looking down on a world they seemed already to have left. In parts of Mombasa you found a medley of mock European and Indian exteriors, copycat buildings which looked false and pathetic trying so hard to be outside Africa in Africa. In poorer areas until much later, Asians lived in cramped homes with corrugated-tin roofs. African homes were indescribably worse, on land with no drainage or basic facilities.

Plagues came to those areas, and the miserable abodes of the poor were burned to ashes.

Not far from this sultry town were cashew and almond plantations. You could pick the fruit off these nut trees, tangy, fibrous and red. It made lips swell and left tongues scratched. *Badam*, our name for almonds, were considered brain food, and my mother used to give me five every morning as I made my way to school. Ten when exams were on, or her almond toffee with a big glass of boiled milk.

Almond Toffee

1 cup almonds

1 egg white

2 oz butter

⅓ cup jaggery, grated, or soft brown sugar

- Process the almonds in a whizzer, then grind in a pestle and mortar until the oil starts to appear.

- Melt jaggery or sugar with the butter.

- Whip the egg white until stiff.

- Knead the almonds, egg and the buttery sugar/jaggery together.

- Roll out so it is flat and thick – use icing sugar to keep the rolling pin from sticking on the dough.

- Cut into squares and leave to dry out.

At the age of five (I think), I went missing at the long beach in Mombasa. In a flowery sundress, barefoot, with red ribbons in my hair, holding a canvas bag, chewing and sucking on a stick of sugar cane, I had set off to collect shells. I found thirty-two, including a perfect conch. It got dark.

Still greedily gathering shells but scared, I came upon a cheery Asian family who insisted I should eat some barbecued maize and squabs before they would help me retrace my steps. I was happy enough to do that until one young man with wavy hair whispered to ask if he could take me to the bushes to relieve myself. I said I didn't go to the bushes but in the sea and went off. He followed me and all I remember is that he opened my plait, stuffed my red ribbon into a pocket and then pulled me into the water. A woman from the party started shouting from the beach – her voice was full of panic as she ordered me to go to her.

By this time the sun had almost fallen into the sea and glow-worms were dancing. When we found my family, a crowd had gathered. There were fatalistic boatmen, an elegant black priest praying for those killed by the sea, half the local mosque, three gormless policemen writing out statements with short pencils, and a white man in khaki shorts. Mum was hysterical and slapped me hard. I cried. There was no need for that kind of reception really. Would she have hit me if I had washed up dead? That was Jena, though; lashed out when she was most frightened and worried for her vulnerable brood.

Mubinabai never got into the grind of housework because she loved the seaside, parties, films and long gossip time. In Mombasa Asian women, *Visi Masis*, supply food freshly cooked in their kitchens in tiffins to families. We have these suppliers in Britain too, but here they use plastic boxes and cheap minicab drivers who sometimes steal one or two delicacies. Mubinabai's favourite cook sent her sulky sons on bikes to the door. These dishes were popular because they were easily carried to the beach or parks.

Kheema Biriyani

Serves 6

1 lb fat-free minced beef (ask an Indian butcher to make it fresh from braising steak)

½ cup crispy-fried onions (you can now buy these ready-made in Indian shops)

¾ tsp salt

2 chopped red chillies

6 whole peppercorns

5 cloves

5 tbsp sunflower oil

1 tin tomatoes

2 mugs basmati rice

½ cup hulled *moong dhal*

4 onions, sliced

½ cup plain yoghourt (not Greek)

2½ tsp garlic/ginger mix

3 tsp *garam masala*

A few strands of saffron

3 cinnamon sticks

5 cardamom pods

2 oz butter

◉ Heat the oil and cook the onions until they turn brown. Miss this stage if using pre-fried onions.

- Meanwhile boil the *moong dhal* in salted water until tender but with a bite.

- Cook ginger, garlic, onions and meat in oil for ten minutes.

- Add *garam masala* and chillies, and cook for three minutes before throwing in the tomatoes.

- Cook for a further five minutes and start adding yoghourt, a tablespoon at a time, until it is absorbed. Cook for ten more minutes.

- Drain dhal.

- Soak saffron in half a cup of hot water.

- In a largish pan melt the butter and throw in the peppercorns, cloves, cinnamon sticks and cardamom pods. Cook for two minutes before you add 1½ pints of water. It will sizzle. Add salt, let it come to the boil, then cook washed rice in this for five minutes without covering. Then cover, lower heat and cook for another five. Sprinkle with saffron and the water in which it has been soaking. Leave to stand for another five.

- In an ovenproof dish, layer the meat with rice and crispy-fried onions. The final layer should be rice. Cover with a double layer of foil and bake for ten minutes – 325 °F, 170 °C, gas mark 3.

 ## Potato Patties – Meat and Vegetable

Serves 6

1 lb potatoes, boiled until soft enough to mash

½ tsp salt

Chilli powder to taste

Ajiwan seeds

2 eggs

2 cups fine semolina

Oil to fry the patties

For meat filling

½ lb fat-free minced beef

2 green chillies, chopped finely

Juice of half a lemon

1 tsp ginger/garlic mix

1 bunch fresh coriander, chopped

¾ tsp *garam masala*

4 spring onions, chopped finely

Salt to taste

For vegetable filling

1 cup frozen mixed vegetables

½ tsp cumin seeds

½ tsp chilli powder

½ tsp *amchar* (a sour powder made
    from unripe mangoes)

1 tbsp sunflower oil

1 tsp crushed garlic

Pinch of asafoetida

Salt to taste

- Mash the potatoes with the spices and salt.

Meat filling

- Dry-fry the meat in a non-stick pan, stirring all the time.

- Take off the heat and mix in the other ingredients.

- Cool.

Vegetable filling

- Heat the oil and fry the cumin seeds for a minute.

- Add all other ingredients and cook until vegetables are done and dry.

- Cool.

- All the above can be done a day ahead.

- Take a palm-size lump of potato mix and flatten it in your hand.

- Place a teaspoon of filling and carefully enclose it to make a sausage or round shape.

- ◉ Beat eggs and season.

- ◉ In a flat plate have some semolina ready.

- ◉ Dip the patties in egg, then semolina to cover completely.

- ◉ Fry these in about an inch of hot oil, turning over frequently until a lovely brown.

—————

Built on seven hills, Kampala was an altogether different place from Mombasa or Nairobi. The ambience was warm and benign in the day, but as the evening sky turned to ink, people stayed indoors or visited each other in cars. Fear loomed even in the boom years. On the coast, life began after dark; in my hometown peril was felt to be lurking and touched your flesh if you dared to walk alone after dark.

Nature in Uganda was shamelessly sensual, the flowers wild and bright and open. Waxy pink frangipani flowers filled trees which from a distance looked like they were hosting butterfly orgies. Jasmine bushes and *Raat ki Rani* (night-blooming jasmine) shrubs breathed out strong perfumes, spreading intoxication. *Champelis*, bold hibiscus flowers which pleated up as the sun set, red and purple bougainvillaea climbing up humble walls – you sometimes felt intimidated by their audacious beauty. This was Elysium, only better.

European administrators of cold blood found such natural sensuality excessive so they made their own botanical garden in Entebbe, with imported trees planted in neat circles of soil equidistant from the next and the next one, their Latin names nailed to posts. It was pretty but without wild colours or the whoosh of heavy floral scents. These gardens were good picnic spots (the grass was always trimmed, and insects seemed almost too intimidated to enter), and you had the best views of Lake Victoria from some hilly spots. Wild animals were disobedient and undaunted by the imposed order. Hippos and crocodiles colonized the water's edge, and other scary creatures were drawn to the gardens by the smells of food.

Once our extended family settled down to a long day in the gardens. Primus stoves were lit up, warming biriyani and *channa masala*. Plates were handed around and salads laid out. Strong upturned boxes with cushions were set down for the very fat folk who couldn't get up easily if ever they let themselves sink down to earth. Diluted rose perfume was sprinkled on white hankies to be used for wiping mouths. I lay down, my head resting on my folded arms, looking at the vast umbrella tree. A branch moved, moved again and stretched. It was a python with a strange lump. It coiled itself round another branch and seemed to be strangling its own long self. I couldn't move as it crushed the creature it had swallowed – possibly a puppy or a kid. Finally I let out a shriek. Chacha Ramzan and Chachi Rehmet, my corpulent uncle and matching wife, were impressively agile as they sped away from the tree, leaving the rest to gather the picnic goods. No python could possibly have had the jaws needed to swallow those two.

Channa Masala

Serves 6

3 tins chickpeas (we used to boil these ourselves over two slow days, but they were still never as soft as the tinned variety – slow cooking to drive you mad)	4 tbsp tomato purée
	1 tsp black mustard seeds
	½ tsp turmeric
	1 tsp crushed garlic
	½ tsp chilli powder
1 tbsp mixed cumin and coriander powders	½ tsp sugar
2 tbsp sunflower oil	1 tbsp tamarind extract

- Heat the oil and add mustard seeds. Cook until they splutter.

- Add all ingredients except for chickpeas, and cook for ten minutes over slow heat, stirring from time to time.

- Add the drained chickpeas and cook for five more minutes.

- Eat hot or cold.

Two parallel roads made up the main spine of Kampala. Asian shops ran along them for miles, most of them like the old *dukans*, stuffed, airless hovels. In the posh bit, opposite the High Court and a fine lawn, were a couple of elegant European shops with white mannequins and carpets on the floor, uniformed doormen keeping out the coloured riff-raff. Apartheid, the discreet sort that did not need to proclaim itself with crass laws and notices, was quietly established.

The Europeans lived at the top of the beautiful hills, the seven hills of Kampala.

They had their own schools, clubs, sundowner verandas, menacing hedges and fences. Dogs too, trained to bark when they saw black and brown strangers. Rich Asians lived lower down the hill in their opulent homes, with gardens, fences, gates and dogs trained to bark and attack any unknown black passers-by. Poorer Asians lived nearer the bottom, too many per room packed into small but decent dwellings. Africans were in the sodding pits. They kept no dogs.

We lived in a tiny flat above the marketplace in Kampala. One day a young man ran in through the open door, carrying a packet of stolen '*chai* toast' – dry, crisp, sweet, orangey baked toast with caraway seeds which was dipped into tea and eaten for breakfast. We heard the ululations of a crowd in pursuit, building up joyously to the moment they would corner him. Leaders of the mob approached the flat and were met by my mother, 4 foot 10 inches tall, round and fleshy like a soft apricot. She smiled and held up the *chai* toast in one hand and 20 cents in the other, telling them in Swahili not to bother her good servant Dawoodi who had simply forgotten to pay. They shouted a bit more, then skulked off, leaving the thief in our care. He was in the bathroom, shivering, his teeth rattling in the midday heat. His sweat was profuse and overpowering. Jena made him milky tea with half a cup of sugar, boiled until it rose nearly out of the pan. He sat on the floor, dunked and wolfed down his hard-earned *chai* toast, eight slices, while my mother lectured him on honesty. The next day he brought her an enormous bristly brown coconut as a present. Nicked probably. A row of shirts hanging on a line in the balcony disappeared.

Small and easily swamped, brave yet jumpy, the settlers reached for the future in fertile and giving East Africa, unaware that within two decades they would find themselves at an abyss, and most would disappear from that promised land. How could they have anticipated the fall? The war now over, business brisk, for most East African Asians things could only get better, or so they thought.

4 *The Sun Drops, 1955–60*

JAPANI HAD BEEN WITH us for years, cleaning, child-minding and helping my mother cook when she took in orders for weddings, births and deaths. His face was round and shiny as a clean plate. Most servants had to surrender their 'impossible' African names when they worked for Asians and Europeans, who baptized them 'John' or 'Joe' or 'Joan' or 'Jean' or 'Mary', short occidental names, easy to shout, sounding like blows to the ear. Christian servants named after virtues – Innocent, Immaculate, Devotee – were relabelled, so too were Sunshine and Moonshine (twin sisters, both ayahs), Jacaranda, Cheetah and Victoriana. Always mindful of his dignity, Japani had arranged his own renaming. His favourite Hindi film ditty was titled 'Mera Jutta Hai Japani': 'My shoes are Japanese; these trousers were made in England; on my head a Russian cap, but my heart is purely Indian.' It was a freedom song he couldn't have understood.

Or maybe he did and didn't want us to know that he too longed for foreigners to let go so Africans could regain their lands and hopes. Indian independence in 1947 showed the end was nigh for the seemingly invincible global British Empire. Too many East African Asians still clung to the hope that it could not happen in 'backward' Africa for another century or so. Across in Kenya, the secretive Mau

Mau movement was determined to remove white rule by any means necessary.

World War II had drained Europe, and an exhausted Britain had to prioritize national reconstruction. France still believed that it could hang on to its African colonies, using élite black 'Frenchmen' to create an impression of change. The British were more pragmatic. In 1946/7 a government committee report recommended a programme for self-government for Africa. It would be organized with the minimum of friction, the maximum of goodwill for the nation and the greatest possible degree of efficiency. The African public-school élite, prepared over two decades, would take over. The report concluded that within a generation, a handover to total self-rule was entirely feasible.

Life, though, did not, never does, follow carefully assessed British political plans. Subject countries in Africa were calling for self-determination on their own terms and within their timescale, and senior figures in the British establishment were forced to accept that withdrawal would be determined by factors beyond their reach. Momentum built up. Rioting in Ghana in 1948 led to a hasty British departure in 1951. Uganda was well managed and resourced, had an enviable infrastructure and no impatient rebellions. Its climate and temperament were mild; the Christian ethos had been embraced by the most powerful tribes, and it made Ugandans patient and less alienated from their rulers. However, here too the calls for freedom were starting up.

In Kenya, white settlers – mostly white supremacists who had grabbed the best land and most privileged lives – were alarmed at both the rise of black insurgency and the British loss of nerve. Asians were held back from purchasing land there as in the other two territories. In the course of the Mau Mau rebellion, led by the Kikuyu in Kenya, both sides were savage. Doom and horror spread through East Africa. The rebels and those suspected of Mau Mau membership were incarcerated, indiscriminately tortured and hanged. In 2005, a shocking new book revealed the scale of the response. A hundred and fifty thousand were herded into gulags and systematically brutalized. Thousands died of ill treatment or of the typhoid rife in the camps.[1] The story was spun in favour of the British.[2]

New evidence has emerged to show that there were some Asian anti-imperialists who joined or tacitly supported the Mau Mau, including the Indian High Commissioner, Appa Pant, and Makhan Singh,[3] who brought trade unionism to Kenya. Most transplanted Asians, however, feared that independence would cast them adrift. They were scapegoats in the story of Empire and also their own worst enemies. Dent Ocaya Lakidi described their position at the time and through to independence:

> The real and proper colonisers of East Africa were white Britons, not brown Asians. The white colonisers were, moreover, culturally arrogant, politically dominating as well as patronising and economically exploitative. Yet in the end they came to be more highly regarded than the politically powerless, culturally aloof, sometimes arrogant and economically weaker though equally exploitative Asians. Why?[4]

Japani had strange carved scars on his arms, and the whites of his eyes were sometimes dark pink when he came back after taking a day off. Once when I had a jigger in my toe, he cooked a long sewing needle on a candle flame until it was black. Then he dug in while I screamed. That was normal – it bloody hurt a lot and had to be endured until broken bits of the whole worm had been hooked out. This time, he licked my blood and chanted in Swahili, '*Mzungu aene ulaya, Mwafrika apate uhuru*' (Let the white man leave; let the African take his freedom). Later I discovered that 'Mau Mau' was an acronym for this wish.

Even though he earned less than the lowest-paid black servants in the neighbourhood, Japani stayed faithful to us, oddly protective of this irregular family. He supplemented his wages making pickles, which he sold to my mother's friends and in the market on Saturdays.

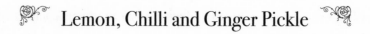 Lemon, Chilli and Ginger Pickle

5 fat limes or lemons (unwaxed)	**A saucepan of water**
5 green chillies, half sliced through	**A dozen or so small pieces of peeled**
½ tbsp turmeric	**fresh ginger**
3 tsp salt	**1 cup freshly squeezed lemon juice**
1 tsp sugar	

- ⊚ Boil the lemons or limes whole for one minute. Leave to cool, then cut into chunks.

- ⊚ Wash hands well. Rub turmeric, salt and sugar into the lemons, ginger and chillies. Handle carefully – it will burn your hands a bit.

- ⊚ Leave on a tray in a warming cupboard for forty-eight hours.

- Place in a sterile container with a tight lid.

- Add lemon juice and sugar until liquid reaches well above the lemons and chillies.

- Leave in a cool place and stir every two days with a sterilized spoon.

- After three weeks the pickle is ready to eat.

~~~~~~~~~~

When men came looking for loan paybacks from my father, Japani was his smiling bouncer. One evening, Papa dived into the large, rusty dustbin. Japani perched on the lid, relaxed and pleasant, as he fended off panting small-town desperadoes on the chase.

'Where's bwana? *Iko wapi*, where's he? Go get him.'

'*Jambo sana*. Would you like some tea? Or special Japani juice?'

'No. Get bwana Kassim, go, quick, tell him to come now, *upesi, upesi*, hurry up, *sala junglee*.'

'Certainly. But where shall I go to get him please?'

'*Aree shenzi*, go into the house, *haraka*, call bwana.'

'He is out, for a very long time.'

'Open the door.'

'What you think I have a key?' Japani then started kicking the bin with his dangly legs, aware that Kassim was shuffling about with terrible discomfort. They left. Papa stank of rank food, his suit was covered in papaya juice, and his fawn leather shoes never recovered.

Ratan the *panwallah* was a fat fool stuck in a hole in the wall he filled to absolute capacity. He spread the story, his voice gelatinous with mucus and spite. 'Did you hear, Kassim fellow again?' as he filled and folded the small leaf with mystifying bits and pastes: '*Sala*, never pays anyone, shows off plenty, you know the guy? I don't give him any credit. The City Bar brothers went looking for the joker for their money, he had to hide in the dustbin. Such a *fujo*. English suit covered in papaya juice.' Laugh, laugh, laugh, until their eyes watered.

Whatever they said, I knew my Papa was smart and often like a hugely entertaining character in a beloved book. He briefly ran a bookshop with an outdoor café festooned with orange and magenta bougainvillaea. A blackboard invited customers to write views on books they had bought or illegally borrowed: 'Jinna book very interesting. English a bit difficult.' Sometimes his creditors chalked up insults: 'Bastard pay up. Wipe your buttocks with your book pages.' I think Papa was happy in his bookshop.

One day he took me to the little park. Bought me a Vimto with a straw. Drops of the dark red nectar splashed my dress. He didn't mind. My mum, I knew, would roll out the endless moans about my bad ways and her sad life. Like sad Hindi songs, they were part of the natural melodies of existence. On Sundays, a small brass band – all polished and smart in black, red and white – played marching tunes in the bandstand. Papa and I sat on a bench as he remembered the beautiful parks in London where people danced and had tea and listened to men of big ideas (like him) given boxes to stand on while they held forth. Papa was wistful that day. He must have known the bookshop was done with, had sunk into a heap of debt.

A sojourn in the pharmaceutical export/import business was briefer – his partner fled the country after some imports were found by doctors to be contaminated. Japani took away thousands of leftover Aspro tablets to spread around his village. Papa's most barmy idea was the Damji Oxford Hat Emporium that never was. An English memsahib's fashion house was closing down, so Papa borrowed money and bought up the stock of elegant headwear. Very cheap, a bargain, he said. The hats languished unsold. My favourites were a brown velvet cap that looked like a squashed dog (cockroaches liked this one too) and a white cloche of swan feathers. I remember others – a neat, red Jackie O hat, a gold turban, and a wide-brimmed purple hat with a violet net veil and a brooch displaying a silhouette of an elegant Victorian lady. These items were eventually dispatched to the drama teacher in my primary school.

Then there were the many jobs with car firms which quickly bored him. In between the bouts of ennui, Kassim got himself a roaring income selling pristine, proud, polished new models. Like beads on a rosary he would go through the brands and models, getting such pleasure just calling out the names of cars he had sold in his life: Standard Vanguard, Humber Super Snipe, Hillman, Morris Minor, Austin, Wolseley, Jowett Juniper, MG, Vauxhall, Riley.

Once, when money came his way, Kassim gave Japani a pair of his English cufflinks in a typical fit of largesse. That Sunday, as always when getting ready for his one afternoon off, Japani polished his skin with soap, greased his hair with lavender hair oil, and put on his best shirt and fixed the links on the cuffs, which until then had been left open. He walked tall. Only before he reached the door, he bumped into my obnoxious cousin Shamsu, who grabbed his arm and accused him of stealing the links.

I hated Shamsu. His neck was thicker than his spindly thighs; his skin smelled of rancid butter. Every night he drank neat whisky, then went off to his black whores, women he said were dirty enough to satisfy him. Then he would zigzag home perilously in his cream-coloured Merc and call for his silent wife, who had to undress him. Sometimes he beat her with clothes hangers until he finally passed out. I had once seen him slap the face of the old ayah who had reared all his children. She, the black drudge, had dared to kiss his baby son, so Shamsu lashed out.

Papa told Shamsu to let Japani go. The brute refused: 'They are all thieves, these *kala junglees*. Mother-fucking thieves, stupid too. Only understand the stick and shoe. No culture, not like us. Kassim Uncle, you are spoiling this one.' He kicked Japani on the shin and I ran to stand between them, crying, an infant protest against injustice, rage without power. Shamsu pushed me away, then stopped abruptly. My mother came upon the scene, the one person who, for some reason, Shamsu genuflected to. She told Japani to go. As he left the house, he was crying. His ironed white shirt was slightly torn at the shoulders. This was an everyday story in urban East Africa at the time. It took *malai* on bread to help me recover, my comfort food, made by Jena to soothe her youngest, hyper-emotional child who could never understand why things had to be just so.

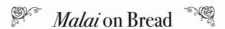 *Malai* on Bread

½ pint full-cream fresh organic milk   **Slices of soft white bread**
Sugar to sprinkle

- Boil, then simmer the milk for five minutes, stirring gently to stop it sticking to the bottom too much.
- Let the milk rest for a few hours. A layer of thickish skin forms at the top.
- Skim this off carefully and plop into a bowl.
- Spread on bread, sprinkle with sugar. It peps up a bad day.

East African Asians have yet to recognize or regret their complicity in the degradation of black Africans in Uganda, Kenya, and Tanganyika and Zanzibar. Most, like old and young British imperialists, prefer revisionist exoneration. Who wouldn't? An Asian businessman in Kampala, quoted in a sociological study, was exceptionally honest: 'We have not been acting properly towards Africans – acting selfishly, calling them "kalas" (blackies).' The author went on to comment: 'What Africans cannot forget is the disdain in which the Asian had been holding the African since Asians came and settled... they know the Asians detest their darker colour and physiognomy. The Asian talks of integration but will he integrate? Of course not. The Asian males had African concubines but no African could approach an Asian woman.'[5] Few Asians knew or cared that, before the British arrived, many of the tribes in Uganda had had a sophisticated system of governance, justice and a profitable agrarian economy.

Shamsu was loaded; his father even more so, his uncles too. Between them they owned thirteen posh cars, twenty racehorses, seventy workers and several businesses. They were coarse, poorly educated and prickly. My papa was cultivated, had been to England and Paris, and thought of himself as a highly bred gentleman. So why were we so poor so often? Oh, he tried all right, but he had no killer instinct. But he did have pride. He hated being patronized, and you could see the flames of defiant self-respect burning in his eyes when one of his ventures delivered what he promised.

To celebrate one temporary success, he bought Jena a gold pendant in the shape of a Chinese dragon, an ivory bangle and an intricate silver model rickshaw, tender, dainty gifts she treasured forever. The neighbours said she was a fool, should have demanded some 22-carat gold instead, that Kassim would soon spend the cash like water from a tap. They knew him well. Instead of paying off debts (which his wife was so very good at managing), he decided to use the bulk of the bounty to fast-track his son into Anglophilia. It was 1955. I was still sucking my thumb and inseparable from a small piece of Jena's old sari, my *lala* (meaning 'sleep' in Swahili). My brother was fun, always sweet to me and protective. I gave him my *lala* at the airport. He promised to bring it back safe. Japani flung himself on to the red dust, wailing and raging against the loud, malevolent aeroplane pulsating on the narrow runway at Entebbe Airport. For years he had loved my brother as his own, never having made enough money to marry or have children. Now Babu, his boy, was off to England. Jena beat her chest and blubbed as her only son rushed elatedly towards the plane. The bird took off and the noise stopped abruptly. Our gathered clan stood paralysed with grief. Papa walked away without a word.

Diasporic folk are prone to emotional excess at travel termini, but here was a moment of something else. The family seemed to have sensed that innocence and optimism had flown off too as the cotton clouds regrouped. In spite of the chaos and perpetual disappointment at home, we still knew hope and joy. After this day, despair came to stay, and our lives slowly began to putrefy. For weeks after Babu left, said my mother, I walked sleepless and speechless around the house until exhaustion overcame me. They found me curled up under the table or behind the sofa or the kitchen door.

Japani suddenly disappeared in 1956, and we were told by a Kampala policeman that our servant was a Mau Mau agent, and that we were lucky he hadn't massacred and eaten us. I refused to believe the liars. I have never forgotten him, my Japani, the sweetest, most loyal man I knew then.

With Babu and Japani gone, and Papa in dire straits again, I was becoming a quiet, glum child. So my mum begged and borrowed cash to send me to a nursery school set up by and for the swanky people in our mosque. A show was announced for *Khushiyali*, our annual July festival, outside our community mosque. It was a lovely event with music, food, nice clothes and performances. And lo! The best-connected kids got all the big parts – impetuous kings, adorable princesses, Bo Peep. I was given a desultory role, to remind me of my place, I reckon. I was the maid in 'Sing a Song of Sixpence', hanging up the clothes and pecked on the nose by a blackbird, a horrid little boy in a black cape. His father was the *Mukhi*, our mosque leader, a big man with a devil child.

On the night, the chosen young ones panicked and yelled for their ayahs, lined up at the back in their pink-and-white uniforms, pretty maids all in a row, paid a pittance to bestow maternal love night and day while the mummies dressed up and went out for coffee mornings. And tea parties. And dinner dances. I put up my hand and said I could do the whole lot. A desperate teacher grabbed me and pulled me away. My day had come. Not before time. I think this is when I became a socialist.

I remember the compound full of flowering trees and shrubs, their bright colours dancing in the sun. The pungent scent of flowering *Raat ki Rani* was thickening the air to syrup. I gazed up at the grand three-sided staircase that swept up and up and up to the beautiful snow-white mosque, which threw its mock Taj Mahal towers to the blue sky. It was covered in necklaces of fairy lights and bunting.

At the bottom of the steps, a stage had been set up and red carpet laid out in the front rows, where the *wabenzi* people with Mercedes sat on cushions. As the sun finally set, crackling music filled the compound and young couples floated on stage to play *dandia* – the stick dance. The tabla player went into a trance; the girls swirled, moved their hips and shoulders with abandon. Their scarves, meant to discourage lewd attention, became inducements. Their breasts jiggled.

I was in a pink taffeta dress with lace and a satin belt. It was noisy, my dress, even more noisy than the rude rustles Papa made with his newspapers when he wanted guests to leave. On my head was a cardboard crown with sequins which shone more brightly than all those real jewels in the crowd. My mummy was given a special place in the front, not far from Masa and Masi, her cousins. They were very rich but so fat that he had to put a towel on his stomach to stop the steering wheel creasing his suits when he drove his big cars.

I was not that poor, wretched little Yassi any more. I was a queen at last, eating bread and honey. I stood up, and just as I began 'Humpty Dumpty', there was a commotion, some bloke shouting under the arches.

It was my father making another scene. I knew that mood – it would grow and grow like the clouds in the afternoon before the daily downpour. Two men grabbed him, and he got even more noisy. But eventually they pulled him away. I gathered myself and found my voice. 'Sing a Song of Sixpence'. And 'The Queen of Hearts'. And 'Jack and Jill'. And they smiled and clapped. Then the *Mukhi* came down to me and smiled – great gold teeth. And into my hands he placed a bar of Cadbury's chocolate. One and a half glasses of full-cream milk.

This was my mother's favourite story about me. She told it to everyone, my beloved ancient mariner.

We were still in the one-bedroomed flat over the marketplace, which I often wandered through with Japani. It smelled African, of sunny sweat and earthy animal flesh and shit, and through these wafted the scent of sexy, musky mango and papaya, or bright, sharp pineapple. The noise of cars and doomed creatures and dust (yes, dust seems to shout in such places) competed with the yells of the traders – 'Come mama nyloni beans, Terylene radishes, better than English.' Japani stopped for smokes and long chats in a language I didn't understand. Sometimes he looked very worried, at other times he picked me up and put me on his shoulders.

Home life seemed infused with despair, the misery of misfits. My brother wasn't around to lift the mood with his upbeat jokes and whistled tunes. At least there was one less person to share the bathroom, toilet, living room and food. My sister moved to my brother's old bed in the living room. I stayed stuck between my parents. The mattresses, older than I was, were lumpy and smelled of babies and unspeakable other stuff. Jena sprinkled Johnson's baby powder over the sheets to make them smell innocent. My ears were peppered with babble from Papa, whose brain never seemed to lie down and rest a little. I was the warning lesson of impetuous sex, and the barrier to any further thoughtless carnal acts. They kept me there until I was almost a teenager, when they had lost all desire for one another.

There were few endearments, many sudden rows and slammed doors. Games of hide-and-seek were played with money, imaginative at first, later grim and full of animus. Papa came home with cash in his pockets – bonuses if he had applied himself or gambling gains snatched from rakish companions. The ecstasy of wine and winnings passed into deep sleep. Jena would then steal a small cut and hide it between the folds of her saris, in her bras or in other sly places. After her death, old banknotes were found carefully concealed in a brand-new bra still in the box.

City Bar was a popular haunt for boastful, respectable Asian men, who gathered in its smoky lounge after they had cleansed themselves of sin in mosques and temples, and dropped the ladies off to be good at home. One day Papa left my siblings alone in the car outside the bar and went in for a drink or a deal. It turned into a long, happy binge. My mother stormed in. No woman had ever entered the place to reclaim her man. An old man who was there remembered the drama:

So small she was, but she made us tremble, your mother that day. She put you on the counter, spoke and her words were her tears. She was telling us we men were fools, failing everybody, ourselves also. She was wearing a simple long dress, and a *pacheli*, a scarf with maps on it. No jewellery, no make up, but so beautiful. She had such lips and eyes, such courage. I left feeling so bad. My wife afterwards said Jenabai should have been born a man. No, I said, she was a perfect woman. My wife didn't like that very much.

Papa was humiliated. He grabbed her finger and broke it. It remained an accusing curve all her life, and Papa, who was never physically violent, gave up gambling in City Bar for good. His wagers moved to life itself.

Jena by this time had started to call her husband '*seth*', 'boss man'. It was obviously ironic. My profligate father squandered money, feelings, family, his own life. He was a news junkie of burning intelligence, a connoisseur of many good things and little business sense, an Anglophile who loved the great writers. He was elegant, frequently eloquent, exciting, yes, but in the end always disappointing.

During the terrifyingly bad times, or when Papa had disappeared, Jena, covering her shame with conceit – 'I will kill my children before begging for money from these people' – would go behind closed doors and emerge with rations or a little money to see us through to the next time. After some of these humbling expeditions, she would cry as if she had been violated. How they talked and blackened her name – what was she doing at the back of the shops? You can imagine the kind of thing in a society in which shame stalked females and sought to trample on their names and hopes. She had to come up with clever ideas to make money go further. We had curried tinned sardines – yuk – and various lentils, sometimes for weeks on end. Serving one chicken over four meals was a feat she was most proud of. When I feel mean or guilty about overindulgence, I still do this with one large bird.

Many Times Chicken

1 large corn-fed chicken	3 cloves
5 peppercorns	2 sticks cinnamon
1 tsp crushed garlic	2 chopped tomatoes

- Skin the chicken and boil whole in a large pot with the spices, garlic and tomatoes, and salt to taste.
- Cool overnight in the fridge.

Recipe 1: Chicken Toast

Meat taken from the legs of the chicken (keep the bones)	2 tins sweetcorn
½ tsp freshly milled pepper	2 fresh, finely chopped green chillies
2 tbsp butter	½ tsp turmeric
	A bunch of spring onions

- Melt butter and fry the spring onions for five minutes.
- Add all the other ingredients and stir-fry.
- Serve on hot toast.

Recipe 2: Red Chicken Pita

⊙   Tear off the breast meat in large chunks and lay down in a single layer in a baking tray.

Sauce

½ cup Greek yoghourt	5 tbsp tomato purée
1 tsp chilli powder	½ tsp paprika powder
1 tsp crushed ginger	1 tsp mixture of coriander and fennel seeds, ground in a coffee grinder

⊙   Mix all the sauce ingredients and cook in a pan over slow heat for ten minutes.

⊙   Spread over the chicken.

⊙   Stick under a grill until slightly charred on top – be careful, you don't want to burn the sauce.

⊙   Serve stuffed into pita bread with a green salad. Back home my mum rolled the red chicken in *rotli* with sliced red onions.

Recipe 3: Green Chicken Pillau

⊙   Take off all the other meat and marinate in green chutney.

Green Chutney

1 bunch of coriander, well washed	3 green chillies
½ cup cashew nuts	A little sugar
Juice of 2 limes	

⊙   Whiz the above together.

1 cup basmati rice	2 cups water
Lots of frozen peas to make up for the small amount of chicken	1½ tsp salt
	1 tsp turmeric

½ cup mixture of cumin seeds, cloves,   2 tbsp oil
    cinnamon sticks, cardamom pods
    and peppercorns

- Heat the oil and add the cumin and the rest of the whole spices.
- Stir for three minutes.
- Add turmeric and carry on stirring for two minutes.
- Add water and salt; when the water boils, add the rice.
- Let it boil for four minutes, then cover and turn down the heat and cook for another three minutes. Add frozen peas.
- Spread rice on a baking tray.
- Spread chicken mix over the rice and cover with foil.
- Bake for ten minutes at medium temperature (325°F, 170°C, gas mark 3).
- Before serving, you can sprinkle with almonds flash-fried in butter until brown. We were too poor for that.

Recipe 4: Chicken Broth

Chicken bones   A variety of vegetables that need using
1 tsp garlic/ginger paste   up (frozen stuff works too)
6 whole peppercorns   2 oz butter
2 chopped fresh red chillies

- Boil all the bones with a mixture of carrots, potatoes, peas, beans, spinach, anything really, plus a teaspoon of crushed garlic/ginger mixture and whole peppercorns.
- Strain the soup.
- Throw away the bones or give them to teething babies.

- Melt the butter and, when it starts to turn brown, fry the vegetables at high heat, throwing in chopped red chillies. Mush up.

- Serve broth in a bowl. On a side plate pile up the veg on thick wedges of baguette. This is just brilliant on those days when you have a sore throat or no will to live.

While we were having to scrimp, other folk around us were amassing wealth, and it piled up in their homes and as soft flesh on their bodies. Food got richer and people eyed the amount of ghee floating on top of curries – less than 2 inches made you low class. (These days you are thought low class beyond redemption if you have any fat showing up in your cooking at all.) Vast mock-silver platters were brought to mosque, garnished and beautiful, to provoke both envy and admiration. *Kuku paka* and fresh bread, goat curry, prawn medleys wafted their expensive smells through the prayer halls, and it was hard to sit still. Sometimes Mum bought a *kuku paka*, and on those nights I went to bed with my nightdress splashed with pale yellow sauce and smelling of coconut, dreaming of the next time, possibly.

Kuku Paka

Serves 4–5

1 large chicken, skinned and cut into largish pieces

1 tbsp crushed ginger
2 tsp crushed garlic

1 bunch fresh coriander leaves washed. Keep half and zap the other half in a
   food processor with 3 tbsp water and chillies

2 hot green chillies

1 tsp turmeric

1½ tins coconut milk

1 medium onion, chopped

3 tbsp oil

1 tin chopped tinned tomatoes or
   4 fresh chopped tomatoes

½ cup unsalted cashew nuts chopped
   (not pulverized)

Juice of half a lime

- Mix together the lime juice, garlic, ginger and coriander/chilli mix. Add a tablespoon of oil and rub this mixture over chicken pieces.

- Lay these out in an ovenproof dish and bake at a high temperature (400 °F, 200 °C, gas mark 6) for fifteen minutes, then lower to medium (325 °F, 170 °C, gas mark 3) and carry on cooking for a further ten minutes. Turn over twice while baking.

- Meanwhile in a saucepan, using remaining oil, fry the onions, chopped as small as possible.

- When these start to brown, add the tomatoes, turmeric and cashews, and stir-fry for a good ten minutes over medium heat.

- Add coconut milk and let the whole lot simmer quietly, humming away and stirring from time to time. It should end up a lovely thick yellow sauce

- Take off the heat and add the rest of the coriander.

- Now pour over the chicken, return to a hot oven, and cook for fifteen minutes.

- Serve with good, crusty white bread.

- The following can be added by top rich, luxury wives:

Hard-boiled eggs cut in half

Hard-boiled quail's eggs

Flaked almonds fried in a little butter

½ cup double cream added to the sauce

The old Indian caste system was replaced by competitive consumerism, less rigid but more crass. From people who had long lived parsimoniously to fend off black criminals and to fool their demanding relatives, canny competitors and taxmen, they turned into the new showy bourgeoisie. After so many arduous years, of course they wanted to have it all and show it all. Cupboards with glass doors became the focal points in sitting rooms, crammed full of things. They displayed unused tea sets, dinner services, brass statues of angels and gods and goddesses, vases, ornamental chests covered in semi-precious stones, incense holders, over-decorated prayer books, carved oil lamps, sandalwood boxes and (for those who were finally able to travel for leisure) cheap souvenirs from Egypt (how they showed off King Tut in plastic!), India and Pakistan. An old man, speaking for thousands like him, told me many times over, 'The fifties was the golden time, the best. We were not worried about anything. Why should we? It was really paradise.'

Public show was everything and there was no space for the sad, mad, broken and possessed. Genetic flaws made you an outcast. The shame of having a disabled family member or mental illness drove people to extraordinary cruelty. You heard the howls of tethered humans from garages and sheds as you had tea and samosas. Sometimes the priests and imams would be called in to exorcize bad spirits in rebellious daughters. There were severe physical assaults, and occasionally the kind gods took the poor souls into custody.

Dowries were no longer simply money; they had to include various goods – velvet settees, full dinner and bedlinen sets, elaborately embroidered Belgian tablecloths, honeymoon abroad, sometimes a car.[6] *Durzis* (tailors) were busier than they had ever been; people now wore clothes not until they tore but until they bored the wearer. The *hajam*, the barber who performed circumcisions, said the celebrations that followed were getting as big as Asian weddings. An astute man, he bought a building which he made into three halls for parties. He became so rich, he started taking Sundays off.

We too had a small glass cupboard, a hand-me-down from Shamsu, always buying bigger ones year on year. Ours contained photographs, my father's precious books, rosaries, and, yes, my school cups and prizes for all to praise and admire. Right in front were Jena's little silver rickshaw and ivory bangle. Mind you, thrift was still considered a virtue, even among those who had accumulated enough wealth for five generations. The four flats along our corridor bought cheap paint together; a sick green oil-based paint was the collective choice in all the years of my child-hood. The whole neighbourhood must have purchased that colour wholesale; you couldn't escape it, slopped on every wall, mushy pea soup pressing in on you.

On the outside the buildings owned by Asians developed their own vernacular, a sort of Asian Art Deco with curves, fin and sun motifs, chalky pastel colours – copycat American movie façades made by Indian craftsmen using black labour. Next door in Mama Kuba's wide glass cupboard were a silver-topped stick like the flashy ones used by Hollywood tap dancers, a whole shelf of fancy cigarette lighters and her gold jewellery. No thief ever dared touch her possessions. She had a bangle made of orange gold, shaped like a cobra, to be worn on the upper arm. It could never get up her undulating and flabby arms, but she displayed it to warn the world of her malevolence.

Mama Kuba, my Ma, my beloved adopted granny, the only one I had, was a formidable woman with large grey eyes at once steely and beautiful. Mama Kuba means 'big mother' in Swahili. And she was. She smoked Player's cigarettes and wore silk robes smoked in *oudh* but was a devout Sunni Muslim, prayed five times a day, fasted during Ramadan, had been to Mecca on hajj twice. Her faith was supreme; all others, she said, were the Devil's webs, trapping the ignorant to be dropped into the burning pits. Shias in particular, who should have known better.

Four husbands had been dumped along the long road in from the coast, where Ma had arrived as a teenager to be married off to her first husband, a distant uncle, much older than herself but good and kind, she always said. He was one of the railway workers, 'but a supervisor, you know. Hard life they had. So many wounds. Died slowly of blood poisoning after foot got cut on broken glass on the track.' He left her with a baby in her belly who also died. She never forgave the British. Then there were three more, each a father of boys and one of Femi, the only daughter.

Femi's skin was ebony, and therefore she was born blighted. (Was her father a *kala*? they all asked.) Ma spread white talcum powder on her daughter's face, which made her look like a scary African mask. Ma's discarded husbands weren't allowed to visit, but they kept her supplied with what she demanded. The most devoted of them, a grocer in Mombasa, sent over dried prawns – stank up the whole building – rice, ghee, oil, flour, lentils and, during Eid, brightly coloured sweetmeats. My mother thought it was deeply unfair. Still married, she was virtually a lone parent, while Ma had all this from husbands long gone. Perhaps Mama Kuba left while her men were still hungry for her.

Femi kicked off her bad-skin karma by capturing sweet Latif, whose cheeks were as pink as pink ice cream. She wore metallic hairclips in brilliant colours. Sometimes she twisted her hair to make two little horns on either side of her head; sometimes a long plait was wound round it, a halo to frame her happy, painted face. Today a grandmother of eight, Femi wears a grey hijab in Bolton and refuses to recollect the vibrant woman she once was. She too says I will go to hell with all the other misguided Shias.

Ma's eldest son escaped at eighteen to live with a tarty woman with gold teeth who wore bright red lipstick and short dresses. On being told this news, Ma's curses could be heard in the marketplace below. Local African traders believed Mama Kuba was a demonic mythical creature who needed to be pacified for the rains to fall and things to grow. They made her offerings. The only beggar who dared to come to her door was gentle George, the *maskini* with elephantiasis who had a host of insects nesting in the deep crevices of his thickened skin. Ma tended to him, softly, with Christ's humility.

Intimidated by their mother, the other two sons, Hassan and Abu, stayed boy-men. Eventually two young wives were imported from Pakistan – Almira, whom we've already encountered making *sev* and *gathia*, and Zubine. They were gentle women, pitifully unprepared for the physical and emotional severity of the house they had been sent to by caring parents who believed Africa would be a gift bigger than any dowry to their daughters. Given the winds that were carrying back such tales of riches and happiness, who could blame them?

The henna on their hands was still deep red when Almira and Zubine were enslaved. They cooked, cleaned, were irreproachably respectful, but that didn't stop the slaps and whippings and humiliation by Ma and her two sons. Almira had children, one after another, and was expected to get back on her feet within the day. Zubine was barren, so paid the more punishing price.

But Ma loved me, gave me money, chocolates, presents when I did well at school, sometimes even passed her hand over my face with intense affection. Don't ask me why. Her own grandchildren got only grief. I massaged her back every day, walked on it up and down as she lay there unclothed in voluminous glory, her copious creamy skin rippling like wax in a lava lamp. Ma was good to Jena too. Every Saturday for years and years, Mum and I would sit on her balcony drinking tea and eating *moong dhal bhajia* while Ma issued repetitive admonitions about our lite Islam, spat into her silver spittoon and cursed the passers-by below.

Moong Dhal Bhajia

Serve 6–8

2 cups *moong dhal*

1 tsp crushed ginger

2 green chillies

¼ tsp baking soda

Semolina (optional)

¾ cup black-eyed beans

1 bunch fresh coriander

3 spring onions

Salt

Sunflower oil for deep frying

⊙ Rinse through, then cover lentils and beans with water reaching to about an inch over the grains.

- Soak for twelve hours until swollen.

- Combine all the ingredients except the semolina and the oil and zap in a food processor. The mixture should be chopped (not pulverized).

- Shape into small flat patties like falafel. If too wet, coat with a layer of semolina.

- Place on clean tea towels.

- Heat the oil until hot, then reduce the heat so the patties fry gently to a rust colour.

- Drain excess oil on kitchen paper.

———

My primary school – Shimoni Demonstration School – was where I found my voice and spirit far away from the heat and dust of my parents' crumbling marriage. I awoke at dawn, shuffled down to the end of the bed that kept me between Jena and Kassim, and went to the living room. Without waking my sister Didi, I got into my red-and-white gingham dress, plaited my hair and packed my little brown satchel long before I needed to. Then I sneaked on to the balcony and sat down, legs swinging, making up stories in my head to get through to breakfast time. As the skies lightened, the shop watchmen wearing blankets stirred, finally free to leave after their long vigil. Then came black cleaners, who swept the streets whistling contentedly. Some knew me and would wave. Servants and ayahs rushed along, fast and silent. Soon the quiet ended with the crashing sounds of metallic security grilles opening to reveal shop windows alive with flies.

Chaturbhai was first to arrive, his face beaming as if it was freshly exfoliated every day. His menswear shop was popular with civil servants and bridegrooms, who paid good money for polyester boxed 'Based on England' shirts, striped ties and suits made by his tailors. Kasookoo, Mama Kuba's grey parrot, cackled and sang for his breakfast, calling to me, 'Yassi Yassi, *khalele sana*, Mama Kuba, *nipe ndisi*' – 'Yassi, too much noise, Mama Kuba, give me a banana.' That thin and spiky Bipul Patel was dropped off at his stationery store opposite. Sometimes when I went in he patted my oiled hair and gave me free pencils and broken, unsaleable erasers. On other days he turned brusque and told me to scarper when all I ever wanted was to spend my 10 cents on something. Papa's Grundig radio started up, BBC World Service, the news at 7.00, and I went indoors for *malai* on bread or eggy bread or fresh fruit salad.

I was always first to arrive in school, walked there by a science teacher who lived in the building nearby. The playing fields still had dew on them, and the classrooms were clean and impatient to get going. It was my time with my place.

There were other teachers too, never forgotten, old now or dead, unaware of how they saved us, their pupils, from a life of the gunny sack. Roxy was a Parsee lady who wore pencil-narrow skirts over healthy buttocks (so said the lecherous male teachers) and adored musicals. She wrote them for us to perform. Here are her lyrics for Scheherazade to sing – played by me in billowy trousers and that gold turban from Kasim's failed hat collection:

> *Scheherazade, we sing in joy for Scheherazade*
> *Scheherazade, she's brought such happiness to everyone*

Our days are now filled with joy and fun
Because of Scheherazade

Transports me to joyland on a magic carpet, that does, and I have loved good, bad and indifferent West End musicals ever since. Harriet Poulson came in from the British Council to teach us elocution and perfect manners. Once a year there would be a contest to find and reward the children who had achieved proper received pronunciation. Hundreds of hopefuls turned up to recite rhymes like this:

It is as well to remember
No elbows on the table please
Nor is a cup, one understands
So heavy that it needs both hands

In my primary school, a new head arrived with his wife – Mr and Mrs Bagchi – from Calcutta. They were intellectuals, actors, passionate about the arts, bursting with ideas and exuberance but dangerously provocative too – testing each other and society. They taught us drawing and painting, poems, introduced us to classical music, to Tagore, to Shakespeare, to the stories of Dickens. They acted, wrote plays and sang beautifully. The Bagchis injected a substance into my blood that has left me permanently high and receptive to art and beauty, with infinite possibilities roaming through my imagination. Remember, Asians were the thrifty, self-controlled, cautious merchants, creatures of family and community, governed by manners and convention. Our parents were bewildered by these two weird creatures. But they would never have thought to question a real headmaster and his teacher wife.

Mr Bagchi was spellbinding, had a voice like melted dark chocolate. She was voluptuous, walked with a wide swing, took up space in the world, had a lashing tongue and inviting eyes. Our mums were unnerved by Mrs Bagchi, yet they copied her walk, sometimes. She has died, but I remain in touch with him, and he can still quicken my pulse.

To be an Asian women in the 1950s in East Africa must have been both exhilarating and confusing. Hindi films were full of pious heroines, sacrificial to the point of madness. Meena Kumari had liquid dark eyes, lakes of pain; Waheeda Rehman, Nutan, Nimi, Soraya were all stunningly beautiful and shamelessly enticing, but when the time came (after the interval), they happily surrendered to a life of marital servitude or had to die. Even today, I cannot sit down at the dining table before my husband has been served his food. These jigger duties get into the blood. Jena loved and remembered the movies in her eighties as if she had just seen them: 'I cut my hair like Nargis. Remember her? And Nadia in *Hurricane Hansa*, smart lady, but too much. Can you remember when I took you to the film shows in Kampala?'

Ah, lovely Nargis, a Muslim beauty who wore shorts and played ladylike tennis, and Nadia, who smoked through a long jewelled cigarette holder, then exhaled in hoops, slowly upwards, stupefying the audience, which always let out a collective gasp. She kissed lionesses and danced to kill. How simply thrilling was the world of fillumy India then: '...heroes in ketchup blood, heroines in glycerine tears and vamps sprawled in garish costumes, legs apart in fishnet tights... Nothing rude, no kissing and generally no loss of virginity. Most definitely no nudity except through the wet sari technique'.[7] Most older men only went to the cinema to keep the wives and daughters happy and protect their reputations; girls without chaperones made themselves vulnerable to bad gossip. A number were denounced as vixens and then no marriage proposals came from the really good families. The girls had to make do with useless drunks instead, rejects nobody wanted even for their most unsightly daughters.

After finishing several paper cones of salty peanuts, the blokes would usually fall asleep until the final 'God Save the Queen' burst into their slumbers. But when Nadia came on, as Miss Hunterwali or Miss Diamond Queen, swigging whisky, you saw them sitting up and calling, 'Come on, shake, shake, shake up more, my bombshell baby of Bombay...' They glistened with desire, their hands pushed down on their crotches, and the wives pretended to laugh. They knew Nadia was a *besharam* – a shameless slut – because she was part white.

Sometimes we went to English and American films. Most popular was that pretty Doris Day, whose bob hair was golden as the early-morning sun. When Prince Aly, firstborn son of our beloved Imam, married Rita Hayworth, everyone in our mosque felt it was their duty to go and see her films. They saw her in *The Lady from Shanghai* and *The Strawberry Blonde* and were somewhat unsettled by the scorching kisses, but they stayed unquestioningly loyal to their own royally holy family. By that time, our leader for all things was urging Ismaili women to abandon their saris, traditional long gowns and headscarves, and get into the dresses, trousers and tops worn by Europeans and urban Africans. Like the Shah of Iran, our Imam was part of the clique which believed that Western values would accelerate progress for previously colonized peoples. Old identities are stubborn, though, and don't give way that fast or that freely. Papa made it clear that he did not approve of his wife getting into frocks (see how complicated he was, himself dressed like a man in Pall Mall!). She obeyed, a rare moment of submission.

Princess Rita came to visit Kampala, looked posh and bored. The congregation in our mosque was captivated. *Durzis* were inundated with orders for dresses with tight, tight belts and outspread skirts. The youngest and slimmest women looked lovely; for the others, being painfully squashed in at the waist meant that their glutted, good-life stomachs were pushed out further in the generous flare of the skirt, like large trays. The Hayworth hair too was copied by fashionable ladies. Imagine a pious congregation of wistful Rita lookalikes...

A daughter was born to the golden couple, named Yasmin. Almost all girls born that year were given the same name. Many years on, these Yasmins (including me) remained attached to each other and to Princess Rita's darling daughter. Nobody mentioned Princess Rita after the marriage collapsed, though, which was all too soon. The dresses were given to the ayahs and the hair puffs flattened. The faithful felt and prayed for Prince Aly, so badly led down by that loose actress.

Meanwhile, education was awakening female autonomy, and fears were growing that girls were getting too uppity for anyone's good. Women's councils sprang up in temples and mosques to restrain the wild mares, return them to the right ways. They had to be retrained to respect husbands, even those who turned out to be useless, inept, ridiculous, loud, demanding, who perhaps burped and farted in public. Most would slap their new wives around a bit and adored their mothers like stupid little puppies. So what? Young women had to remember not to demand or contradict their spouses but to loop invisible ribbons round their heads, to turn them round while appearing docile and willing. A man had to believe that both a decision and its abandonment were final and entirely his own. The technique had to be learned. This was the secret of a long, if not invariably happy, married life. Hardly a handful of Asian marriages in East Africa ever arrived at the last post of a formal divorce. The families intervened with buckets of blackmail and, in our community, the backing of the indomitable Marriage and Morality Council. Warring couples were put back on the road to fatalism. A family's *khandani, izzat*, honour, mattered more than happiness in marriage. If the odd couple did part, disapproving tongues lashed the woman who had so carelessly allowed her man to escape.

Jena had never mastered the required skills, but her friend Zerabai from the small hamlet of Masaka was a famously good wife, a domestic legend, super-skilled at managing her husband. One example: Zerabai wanted to go to Zanzibar for a holiday. Her husband, Sultan, never left his shop, didn't even to go for a pee, in case he missed selling a box of matches or bottle of groundnut oil. Once or twice Zerabai had had to rebuke him after finding smelly patches on the insides of his trouser legs.

For six months Zerabai reminded him of sudden tragedies and brief lives: 'Are we taking anything when we leave the world? Empty hand when we come and empty when we go, nothing in the hands, see? Should see things, do things.' 'That's the trouble with women,' Sultan grumbled. 'Just talk rubbish all day. Us gents, working like donkeys so the monkeys can spend our money. Mine wants holiday, in Zanzibar. Our fathers were right to be strict with their ladies. Look at me, not even ninety pounds now. And she can't climb ten stairs any more without the *gola* boy helping her. Am I paying him good money so he can push her up the hill instead of my Morris Minor?'

Next, Zerabai bought a hand-painted picture on black velvet of dhows waiting in the sea of the coastal town. An unnaturally effulgent evening sun, the colour of marigolds, was setting clumsily in the background. The surf came in and looked like a line of toothpaste on the shore. She hung the picture so her husband's eyes found it when he was eating.

'So peaceful, na? Look at it, the sky is colour of fresh passion-fruit juice.'

Sultan's eyes glazed over.

'Coast is the best, healthy air, people there live for one hundred years, I am telling you. Water so nice, cheap lodgings, clean *dharamsala* costs less than living at home.'

Later she dwelt on the mysteries and secrets of Zanzibar, the dark-skinned Bai who wore *bui-bui* and lived alone by the sea. A circle was drawn in the sand around her hut, and people swore the capricious sea never rubbed it out. No one would cross the line. They would call to her gently. Her eyes were as obscure and lightless as a swamp. 'Aree, listen, Mama Sukasuka has special magic cures for empty wombs, flatulence and fastest heartbeats.'

Sultan suffered terribly from digestive and other health problems. He was getting nervous too that if there were no children, the black customers would one day occupy his shop. Exactly a year and five days after Zerabai's campaign started, the holiday was fixed. Sultan started talking fulsomely about Bai and her powers, cheap lodging houses and the undoubted virtues of coastal air.

Zanzibar worked its magic. Bai gave them potions; Zerabai bought perfumes and satin duvets, and did what they needed to many times over to make the promised baby. When they got back their old dog was dead, the *askari* gone. Thankfully the general goods were intact except for the dhals, which all had weevils and would have to be sieved before selling. A son was born eight months and nine days later, a miserable, mean boy who inherited the shop and got rich after his father died.

Jena, inspired by Zerabai, took me twice to Zanzibar. I remember the narrow lanes in Stone Town, the gorgeous seafront with coconut sellers and street barbecues, the sparse and clean *dharamsala* with a ladies' section where we stayed. Food was brought in by the mosque cooking committee, and Mum talked about the holidays for years afterwards.

Other ladies were as canny. Parveenbai got the Electrolux 14-square-foot fridge from Gailey and Roberts, where hardly any Indians ever went to shop. And the Lakha ladies knew how to get their mean men to carpet the whole house, English carpets they were too, eye-wateringly expensive, and then they were walked upon, what an impressive waste of money.

Khadija's story was brought up as a cautionary tale. Without forethought she asked her husband if she could learn to drive, like so many modern Asian ladies and European memsahibs. Big mistake. She asked directly, thinking he would be too shy to refuse because they were all at the Sayanis' house, eating samosas before going to a music party.

Mrs Sayani had her own car, which made her more envied and important than all the other women in our community mosque. Khadija expected Mrs Sayani to add her bit of support. But she didn't. She couldn't. Before she could chip in and say, 'Yes, brother Alnoor, why not let her drive? More better than paying those lazy drivers who sit and smoke all day doing nothing', Alnoor went off, like the whistle on their old pressure cooker. Mrs Sayani kept quiet and let him blow up. She knew she had to be careful too, not to make her husband question his own laxity over this matter.

'Women driving?' yelled Alnoor. His small body tightened, he turned his head right and left and almost all round. Then he started rocking with laughter, sending spit and samosas flying: 'Your brains can't even add the receipts without pen and paper or point to the north, show me, show me, which side is Lake Victoria? And you want to drive? Roads will run away if you start. I can teach a boy five years old to drive, but no, please, not a lady. Brains made of *ladoo*. They will never be at home if we give them the cars – already they are out too much.'

Khadija had to laugh along merrily with the rest. She slapped her husband's back to show there were no hard feelings. (He almost fell into the chilli-tomato chutney.) She had been making such exciting plans. How she would drive the boy to the market and stuff panicked chickens with their feet tied tight in the boot instead of walking there and back. This was not how you convinced a man to agree to your plans.

Her rival Gulla Bol-Bol (her nickname, 'Talk-Talk', because she never let anyone else speak), the missionary's wife, did get her driving lessons. Then Gulla Bol-Bol was observed cuddling the instructor on the hill where stood the enormous Anglican Cathedral. Someone claimed to have seen her feet flat against the windscreen. Her husband was unimpressed by the gossip. Yes, life was changing all right.

Our mosque lurched between the irresistible pull of the new and the insistent calls of the eternal. In 1955 the Aga Khan decided that his East African flock needed more of a push towards the West. He built hospitals, introduced the British curriculum, instructed mothers to learn English, already a global means of communication. But always looming behind bold steps forward was the voice of Allah reminding us of our duties and submission to Him.

We knew a woman who ran a nightclub and freely distributed opium, whose sister was a dancer in that nightclub and was, they said, a mistress of a powerful Hindu industrialist who plied her with much gold. The sisters went to mosque every single evening and before sunrise at five. Their invocations were intense and sincere. At prayer time, most young kids got into trouble even if all we were doing was chewing gum loudly or grinning quietly. We had to keep ourselves amused, especially during the long hush when adults shut their eyes tight and pleaded fervently for rain or an end to rain, for a reduction in road accidents and recovery for all those sick people who were too ill to come to mosque, for miraculous relief from growing debt problems and for more money. Always more money. Then the congregation would chant as one to add power to their prayers: give us *barkat*, good luck, in all these things, and make us bring up children who will have faith and always stay under our heels.

The Sun Drops, 1955–60

A thin carpet in the middle separated the males and females. Men were starting to wear dark suits and shirts in mosque, and Chaturbhai's business boomed. Fashionistas balanced enormous bouffants, backcombed and then stiffened with beer. The flat odour spread through the aisles. They wore hooped or stiff under-skirts, and when they bent over, it was not nice. Old men and women sat on chairs, and sometimes one fell asleep and snored loudly, setting us off. Loaded Ismaili men liked their women to be adorned and exhibited, their precious, ornate figurines too big to fit into the display cupboards at home. No different this urge from the house-holds of manufacturing families going places in Victorian England. Pearls, pearls, pearls, some strings with diamond clasps, emerald and ruby lockets, more garish every year. The nouveau riche looked down on their traditional sisters still wrapped in their modesty. My mother was one of them, determined to wear the sari to death. (In her coffin I placed her favourite old sari, purple silk with painted wild flowers.)

It was a forgiving place, our mosque. The nightclub sisters were never rebuffed though gossip buzzed around them like flies. When sinful devotees died, how sincerely they were mourned, even that *chafu*, dirty Vallibhai. He enjoyed pushing his long forefinger right into the middle of women's bottoms as a stick might probe a thick jasmine bush. Every Friday shoes went missing, stolen by the poor or envious; barefoot victims would bend over, desperately seeking their lost footwear. That was when Vallibhai would send in his hand, then sniff the hidden odour with his enormously long nose. They called him '*mendho*' – a cockroach who got into dark places. His daughters, they whispered, had never married because they were spoiled by their sex-mad father. But when he passed away, all was washed clean on the funeral slab, and the congregation wished him on to paradise. Death suited him. His daughters wept, and his impoverished widow set herself up near the back exit of the mosque to sell hot *channa bateta* in rusty bowls washed with a cursory dip into a vat of dirty water.

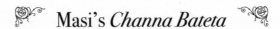

Masi's *Channa Bateta*

Serves 6

3 tins chickpeas	1 lb potatoes
2 tbsp dried tamarind	6 dried dates
½ tsp turmeric	Red chilli powder to taste
1 large dried red chilli	2 tsp *channa* flour (*besan* –
2 tbsp oil	chickpea flour)
1 tsp black mustard seeds	½ tsp sugar

- Pour boiling water over dates and tamarind, and soak overnight.
- Heat oil in a pan with whole chilli and mustard seeds till they crackle.
- Add turmeric and chilli powder and cook for a minute, stirring all the time.
- Add 1 pint of water and salt to taste. Bring to a boil.
- Now add diced potatoes and cook until nearly soft.
- Chuck in chickpeas and simmer.
- Meanwhile crush tamarind and dates with your fingers, then strain into the pot with the sugar.
- Stir the *besan* into a little water to make a paste, then stir into the simmering pot to thicken the mixture a little.

- Cook for another five minutes.
- Serve in bowls topped with Bombay Mix if you like.

———⌣———

Papa remained excommunicated. After the time he wrecked my performance and *Khushiyali* they never let him into the compound. He could have been accepted back in with the smallest of apologies. Or he could have walked away from his people forever, like Spinoza, one of his favourite philosophers. Papa chose instead to harangue folk going in and out. I watched him picking on the wife of a car mechanic, a family friend. Short and voluptuous, she imported and sold coconuts from Mombasa. Her plunging neckline offended Papa: 'You look cheap and foolish. Has your husband no self-respect?' She laughed at him and wobbled off on her way. Papa was both a rolling stone and a stubborn, sullen crag, a bohemian who hung on to old values buffeted by the sea of modernity. As a child these moments were sometimes embarrassing, at times achingly funny, exhilarating even.

My brother was made to come back from England prematurely because Papa whimsically decided that my sister should be packed off instead, too young, too naive, just as thrilled at the chance she was handed. Babu was dazzling when he came back. Cool, a jazz buff (the instrumentals, which sounded like screeching cats, made us crazy in that small flat), daring, fashionable and still as loving, though he had lost my *lala*. He looked happy enough, but it must have cut him up to be hauled back and then pushed young into work as we were passing into irreversible penury. We no longer speak, but there was a time when he was a brother like no other. Papa nagged and harassed him so Babu stayed away from home, sneaking back in the dead of night when the hungry dogs howled.

Living in the middle of equatorial Africa, in the post-war world, Asians were pulled both to the East and to the West. No wonder we ended up confused and adrift. Ladies from the English Women's Institute ran child-craft classes for Asian mothers. Baby shows were organized, and the fattest light-skinned tots got all the prizes. Asian mothers were advised to stop breast-feeding. The elegant (if a little too thin) English nurse Mrs Penelope Thwaite sold them dummies, gripe water, dill water, safety pins, bottles, teats, cute bibs with pictures of pink bunnies and brown teddy bears, baby oil, baby powder and tinned milk. All imported from England. My cousin Moni, new mum, took me with her to these sessions.

Mrs Penelope had stuck up on one wall pictures of gorillas with suckling babies and pictures of various half-naked black tribes with sullen expressions and unreliable, flinty eyes. Standing before these images, she was beauty and truth itself. Her eyes were half closed. She hated the light more than the dust and the heat because it exposed her dry and pleated skin, which flaked and itched horribly. Penny Thwaite had an unsteady voice. Her walk too was cautious, as if she was trying to protect herself from grabbing thorns, demanding black hands, animals, insects, sticky tree sap and malaria.

'Now, ladies, I want you to forget what your mothers did. Nature doesn't know best. Do you understand? Once nature has done the business and you have your baby, you have to learn to nurture. Hands up anyone who knows what that means?' No hand would shoot up, as the women couldn't hear the difference between 'nature' and 'nurture', and they were too shy to ask. Some shrugged their shoulders and muttered in Kutchi or Gujarati. Mrs Penelope hated foreign words and said so. When they had been particularly bad at answering her hard questions, the mums thought it best to smile at her instead in a very friendly way.

'And in the UK, ladies want a better future for their babies. Now, you want the best for your sweet chocolates, don't you? And look here at my figure, you see, no drooping breasts?' Penny turned sideways at this point to give the incredulous women a good look at her pointy, tight breasts, still only a size 32A. 'Any questions?'

'Please Mrs, tin milk too much expensive, no?'

'No, my dear, just think. You go to the doctor less, your children are healthy and catch few infections. How much do you girls spend on saris and those gold bangles, eh?'

Laughter and then the rush to buy, with new anxieties that the goods would run out. Today the same persuasion carries on. In an article in the *Guardian* exposing hard-sell techniques by Nestlé of its powdered milk, a doctor in Bangladesh said this: 'Putting white people on posters sends out the message that it is the western way, the best way.'[8]

The WI enthusiastically organized a march to mark the coronation of Queen Elizabeth II. All schoolchildren in Kampala lined up waving little flags in the hideous midday sun. A small band marched past, then some policemen – black and brown – escorting a big white man in a white uniform and a white hat with a white plume riding proud on a white horse. We got the point. White was great, white was in charge; we submitted to this. And even when we grew up and became anti-colonialists, post-colonialists, anti-new-colonialists, that reverence remained for our Mother Imperial.

How come, I am often asked by indigenous Brits, how come you can make such splendid scones and Victoria sponges? Because we were taught English cooking in our schools, the best and the revolting. Sausage rolls were, for me, the most disgusting. I can still recall the grey stickiness of sausage meat as we pushed it out of skins, the terrible heat of the midday sun beating down on the hot tin roof of the cookery block. The pastry melted to soggy in an instant. (My poor mother, who barely had any cash, had to get the ingredients on long credit.) The rolls, stuffed with pig meat, were *haram* and had to be thrown away. Another classroom recipe contained more possibilities; it tasted like milky newspaper.

Shepherd's Pie

Leftover cold mutton

Dried herbs

Onion

Potatoes

Salt and pepper

Butter

Milk and water or stock made with Bovril

Some boiling milk

- Chop the meat and season with salt, pepper and herbs.

- Into a buttered pie dish put a layer of the meat.

- Sprinkle chopped onion over that and the liquid to cover.

- Bake for twenty minutes.

- Mash potatoes and spread over the top.

- Brown in the oven (325°F, 170°C, gas mark 3).

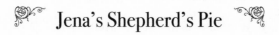

But it gave my mother ideas. 'Now, *beti*, wait till I make it,' said Jena as she threw the pie into the bin. 'Next time. This will be my Indian shepherd's pie. With bit of *garam masala* and magic we can repair this dish.'

Jena's Shepherd's Pie

Serves 6

Filling

1 lb *very* lean mince	6 spring onions
1 bunch fresh coriander	Salt
2 green chillies	1 small lime
¾ tsp *garam masala*	¾ tsp crushed ginger
¾ tsp crushed garlic	¾ tsp mint sauce
5 chopped tomatoes	

Mash

8 medium-sized potatoes	**2 oz butter**
¼ tsp crushed garlic	**2 tbsp milk**
Salt to taste	**¾ tsp paprika powder**

- Peel and halve potatoes and put them to boil in salty water.

- Using a non-stick frying pan, dry-fry the mince with salt, ginger and garlic.

- Add *garam masala* and cook for two more minutes until dry and aromatic. Allow to cool.

- Stir in finely chopped spring onions, coriander, green chillies, lime juice as well as the mint sauce.

- Transfer into a pie dish and layer tomatoes over the top.

- Melt 1½ oz of butter and add garlic, frying over gentle heat for a minute.

- Mash the potatoes with this butter-and-garlic mixture, then add the milk, paprika and salt.

- Spread over the meat-and-tomato mixture.

- Melt the rest of the butter and brush over the top.

- Bake for twenty-five minutes in the oven at medium temperature (350°F, 180°C, gas mark 4) until nicely brown at the top.

And as we learned more about English food, we found new ways to appropriate it, lead it away from itself. We were in awe of the great old country and had come to believe she had built up invincible power on a devilishly potent diet. But too much of it was bland and tepid. So began a whole new adventure. Victoria sponges were lifted with lime juice or saffron; shortbread was pepped up with grainy cardamom seeds; grated cheese was added to kebab mixtures; roast chickens were stuffed with pistachios, figs, almonds, green papayas, spicy eggs or spicy mashed potatoes. We made a wonderful creamy pudding using wild dried apricots and carrots to resemble trifle, but it was nothing at all like it. Strange but true: England gave us an exciting new food emporium to pick and choose from.

Some English tastes were taken up unadulterated. Mysterious-tasting HP and LP sauces, blanket-warm Ovaltine and cake icings gave us imperial cachet. As Stuart Jeffries put it, '...our puddings were the terror of the earth. Our bottled sauces alone made foreigners tremble so much it proved quite easy to subjugate them and plunder their ancestral homelands.'[9]

I have a copy of *St Andrew's Church Woman's Guild Kenya Settlers' Cookbook and Household Guide*. First published in 1928, my copy was the twelfth edition, out in 1958. Most of the recipes use imported ingredients, from tinned French anchovies to Bovril, excellent, they say, for curried vegetables, which I confess I have not yet tried. The custards and hot steamed puddings must have evoked longings for home, and the jam and pickle recipes were delightfully inventive – Pineapple and Vegetable Marrow Jam, Tree-Tomato Jam, Military Pickle, even Banana Chutney. For the Military Pickle various vegetables are salted, then boiled with turmeric, vinegar, salt, sugar and chilli – clearly the Asian influence. But then the pickle is thickened with a whole cup of flour – it must look and taste like flavoured cement, I reckon. Waste was frowned on, and there are scores of handy hints for leftovers. White memsahibs got essential Swahili on the back page: 'You have stolen the sugar', 'This soap is sufficient', 'You are free every day from 2 to 4 but at any other time you must be on duty on the premises', 'Do not be sulky', 'You are insolent! You must look pleasant.'

Vegetable Marrow Jam

Enough marrows to weigh 6 lb after being peeled and cored
Juice and rind of 2 lemons

¾ lb sugar to each lb of marrow
1½ lb preserved ginger
2 oz fresh root ginger

- Cut marrow into cubes.
- Place in a bowl and cover with sugar, leaving until the next day.
- Strain off the syrup and boil with the juice of lemons and fresh ginger (tied in a muslin bag).
- Cut preserved ginger into small pieces and add with the marrow to the boiling syrup.
- Boil for another hour or less if transparent sooner.
- Remove bag of ginger and pour into hot jam jars.

In February 1960, Harold Macmillan made his famous speech in South Africa, the first British Prime Minister to travel there: 'The wind of change is blowing through this continent,' he intoned, 'and whether we like it or not, this growth of national consciousness is a political fact.' For Asians the wind carried a warning chill.

5 *Children of the Revolution, 1961–67*

Bᴙ 1960, UGANDAN ASIANS had turned Kampala into a conspicuous statement of our presence, a street theatre parading wealth and vanity,
religious spectacles too with jousting deities and conflicting band *wajas*, any excuse
to show off and compete. Cradle-to-grave capitalists, East African Asians do both
consummately, on this earth and in preparation for the next. Diwali brought out the
drummers and soulful accordion players accompanying young Hindu women – lit
up by sequinned saris and sparkling chandelier earrings – who danced in lines and
circles beating bells and sticks, creatures of wispy light to enrapture and confuse.
The virgin sirens knew how they tortured unmarried men (and married ones too, I
suspect) bursting with unreleased sexual longings. At midnight the town blazed
with fireworks, and any surreptitious stroking of female hair and flesh would
suddenly be exposed by a mighty flash, an instant photograph of sin.

Rival groups hurled bangers at each other (miraculously there were no serious
injuries) while shopkeepers dodged the crackling energy and passed around sweetmeats: perfect round *ladoo*, creamy circular *penda*, fudge-like *monthar*, sugary
almond slabs, pink copra squares (Bounty bars without the chocolate), and white
vermicelli nests soaked in rose water, their centres filled with nuts. Best of all were

the ricotta *burfi* decorated with edible silver paper. Sweet indulgences, they hoped, would bring in a sweet year. The crowds gorged and surged, high on a mass sugar rush. Holi, the other Hindu festival, was mischievous; coloured water and powders were hurled at passers-by, who minded very much. It was hard to tell who was a Hindu so all got soaked and had their clothes ruined.

Ricotta *Burfi*

1 lb ricotta cheese

4 oz caster sugar

½ tsp cardamom powder and the same amount of cinnamon powder or nutmeg

3 tbsp butter

6 tbsp full-cream powdered milk

A few sheets of edible silver paper (you can get these in well-stocked Indian food stores)

- Melt the butter over low heat, then add the ricotta, cooking slowly for approximately nine minutes.

- Add sugar and carry on cooking and stirring, adding powdered milk and flavourings a little at a time.

- The mixture should start to form into a neat ball.

- Pat into a low, greased baking tray about 2 inches deep.

- Lay silver paper carefully on top – a lovely but fiddly job – and cool for several hours.

- Cut into small pieces. It keeps in the fridge for a fortnight.

On the Hindu day of *Rakhi* sisters tied shimmering thread bracelets on real and casually adopted brothers, who had, in turn, to give them lavish amounts of money. Canny girls used *rakhis* to thwart pesky Romeos, who then had to lay off. Manu, the town's most persistent romantic chaser, was handed many such glittering brush-offs. He wore them all on one arm as he drove patiently up and down the main road on *Rakhi* day. Once he knocked over a lovely but unmarriageable woman with a glass eye and sped her off to hospital. Guilt made him receptive to her charms, and she moved into his vacant heart. They lived happily ever after. How I envied my Hindu girlfriends on this day.

Then there were the raucous turbaned tribes. To mark their special festivals, Sikh men, many of them muscular carpenters and heavy-metal workers, burst into *bhangra* and pounded the streets heavily. Their traditional daggers were brandished, moustaches dripped, turbans fell off, and hair tumbled down to their waists. It was a scary and thrilling show of sweaty, alpha manhood.

Eid had Sunni Muslims promenading in a dignified line on their way to mosque, not for them raffish stunts or antics. Their God was very solemn but liked fine clothes. The men and boys were dressed in new brocades and velvets, hats and jewels. They looked like mini Moghuls and behaved with princely decorum, from the youngest to the oldest. The largest Shia sect – the Ithanasharis – marked *Mohurrum*, days of atonement and grief for their murdered imam Husayn, grandson of the Prophet. Men and boys had sharp blades hanging off long dog chains, and with these they flagellated themselves in a procession along the main road. The squirts of blood and curdling wails put off customers in the Greek Christos coffee shop, Drapers,

General Motors, the Athenaeum bakery, *mithaiwallas* and my father's old book-shop, now in the hands of a spindly Goan whose very dark-skinned wife wore white court shoes which left chalky marks on her busy ankles. Pure vegetarian Hindus lurched and vomited as the blood squirted outside their shops. Papa was always brutally unforgiving of these masochistic worshippers: 'Making so much *fujo*, commotion, giving us all a bad name. *Sala*, stupid they are, never read the Islamic books, like I am doing all day. Where does Allah tell them to do this devilish dance of blood? Who will clean it from the streets? Will they? No. Go off and stuff them-selves with biriyani.'

On ordinary Sundays you felt you were strolling through Bombay. Hindi films were on in every cinema, Hindi music blared out from cars, and we filled the streets. Dressed in best, all made up with nowhere special to go, we roamed pointlessly, stopping briefly for passion-fruit ice cream or roasted corn on the cob. Indian cafés fried and stirred, releasing their aromas on to the streets and our clothes. The air itself was commandeered. Innocent fun, we thought, unaware of the shadowy figures who didn't, couldn't, share it.

Even now, East African Asians will tell you that that was the life, when the social order was accepted, no one was silly enough to cross the boundaries, and they held the streets of Uganda's capital. 'Who needs heaven,' they would ask, 'when we have it here, even after death?' Sad, a lugubrious third cousin (his name shortened from Sadrudin), will never forget: 'We were so happy and having a *badshai* life of kings. Servants to do everything, costing nothing and after work and good meal, sitting on the veranda, taking the air, a little good whisky, listening to filmy songs. Walking on Kampala Road on Eid and Diwali, lost it all.'

Few ordinary Africans stayed on in town after dusk, unless they were all-night servants or had quarters provided by their masters. (Many chose not to use these because they would get no rest or respite if they were around all the time.) Their blackness was always suspect, a sign of criminal intent except when twice a year the *sanene* came, swarms of plump green grasshoppers. Black Ugandans thronged the main streets of Kampala late in the evenings when the bounty flew in. The insects clustered noisily around street lamps and were gathered up in sheets with whoops of joy and songs of praise for the delivery of free protein. Some overjoyed consumers were reckless and got run over by cars whose drivers never dared or cared to stop. The grasshoppers were fried or cooked with tomatoes, sometimes eaten raw after the heads had been snapped off. Better than chicken they said.

The rest of the time the Africans stayed away. Around the small fires in their compounds, in shanty towns or neighbouring villages, families sat around every evening, as they had done for thousands of years. Electricity belonged to their rulers and the brown classes. Here the lucky had paraffin lamps. A drum or wood pipe would play, women would hum softly as their babies fell asleep. *Pombe* – lethal hooch made from rotting bananas – was drunk by the men to bring some cheer. Like native Canadians and Americans and Australian Aborigines, it made them forget their perpetual humiliation. Cassava was slowly roasted under fires. Once they might have softly told fables and stories about the ancestors. Now the low voices and murmurs circulated tales of resentment. Day after day following Macmillan's 1960 speech, Ugandan Africans were observed getting restive. They demanded increased wages and respect. Political rallies became frequent. Oddly it was also the time when tribal divides intensified. The tribe despised by all factions was brown. We were of course blissfully unaware of the hot lava building up beneath our dancing shoes.

Then the counter-culture burst forth in the West, and we began to listen in on what was going on. I entered secondary school as the crosswinds wafted over Op art, Twiggy, the Beatles, Blue Hawaii, Kid Galahad, various rubbish Elvis films, drainpipes, miniskirts, the Twist, backcombing, teen age itself. Hooked fast on sing-a-long-love we caught up with the 1950s backlist – early Cliff and Elvis, Ray Charles, the Supremes and, in my case, Jim Reeves – Gentleman Jim, as he was known in Africa. On Radio Uganda deep into the night plaintive lovers sent beseeching messages.: 'Marybeth wants "Am I Losing You" by Gentleman Jim and is asking her fella: Is there somebody new? Tell me what to do?'

My school, Kololo Senior Secondary, motto 'Lead Kindly Light', cheap shacks and hot tin roofs, built halfway up a hill, was a sanctuary and a powerhouse for misfits like me. In the last year, though, I was caught up in a firestorm. The scars have never healed; they were the making of me.

After 1960, informal apartheid had started to give a little.[1] The first lot of black kids were admitted into the school, and I remember little African and mixed-race children in mosque at this time too. Scrubbed clean and in lovely clothes, they were shown off, the adopted few, some the children of loyal servants, taken in by charitable families and converted to our faith. Some things didn't change until they had to. English school inspectors still came in to impose the old order into the very last hour of the Empire, sticking up notices like 'No Vernacular in School' and 'Malodorous Lunches Not Permitted', by which they meant our delicious Asian wraps.

 ## My Malodorous Packed Lunch

Roti

1 cup *chapatti* flour   ½ tsp salt
1 tbsp vegetable oil   Warm water

- Rub in the oil and add the water slowly until you get a dough that is neither too soft nor too stiff; add water or flour if you need to.

- Heat a griddle – a gas cooker is best for this.

- Break off small balls and roll out into thin (perfect or imperfect) circles.

- Slap on to the griddle and cook, turning over several times.

- Lightly butter each *roti*.

- Spoon along the middle dried potato curry, spicy mince with egg, boned chicken taken from a chicken curry – anything that isn't runny.

- Add sliced cucumber or radishes and roll up.

My mum used to freeze the rolls the night before so by lunchtime they would defrost and be ready to eat. There were some kids whose rolls went off, and then they truly were malodorous. Never stopped them eating, and never made them ill. Our stomachs were not prissy.

Spicy Dry Mince with Egg

1 lb lean minced beef

3 onions, chopped

1 tsp crushed garlic

1 tsp crushed ginger

2 tbsp tomato purée

1 tsp *jeera* powder

1½ tsp *dhania* powder

1 tsp chilli powder

Salt to taste

1 tbsp vegetable or sunflower oil

3 eggs, beaten and seasoned with salt

- Fry onions in the oil until they start to brown.

- Add the meat with ginger and garlic, break up and cook slowly until dry and brown.

- Add spices and stir while they cook over low heat for four minutes.

- Then stir in the tomato purée and salt, cooking for two more minutes.

- Put this mixture into an ovenproof dish.

- Pour the egg over, cover with a 'lid' made of double-layered tin foil, and bake in the oven (medium heat – 350 °F, 180 °C, gas mark 4) until the egg sets.

- Take off the foil for the final five minutes of baking.

- Cut into squares and eat with *roti, paratha* or other Indian breads. You can serve these on thick slices of white bread too.

By this time we were starting to copy some of the whitie unruly-youth stuff – never sex or drugs, never that, not until a little later, and then only the handful of hardcore rebels. But just enough to set the old on edge. Mrs Bose, the shuffling science teacher who looked like an old turtle, didn't care for this hanky-panky, not at all. In her plain *khadi* white saris and lace-up men's shoes, she was everywhere, all the time, spying, disapproving, imposing sudden, crazy rules to whip us into shape. No pointy bras, no knees showing, and plaits had to be pushed to the back. And we had to wear thick vests over our bras. She thought if plaits were hanging down the front, hair oil would seep through the blouses and reveal the shapes of breasts, leading boys into a frenzy of silent masturbation or worse. 'The boys will jump on you, spoil you, put a baby inside you before passing your Cambridge,' she warned us.

Mr Banya agreed and had his own rough ways to hold back the hedonism of the new degenerate England: 'Really that country finished now, not as it was once, greatest Britain.' He was like Bottom in *A Midsummer Night's Dream*, wanting to play every part in the school, teach any subject, the self-believing, all-round man. Boys feared his Coca-Cola tests to stop them wearing tight 'rock and roll' trousers. If the empty bottle got stuck passing through the outside leg, the poor blighter was made to walk around in his 'undering pants'. The head, Mr Raval, had a collection of fancy hair clips which he snapped on boys if he thought they were trying to copy the Beatles. It was a long and exhausting wrestle between the old and the young, and as ever the latter proved unbeatable.

Mr Raval was ferociously conservative, had a black-and-orange smile (he chewed *paan* all day long) and teeth like old stones in a graveyard. His face contorted with sadistic pleasure when his thin stick whistled through the air and landed sharply to draw lines of blood on calves and forearms. Thirty-five steps led up to his office, which smelled of pain and looked down on the wide open-air space where we stood every morning for sombre assemblies. The beaten were put on display, snivelling and contrite, and the top cream too when they did well in exams. One corner was for the bad, the other for the good. I was up there a number of times both for punishment and for praise. But I promise I never snivelled. Mr Raval had decided I was very bright and much too wayward. He said he wanted to kill the thoughts he thought played in my head. Yet he was the one who pushed me hard to be what nobody ever thought I could be, given my circumstances.

Our school staff sailed over from India and Pakistan to take up noble jobs most East African Asians thought were beneath them. These imported pundits were respected as teachers but also despised for choosing an occupation that paid so damn little. They were embarrassingly more foreign than even we were in Africa. And they were undoubtedly confused.

Never forgotten is poor Mr Kavi, the history teacher whose own eight children walked up and down the hill carrying their shoes so as not to wear them out. His history was simple and unfailingly supportive of the powerful. The Tsar warned revolutionaries, 'Do not do mischief in my kingdom,' and the French Revolution was led by 'misbehaved peasants who couldn't know their place'. A pukka British loyalist, he had us cheering when the Indian Uprising (Mutiny to him) was finally put down.

Then there was Mr Das, who inexplicably taught us both physics and English.

His logic was strange and compelling: 'Chair broken? Sit two each on one chair.' 'We need two projectors therefore we have none.' When he taught us physics, he spoke in a monotonous voice while scribbling hieroglyphics on the blackboard. We copied what we could. Any interruption of the dreadful silence and he would bark and pronounce us idiots. But Das the literature teacher was voluble; too many words, too big for his mouth, filled our ears and bounced off the wall, deeply felt. He played Juliet and Hamlet, climbed on tables, reached the eaves where birds nested and mice played.

I mock and I shouldn't. They deserved homage, do so now. As does Mr B. K. Patel with his rodent face and panicked, bright eyes caught forever in the headlights, who had been on a warship off Burma when it was bombed. During thunderstorms he would paddle over the same sentence again and again, as if he was on a raft. But he instilled application and forbearance. Imagine what you will one day be and stay on the hard road to get there, he advised.

Around this time arrived exhilarating rule-busters who carried off those of us never made to be doctors, scientists, businessmen or nerdy lawyers. Edie Garvie, the energetic Scottish dancing lady, turned up in 1961,[2] was an educationalist free of the worst of colonial hubris and genuinely excited by the emerging liberated Uganda. Together with Ganesh and Kuku Bagchi, she swept us up further into the excitement of the performing arts. They set up drama festivals (with support from the British Council) and joined the company of actors at the new National Theatre of Uganda. I played a fairy in a terrific production of *A Midsummer Night's Dream*. We wore tight tops over pubescent breasts, and our midriffs were on display. Imagine that. Papa never came to the show; I was thus spared the shame of another public rant. Ganesh and Kuku were Oberon and Titania, playing out their own tempestuous marriage on stage. We Kololians were taken into the worlds of Chekhov, Shaw, Arthur Miller, Ibsen even, and – my absolute favourite – Shakespeare.

There was an empty storeroom underneath our flat, full of rubbish, merry mice and insects. There, sometimes, alone, I tied ribbons under my bust and round my forehead and played Miranda, Desdemona, best of all Cleopatra – a melodramatic fest sometimes producing real tears. I was in mid-flow one day when Jena came banging on the door, sobbing and screaming as if she had been bitten by a dog. Marilyn Monroe had just been found dead. It was August 1962. That same year the Beatles arrived with 'Please Please Me' and got us, the young, or at least some of us, into the Swinging Sixties proper. We became conscious of the self within, of that singular voice and longings that make us special, of choice and new openings, of liberty from social constraints. These stirrings of personal freedom coincided with the shackles of Empire falling away.

I look back and realize that these tremors affected some Asian adults too, including a few dedicated guardians of organized morality. They started to push against the walls of their subscribed lives. I became aware of the buried passions of those around me, men and women who felt imprisoned in loveless lives and secretly tried to snatch pleasures which, if discovered, would ruin them. Asleep (or so they believed) in the back seats of cars, children were driven to dark places, to hilltops, where desires were satisfied repeatedly, clumsily, leaving the adults more upset than ever. We peeped and knew (though never said), and even now I would not name them, the bold romantics, some in heaven, who risked so much.

Our languages have no words to express sexual longings, to name an orgasm or the erogenous zones or adultery. Until the 1960s, married couples expected the slow maturing of affection into the twilight years. Some, you could tell, had marriages that also gave them physical pleasure; most met the requirements of duty. You never saw any body contact between couples, and discretion prevailed. Living among Africans at ease with their bodies and sex made Asians even more uptight than Indians and Pakistanis were on the subcontinent.

The very few who transgressed remained unforgiven. There was a young woman in our neighbourhood who had dark, hairy spots like those on a jungle cat. They whispered when she walked by that she was the child of a sinful union between two married lovers. Then there was the albino girl, waxy white with red eyes, a living reproach to the evil two – a man and his cousin – who were doing it under a tall tree near the forest. Lightning struck the tree, which died soon after.

In 1961, non-Africans made up 1 per cent of the population of Uganda. They owned most of the wealth of the country and occupied almost all the high-status jobs. The equivalent of £600 per annum was spent on the education of a white child, £150 on an Asian child and £15 on a black child. Britain had been in charge since 1893.

Racism was seeded by the colonial system and would in time yield a bitter harvest. Yet, as Uganda moved towards independence in October 1962, there was little indication that the country was headed for disaster. On the contrary, it appeared a model of stability, well prepared to handle self-rule. In comparison with Tanzania, which possessed few natural resources, Uganda was blessed with an array of cash crops. African producers grew cotton and coffee, which brought them incrementally higher standards of living. Many could finance the basic education of their children and had better expectations for the future. It is true that plantation owners were never black and that payments to workers were kept low. However, labour rebellions were rare because nobody starved and people could track some progress. Development projects also were flourishing. Makerere Technical College, set up in 1922, became a prestigious university in 1963, and the gleaming new Mulago teaching hospital opened – gifts of the departing British.

Uganda's political parties formed more to compete for the right to govern after independence rather than as a means of winning it. The national government was expected to be presided over by pragmatic elected leaders who would broker expenditure on roads, schools, dispensaries and other facilities to satisfy local or regional interest groups in return for political support. Milton Obote, head of the Uganda People's Congress and the man expected to head the new Uganda, though not charismatic, had the political acumen to balance the various demands made by competing regions and tribes.

The other two East African nations had more ideologically driven leaders in Jomo Kenyatta and Julius Nyerere. Nyerere was a committed socialist and in some ways an admirable leader. He never amassed a personal fortune, and systematically built a sense of nationhood and mutuality to unite his people. That ensured Tanzania could deal with conflicts without the tribal bloodletting of Uganda and avoided the levels of corruption that have brought down Kenya since independence. Nyerere even translated *Julius Caesar* into Swahili so that citizens could understand the dangers of concentrated power. Ironically he was himself was the megalomaniac he warned against. In 1961 he wrote an article outlining a vision found menacing by most Asians:

> African countries are usually countries without natural unity. Their 'boundaries' enclose those artificial units carved out of Africa by grabbing colonial powers without any consideration of ethnic groups or geographical realities... in the case of East and Central Africa, you must add the new tribes from Asia, the Middle East and Europe. Here are divisions enough to pose a truly formidable task in nation building... Ours is a patriotic struggle which leaves no room for differences and which unites all elements in the country.[3]

Kenyatta and Obote, heading in the same direction, applauded and promoted this spurious definition of 'African democracy' which disallowed debate and dissent and saw diversity as disloyalty or, worse, provocation. Meanwhile white administrators, educators, civil servants, army and police personnel, and big-business managers briskly prepared their retreat, showing no signs of despondency. Their stiff upper lips never quivered or twitched, and sentimentality was packed away even though many had never had it so good and never would again. Our imperial protectors seemed to be in an unseemly hurry to leave.

At Ratan's *paan* shop, Asian men gathered to digest the upheavals. I was often there to buy some chewing gum, a pleasure forbidden by my mother, who said it was made of dog shit. 'What is the haste, I am asking you?' shouted a worried Jamu, the car mechanic, husband of the buxom coconut seller, whose loyal *mzungu* customers paid him what he asked for without ever wasting his time haggling: '*Jaldi*, *jaldi*, can never understand these British. Did the same in India also, leaving too quickly and what for? Lakh people had to die.' 'Very true,' agreed Sajad, the barber next door, as his blade whipped rapidly round the face of a tense customer. 'They want to rush, run away faster than an impala as if forest fire coming. What will they get in England? *Alishaan* life here, yaar, living like princes, even the teachers are having five servants. Over there will have to polish their own shoes, then they will be sorry. Should have bribed the blacks and kept the country. Don't know what will happen now.' 'You are completely and absolutely and totally right,' said Ratan. 'Give these *kalas* a few thousand pounds – we also would have given our share – and would have bought back the Empire. Just to go like this, damn fools.' Mama Kuba seemed afraid for the first time ever and tore down the calendar picture of the Queen hanging on one green wall in her sitting room, hurled it on to the street below. Then she sat down and cried; her glassy grey eyes seemed to break into pieces. I had never seen my Ma cry. Desolation, loss of verve, trepidation, confusion infused homes and communities. Whites moved like manic images in a speeded-up film scene,

Asians like in a slow-motion sequence. Africans watched both spectacles with little sympathy and bided their time.

In 1962 independence arrived. A handful of Ugandan Asians – exceptional people – welcomed liberation, joined political parties and entered parliament. Sugra Visram, who sometimes wore the *busuti* – an African dress with a Victorian bustle – was one, and Sherali Jaffer, an ambitious and wealthy man, was another. Both were Ismailis, people from our mosque. They gossiped endlessly about Mrs Visram's close friendship with the handsome Bagandan king Mutesa II (nicknamed 'Freddie'), first President of Uganda, not good thing for our women to be photographed with a *gola*, they said, even if he is a king and really quite handsome, for a *gola*. Asians tried to rejoice or at least pretend convincingly when what they felt was vulnerability and loss.

The Union Jack quivered down the pole, and the Ugandan flag with its cute crested crane was raised. The fireworks display was forgettable, nothing like as fancy as Diwali night (new black leaders hadn't yet caught the African disease of extravaganza). Canny Asian industrialists had contributed DIY floats to the celebratory procession, mainly to advertise their products. Their spoiled daughters waved from delivery lorries dressed as fairies or the saintly Sita. I watched jealously. Why couldn't my father have a sugar plantation or flour factory? Bands played loud and marched with their heads high. The anthem was rousing:

Oh Uganda, the land of freedom
We hold your future in our hands

United Free

For Liberty and so on and on...

Like milk turning in the tropical sun, these hearty expectations soon were sour. The anthem was a lament before long, for what might have been. Obote turned out to be an unsafe pair of hands who won the election by doing a deal with Mutesa II. Mutesa was given the role of President, and for a short while everyone was content. Idi Amin was appointed deputy commander of the army, an ominous choice. All too soon after coming to power Obote abrogated the constitution and by 1964 had turned against the proud Baganda.

On 22 May 1966, Mutesa's main supporters were arrested. The Bagandans rallied round their king, building barricades around the palace. Amin was sent in to demolish the resistance. Mutesa escaped, ending his days as an exile in London. Using his willing general Amin, Obote then launched a reign of imprisonment, torture and killings to tame dissenting Bagandans. Credible observers believe as many or more people were killed during Obote's times in power as were during Amin's reign of terror.

Both Amin and Obote were from marginal tribes; both suffered from feelings of inferiority. Obote had been expelled from Makerere University and could not abide those who were better educated than he was. Amin, semi-literate and a Muslim convert, had been trained in extreme brutality by the British army. His officers had had him poked and prodded with sticks when he boxed – he had been a Ugandan boxing champion from 1951 to 1960. And before he played rugby with his Scottish officers, they hit him over the head with a hammer. Amin's reward was rapid promotion to 'effendi', the highest rank for a black soldier. His British commanders found him amusing and useful, believing that he was easily manipulated. As one of them put it, 'A splendid type, and a good rugby player, but virtually bone from the neck up and he needs things explained to him in words of one letter.'[4]

First the leaders of East Africa turned on their own, and last they turned on their own. In between, others of us got caught up in their inescapable machinations. Oppression becomes a habit, and both perpetrators and victims adjust to it. Even more astonishingly, the human spirit can stay upbeat through it all. In the early days and months we, the people of Uganda of all races, still found reasons to be hopeful and buoyant.

Edie Garvie started up a youth club for Asian boys and girls – the first of its kind – where we could socialize and play at romance away from the penetrating eyes of the old guard. She persuaded wary parents that the kids were safe with her. Soon some white and black youngsters joined in too. Up on Nakasero Hill at the All Saints' Church Hall she got us doing the Eightsome Reel, the Highland Fling, Do-si-do, Canadian barn dances and the Dashing White Sergeant, and belting out camp songs about the American Railway and She Who Sat Neath the Lilacs and Played Her Guitar. At the end of every joyous gathering we sang 'Auld Lang Syne' as if it was the last night of revelries, for who knew what would happen the next day? I made a cotton tartan skirt and waistcoat to wear to the club; having a seamstress mum meant I could sew at a young age. Now that we were twirling, I made myself some pretty knickers too, laced and ribboned. Until then Mum had made mine from leftover fabric, 10 inches down the thigh and elasticized at both ends, to keep me chaste.

The Bagchis had a young African, Charles Kabuga, staying with them, a new member of their open family. I danced the reels with Charles; he held my hands, which didn't turn black, as we were warned they would by our elders. Oh, the agony and ecstasy of transgressive acts! Garvie's club was never as safe as she believed. Palu, our neighbour, whose daughter went to the club, always picked us up. Then on the way home we stopped over to eat pomegranate chicken and coriander sweetcorn, a specialty of the café near the Odeon cinema.

Pomegranate Chicken

4 lb chicken pieces, unskinned (leg and thigh joints are best)
½ cup pomegranate sauce or paste (you can buy the dark brown, tangy paste or sauce ready-made in Arab-owned stores)

⦾ You simply half cook the chicken in its skin, then insert some of the paste under the skin and on top, and return to the fairly hot oven (400°F, 200°C, gas mark 6) or barbecue.

Sweetcorn with Coriander and Pepper

2 tins sweetcorn kernels, drained	2 oz butter
Salt and freshly ground pepper	2 tbsp finely chopped fresh coriander

- Melt the butter until it froths.
- Add corn, the seasonings and the corriander, and cook for a couple of minutes.
- You can add a squeeze of lime if you want.

My hormones were now rocking, and it didn't take long for me to throw myself into teenage angst and daring romance. I got myself a real boyfriend who didn't look much like Cliff or Paul McCartney but was still a catch. Vinod, nicknamed 'Kid', a skinny lad with a big head and curly hair, was indolent, smart, cool, supercilious and a great dancer. He later broke my tender little heart, two delicious years after I tasted my first wet kisses under the vast, dark, winking sky.

Kid took me to watch *The Young Ones*, Elvis films and any that featured the sexually and culturally androgynous Omar Sharif – very male yet with the most tender, clear, pool-like eyes, unmistakably Arab yet smooth as Dean Martin. The trips to the cinema cost Kid. He had to buy tickets for my mates Lilly and Vira, who came along as chaperones, only they too were a little crazy about Kid, who was unusually audacious for the son of a hard-working small shopkeeper. We were going steady, and the struggle was never to go anywhere near all the way. Did we really snog in the back rows of a dark cinema? Such behaviour had never been seen before, was most definitely not allowed. Besides, he was a Hindu, I a Shia Ismaili Muslim, and although the various Asian faiths worked and played together, when it came to crossover sex and marriage the old taboos came down with swords in hand.

Two lovers fell victim to this vicious intolerance to become the salutary lesson, the warning writ in scalding ink. Dinker Mehta was our chemistry teacher, Mr Dinker, young and trendy, who wore drainpipes and had an Elvis hairdo. He too was a Hindu, who had fallen madly in love with a young Sikh trainee teacher and she with him. And they were not careful. When word got out she was taken out of the school, never seen again. A few weeks later, Mr Dinker was found dead in the chemistry lab, in a pool of vomit. He had swallowed concentrated acid. Our grief and shock were indescribable. It was 1963. Then, a few weeks later, on 22 November, John F. Kennedy, general hero guy across much of Africa, was assassinated. Asian shops, open always, stayed closed the following day. Despondency and pessimism made the bones feel unnaturally cold. The sun still shone every day, but we couldn't feel its warmth.

A mere two months later came another cataclysmic shock. Zanzibar had only just become independent when, on 12 January 1964, a revolution shook the idyllic island, led by John Okello, a rabid African soldier of whose kind there are too many on the continent. Centuries of black anger buried like landmines exploded. His men beat up and looted Asians, shot Arabs and stole from some their young virginal daughters, the youngest only eleven, taken to be raped in vengeance for Arab racism and slavery. 'Arabiani Biriyani' they shouted as they grabbed and held aloft the tiniest screaming lasses. Soiled goods, they would never be taken back if and when returned. Blood ran down the small lanes of the old Stone Town. Occupied buildings and nationalized businesses could be borne, but how could the sacrifice of young girls ever be forgiven or forgotten? The royal clan and thousands of ordinary Arabs fled; those who stayed never recovered. Tanzania was born, red in tooth and claw. Unspeakable fear swept through the three East African territories. Asians were thrown into panic that the same fate would befall their girls one day.

Shamsu was agitated to the point of dementia: 'They want our girls, the *junglees*. They will take them too, so buy some guns, get some military training. We will have to fight them.' He bought a gun, got some training and one night, drunk as ever, shot his driver, Livingstone, while the faithful man dozed in the chill of the night, wrapped in a blanket. Shamsu was rich enough to pay off the police, the detectives and Livingstone's old widow, who seemed grateful to get more money than her husband had earned in a year. Some, a few, black men played on these fears. In public they baited us: 'Hey, you daughter of Shylock, how much money has your father sent out today? We know what you are doing. This is our country, you will be ours too.' When Asian men were about, they got bolder still. 'Hey, *mzee*, old man, tonight I come to your house, and you be giving me your daughter. Then we will do it, jigi-jigi, you know we African men do good jigi-jigi, and you can give me your big car, eh?'

The new menace was impossible to bear, and more Asians lost the will to remain in Africa. So much was happening so fast, the film reel itself seemed to have escaped the spool. It might have helped post-independence progress if schools, the media and political discourse had reminded the people of the contributions made by the imported subcontinental minority. The trade unionist Makhan Singh and the liber-ationist Pio Gama Pinto had given their lives in the pursuit of social justice and equality. Others, like Amir Jamal and Ambu Patel, were indispensable allies of the black leaders who took over after independence. Our children know nothing about these figures; East Africa has erased them from collective memory.[5]

It got worse, and fast. Asians saw an increase in snide insults and provocations appearing in print and speeches. Letters in newspapers got openly xenophobic: 'The government was neither instrumental in bringing these disgruntled Asians into the country, nor it is bound to stop their exodus.' 'They have stuck to their British passports like leeches...' 'The harvest of bad seeds was sown by Asians them-selves.' If Asians praised African politicians, they were despised as pathetic and insincere; if not they were damned as treacherous. True, Asians handed out bribes, but Africans expected and accepted them. It was how it was, had been for a long time. We found an erudite champion in Paul Theroux, who wrote a scathing essay on the way we were being treated:

In East Africa nearly everyone hates the Asians. Even some Asians say they hate the Asians. The British have hated the Asians longest and this bigotry they passed on to the Africans... Racial insult against the Asians now approaches the proportion of a fashion. According to popular East African opinion, the wahindi are responsible for flagrant racism, the failure of African socialism and progress, all the bad driving and motor accidents, sins of pride, envy, scandal, gluttony and lust, monopoly business, African neurosis, subversion of ruling parties, the success of dissident parties, the bloodshed of such terrorist groups as the shifta, a high birth-rate and bad food.[6]

Bad food even? It was not looking good for us.

The big Asian houses up the hills were darkly melancholic. Oh, those dazzling chandeliers, the roving spotlights to catch intruders, the fairy lights round trees and bushes all gone too, swallowed by the black around them. Wealth made the owners enemies of the socialist fervour building up around East Africa. Remember this was the Cold War playing out in countries which had no historical connections to either the US or the USSR. (Until I came to the UK I didn't know the name given to this long, malevolent, secretive conflict fought by invisible spies and diplomatic bribery.) Our leader the *Mukhi* made sober, coded speeches: 'In Islam, modesty is everything. Be modest in attire, in manners and do not provoke the envy of the locals. Allah wishes that. You sometimes forgot His message. Eyes are everywhere watching us.'

Servants who had used to stay with families until they dropped dead now came and went before they got to know the family secrets. In mosque women dressed simply, their many strings of pearls, chunky gold and shouty diamonds (big bling before the word) were buried deep (some in a vault in mosque) or smuggled away to Swiss banks. Like barren Christmas trees, they made us kids sad. No more *Khushiyali*, no more *dandia* and sweetmeats, and – most upsetting of all – Vallibhai's widow lost her *channa* corner. The glamour and colour disappeared; worshippers had lugubrious faces, their fingers rapidly running through the *tasbis* in their hands. They spoke with forked tongues, saying the right things to the new masters while in private, in the Asian languages, they abused and cursed the new politics.

Inexpensive dishes of penance were brought to mosque. But, and this was an open secret, in the homes of the big people, with the curtains drawn, the feasts were getting more outrageous, food absurdly richer, as if they were living through the last days of a hedonistic civilization – which in some ways they were. They had to eat up their wealth before the blackies got to it. In the home of my rich relatives, this dish was cooked every week, when previously it would be made only during Eid.

Creamy Lamb

Serves 6

3 lb leg of lamb, fat taken off and cut into small chunks

6 each whole cinnamon sticks, peppercorns, cardamom, cloves and star anise – usually called 'whole *masala*'

1 bunch of fresh mint, chopped

1 tsp chilli powder

4 tbsp oil

Flaked almonds, flash-fried in a little butter

1 pint whipping cream

3 tsp each crushed ginger and garlic

3 dried whole chillies

3 tsp mixture of ground cumin and coriander

1 tbsp *garam masala*

1 tsp paprika powder

4 onions, sliced

⊚   Heat the oil and add the chillies and whole *masala*. Let sizzle for two minutes, then add onions and fry until light brown.

- Add ginger, garlic, ground coriander and cumin, and fry for another three minutes.

- Add meat, cream, chilli and paprika powders and half a cup of water.

- Lower heat so the lamb can simmer.

- Cook for an hour and ten minutes, or more until the meat is very soft. In the last ten minutes open the lid so the sauce can thicken. Stir regularly.

- Add *garam masala*, mint and nuts.

- Serve with *roti*.

The mosque caretakers, known as *jamatbhais*, were pious though cantankerous men who gave up their whole lives to keeping the place pure and pristine. Holders of keys and secrets, they knew every member of the congregation, what illnesses and misfortunes befell them, what their daughters were up to, where the tithe funds were spirited. Their sharp eyes could pick out any non-Ismailis trying foolishly to sneak into the holy enclave. They lived in the compound and survived on the food brought in every day by the faithful. Hadi, our *jamatbhai*, loved Jena's coconut dhal so she always remembered to take in some for him in plastic containers, wrapped in muslin, sealed with tape and with her name scrawled on the cream cloth.

 My Mum's Coconut Dhal

Serves 6–8

½ cup red *masoor dhal*

½ cup *channa dhal*

2 tbsp vegetable oil

1 tsp turmeric

1 tsp crushed garlic

1 tsp cumin seeds

Salt and lime juice to taste

½ cup hulled *moong dhal*

½ packet coconut cream – the block variety

2 green chillies, slashed open

1 tin chopped tomatoes

Lots of chopped fresh coriander

4 hard-boiled eggs, halved

- Boil the *dhals* in salted water until cooked but not totally mushy – the water should stay to about 3 inches above the lentils.

- Add the coconut and simmer further for about five minutes (the block will start to melt).

- Heat the oil in a small pan.

- Throw in the chillies and cumin. When you hear the seeds cracking, add all the ingredients apart from the salt, lime juice and eggs, and cook gently for fifteen minutes.

- Meanwhile, with a hand whisk, mix and mash the dhal until it looks a little like porridge.

- Add the tomato mixture and simmer for ten minutes.

- Add lime juice and salt to taste, then float the eggs in the mixture.

- Eat piled on to thick slices of bread or with plain rice.

The snootiest families had to submit to the will of the humble, impeccably honest *jamatbhai*, possibly the only untainted worshipper in that house of God. Hadi had married and produced six fine boys, one of whom, Farooq, was given into the service of Allah soon after he was born. The child would be the next *jamatbhai* come what may. Farooq declined to honour the promise and is into real estate in Texas. His father died a wretched man, terrified of the punishment waiting for him in the hereafter.

Feelers were put out so due arrangements could be made to protect hard-earned, untaxed piles. The sons of poorer Asian families, previously employed by the rich to mind shops, became daring runners and mules. They were sent on air trips to Europe, loaned winter coats, paid enough to sneak out jewellery and sterling. Hadi's second son grabbed the opportunities thrown up by this gold rush out. Cobblers hand-stitched what they called 'hugger mugger' ('HM') shoes with ingenious hiding cavities in heels and platform soles. Best-selling bags were made with many secret compartments. Some couriers never came back. Somjibhai, a friend of my father who lived in Harrow until he died, was still looking for one missing black-guard: 'One day I will find him that Badrudin and denounce him in the mosque. Allah will surely put him into hell. *Sala badmash* took everything – I turned from prince to worse than pauper. Do you know how many pounds were in the shoes? Plus gold bar big as shoebox in his suitcase.'

Meanwhile more and more spoiled-brat London returns were coming and going to torment us. These were the children of the most show-offy Asians, sent out to be educated at D-list English boarding schools which taught them only cheap conceit.

Yasmin Walli from my old school said Africa was boring and backward. She brought pictures of herself in winter coats next to a snowman. (Do you know how much we wanted to touch snow?) Their clothes were fabulously ready-made with labels stuck on the back of the neck. Their older sisters wore nylons and hair coiffed to make them look like stickler stenographers (which most were). Not Nadya, though; she was an artist, a choice as outrageous as career prostitution. She wore silver-paper dresses one year – all the rage, she said, in Carnaby Street. The young men returnees had become dull pharmacists or accountants, or property solicitors. They spoke Hindi, Gujarati and Kutchi with English accents, looked down on us and spoke of steaks and prawn cocktails, claimed they no longer had the stomach for spicy food. Well, it didn't take long for the little people to catch up and subvert these *malai barafu* (our nickname for them, meaning 'creamy lollipops'), often by spicing up the recipes they said were thoroughly, properly, tastelessly English.

 Chilli Steak

6 slices fillet steak, beaten flat with a
    meat hammer

A small amount of oil for frying
1 tbsp malt vinegar

Marinade
4 tbsp thick yoghourt
1½ tsp ginger/garlic mix
3 green chillies (hot)

Bunch of fresh coriander
1 tbsp tomato purée
¾ tsp salt

⊙ Zap the marinade ingredients together in a food processor for two minutes, then spoon a little in the middle of the meat slices. Roll and tie them with thread, as for beef olives.

- Pour vinegar on the rolls.

- Leave covered overnight in the fridge.

- Heat the oil till sizzling, and lift the steaks from the juices to fry three minutes on each side.

- Place in a warm dish.

- Cook up the leftover marinade on high heat for three to four minutes, and slap the paste back on the meat. Serve with iceberg lettuce leaves.

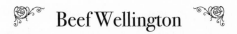

Beef Wellington

A hunk of fillet steak
Ready-made puff pastry
1 beaten egg to glaze

Marinade as above
A little good-quality butter

- Slice the steak lengthwise and submerge in the marinade.

- Cover and leave for twenty-four hours in the fridge.

- Remove the meat and pat dry.

- Cook the marinade down until the mixture thickens.

- Sandwich the meat slabs with the paste – not too much, mind.

- Roll out the pastry big enough to completely enclose the meat.

- Spread butter on all sides of the meat, place in the middle of the rolled-out pastry, fold over to cover and seal with egg.

- Brush rest of the egg all over.

- Bake in a medium-hot oven (350°F, 180°C, gas mark 4) until nicely brown, about fifteen to twenty minutes.

- Serve with a salad.

Chicken *Ishtew*

Serves 6

1 large chicken, skinned and cut into pieces	4 each carrots, parsnips, large onions, tomatoes, potatoes and leeks
3 oz butter	
Chicken stock, enough to reach 1 in. over the chicken and vegetables	3 sticks each cinnamon and cloves
1 tsp *garam masala*	6 peppercorns and cardamom pods opened up
1 tsp grated ginger	1 green chilli
1 tin coconut milk	Salt to taste

- Melt the butter and add the whole spices and ginger.

- Sweat all the vegetables in the butter over low heat.

- Add the chicken and stir for five minutes.

- Add the stock and simmer uncovered for fifteen minutes.

- Stir in *garam masala*, chilli and coconut milk.

- Cover and cook for another ten minutes, then add salt.

- Some of the vegetables will turn soft – that is fine.

- Eat with fresh French bread.

Modernist buildings were going up everywhere, as hideous as the ones in England only we never thought so. The old Art Deco architecture was so embarrassingly yesterday. Most proudly modern, all sharp edges and futuristic, was the new parliament going up close to where we then lived in Century House, a block of spanking-new flats which had bathtubs and tiles, rented by the up-and-coming, sign of Babu's growing prosperity.

In the daytime, back doors were open in most of the fifty apartments, and women bellowed to each other, whacked their kids, complained about men in a chorus of despair broken by grating laughs. Sometimes a voice would go silent, and you knew the man or his doting mother had arrived to enforce compliance. When the heat and noise got too much, my girlfriends and I escaped to the roof, and there among the water tanks we pretended we were ballerinas. One was the daughter of one of the opium-nightclub women. Papa thought the girl was the devil's spawn and forbade any contact. So she became my new best mate.

I have problems working out what exactly happened to my sister around this time. She was also an England returnee for a while, turning up in glam clothes and matching shoes and bags, looking better than Twiggy definitely. The last time she had shown up in Kampala was soon after we had moved to Century House. Everything had turned silently gloomy. Jena wept day and night. A photo was taken of us all on the day my sister flew back to London. The women look grim, and the men seem to have slaughter on their minds. I didn't know then that she was young, unmarried and pregnant, and determined to keep her child whatever they threatened. Such a scandal would have shocked England of the time. Imagine, then, the response of an already troubled Ugandan Asian family.

Then she vanished from my life. Her photographs were taken down; my mother's voice sounded high and false when she told people her older daughter was doing so well in England. Years on she did visit for a few days with a beautiful young daughter, married and happy. Papa never spoke to the child. When we met up properly again in the early 1970s, my startlingly beautiful sister was beginning to show signs of mental illness. It slowly took her over. What a book she might have written one day.

Papa went through more bouts of depressive withdrawal from work and life interspersed with manic episodic activity. Always forgetful, he was stuffing too many live cigarettes into his pockets, and we all learned to keep an eye on him. The bizarre spurts of adventuring were harder on us than the times when he sank into hopeless silence. Maybe he was bipolar. Maybe he was truly a dreamer who fell to earth and took off again and again. I wish I had understood his dreams better. In 1966 he took part ownership of the Chinese restaurant downstairs in Century House. This for a man who only ever wanted one egg on toast for supper each night, who had all his teeth removed at forty for good health, he said, who was indifferent to food, except for *paya* – goats' trotters – on Sunday mornings, stewed with subtle spices and eaten with crusty bread.

Back at the Canton he was quite the gentleman – suit, cigarette holder, chain watch in his waistcoat. He ambled from table to table, engaging the customers in bouts of political conversation. In the first months, the books showed a little profit, but all too soon the affluent regulars and anniversary couples disappeared, and the place was filled with his City Bar comrades who never paid for anything but loved verbally jousting with Kassim, their very good friend. You can guess the end. It only took eighteen months. When I went back to Uganda in 1999 to make a radio programme, the sign for the Canton was still flapping; the place was a fax bureau, now is probably an internet café.

A new flock of white people had been flying over through the 1960s, mostly Brits but some American draft dodgers too and a few continental Europeans. They were much nicer than our copycat England returns and thankfully different from the old imperial sort. The newcomers were free, flowing, easy, wore crumpled cheesecloth and cheap sandals, and their white feet were dirty – a novel sight that, dirty white feet.

They came to teach in our school. Miss Lachlan, from Paris, was nursing an irrecoverably broken heart and wore her dresses with the zip in front and pointy darts at the back. She taught us sad French poetry and Camus. And we compliantly fell into existential angst in her lessons. Jim Ball, the handsome American, was tall, muscular and sneering, and said he was one of the divers in *Dr No*. How could we not believe him? He drove an open-topped black car and broke the heart of poor Miss Mary, our Goan domestic-science teacher, who had gone from mousy to sexy in no time at all, turning into a coquettish vixen in miniskirts and Hollywood-heroine sunglasses. Jim Ball left her for another Mary, a sensuous black singer at the local nightclub. You could have crafted four Miss Mary's from this rival's bountiful flesh.

My brother was married now and the man of the house but still having to provide for his parents and sisters. It must have been so difficult to launch his own life. Mum, Papa and I were tied to him like those noisy tin pots on a string pulled by street vendors. To me his wife was a surly interloper; to her I must have come across as an unruly and wilful teenager. There never was any affection between us, only awful, poisonous antipathy. I remember exactly the day we met. She came into our home wearing a tight satin dress with jumbo scarlet roses and a bow across her ample hips. She pretended to smile. Her eyes roamed round the flat as if she was surveying her own territory, which she was. Jena offered her tea and snacks with a voice getting smaller and weaker as if she was already beaten.

My mother felt usurped, and for many years our home became a frontline where females battled as only they can. Babu was caught (he conveniently claimed) in the middle. He decided I was a no-good hussy who needed to be disciplined. It was often desperately hard, and I took refuge with neighbours when tempers erupted and violence engulfed the flat. It felt as though the political storm clouds and the squalls in our home were reinforcing each other. The sun cast only shadows. I cried a lot.

School was different. There life was brilliant, especially after the tall, blonde Mrs Mann, Jim Ball and other free spirits came in to rock the place. Our head, Mr Raval, had an imperial mindset – he was flattered white teachers had come to his school. Maybe he should have been a little more circumspect. These were strangers who didn't understand our divided lives, our divided selves. Looking back, although I paid a heavy price for their libertarian ideas, I am glad they took risks with their pupils and refused to conform.

Joyce Mann decided to overturn the social order, stir things up, using a school play. She announced a production of *Romeo and Juliet* for a major British Council drama competition with the Capulets played by Asians and the Montagues by African pupils. Off I went to the audition, bursting with hope and expectation, desperate to get the part of Juliet. But no other girl even put up her hand. There was no competition. I got the part. Wise girls. Romeo was played by John Abwole, a graceful, idealistic young black man with treacly eyes.

My memory played safe and wiped out the truth, the dangerous truth, that we touched and kissed on stage. Until now I believed we only spoke of love, and that was daring enough. I had to erase the rest, possibly because I was aroused by this gentle, alluring boy. Writing that, even now, sends shivers of fear through me. Remember – I existed in that space between superior whites and the beasts of burden. And from that space you did not reach across to touch black skin or kiss black lips or give your heart to a black man. Even in a school play.

How did John feel? Elated that we were living in times when this was allowed or terrified that he was trespassing on dangerous ground? He never said. A few years on I had a letter from him from India, where he had gone to join the Ugandan consulate and hadn't had the right jabs, so was in quarantine. He wrote, 'I can see India from my window, the lovely women in their colourful clothes. I am dying to get out there.' Soon after he was killed in a car crash. So my African Romeo is buried in India.

Vinod, the cool boyfriend, was Tybalt. Watching me on stage with John turned his stomach. In his eyes I became an easy miss, available, shameless. He tried and failed to get me to surrender my precious virginity just as we were working up to first night. This meant that the tension between Romeo and Tybalt was as real as was the animosity between the Montagues and Capulets. Mrs Mann encouraged them to bring in mock weapons, and they did. And oh the fights, swagger, jibes and blades. It was as if both sides knew the universe was changing. The Capulets knew their wealth was no longer enough to protect their status; the Montagues strutted, looked us in the eye. They were never going to be our servants again, these future lawyers, ministers, judges. As they went for each other, it was the past battling with the future in Verona.

Our play won first prize in the British Council drama competition. I was pronounced an 'enchanting Juliet' by Betsy, the adjudicator from the Council, and awarded a scholarship to study at a drama school in London.

That incredible evening a teacher drove me home. I rushed up to the dark stair-well leading to our flat. I could smell the redolence, the deep fragrance of jasmine woven into my long black plait, and my lips were painted bright chilli-red. I was wearing a white-and-gold gossamer sari. On my arms dozens of glass bangles jangled jubilantly. I had my silver-coloured cup shaped like a Babycham glass. It held my joy, radiance, liquid gold. As I stepped into the dimly lit living room I saw a crowd of people – my mother, my father, my brother and his wife – whose face was hard as granite, uncles, aunts, my cousin and his box-shaped wife. They appeared so deadly serious, I thought someone had died. My father was looking down, his long arms dangling, his smoky breath rattling. My mother wept into her *pacheli*, her chubby frame wobbling with terrible grief. My cousin's wife smiled. There was lipstick on her teeth like blood on a hyena's jaws. And then one of my cousins moved towards me, his eyes like knives. He grabbed me and there followed a frightful beating. I still carry some indelible marks. My crime? Romeo was black, and for an Asian Juliet this was forbidden love even in an innocent school play. One male cousin grabbed my shoulders, banged my head against a wall, slapped, scratched my face. Another pinched my arms and broke the glass bangles I was wearing. They called me a *vaishia*, a slut, a polluter of their good name. What good name? This was not the first nor the last time fists were used instead of words in my family.

Kassim didn't hit me, but he still didn't look or speak. My mother's voice shouted in vain to stop them. A story had blazed around Kampala that I had tried to elope with an African and a young Asian man had to fight him off with a knife to save my honour.

My mother eventually forgave me. Kassim couldn't look me in the eye, couldn't talk to me, never explained what I had done that was so wrong. Perhaps a lump of hypocrisy was stuck in his throat. He never ever spoke to me again after that night.

Yet Kassim had always claimed that he was a socialist and egalitarian. He impetuously gave his best clothes (ours too sometimes) to African beggars, and always shared his cigarettes and money with the neighbourhood servants who approached 'bwana Kassim' easily, without fear or exaggerated humility. He was also acutely aware that in the changing political landscape made us vulnerable. Did he mean any of it? Or was he incapable of practising the racial equality he preached? I'll never know.

After that night he lost any remaining authority. Papa crawled permanently into his pyjamas, withered into self-pity. I realized then that he mattered, that I needed him. He had guided me to the great writers, to Shakespeare, Dickens, Orwell, Hawthorne, Wordsworth, and made me read about leaders who had changed history. From about the age of nine, thanks to him, I was already an avid reader and politically aware. I idolized his stimulating, independent mind, but Papa was not someone you could love or who loved back conspicuously. He never hugged or kissed any of his children. As I watch my husband crushing our daughter to his heart it brings out envy, sorrow, regret, longing, sometimes flashes of anger in me. What I do know, though, is that after my sister disappeared and as my body matured, Papa had grown suspicious and controlling. And although he was never physically violent, I became more apprehensive of his moods and demands. A man who sought freedom all his life feared any signs of it in his children. Perhaps because he knew it would make us too much like him.

I couldn't breathe at home, so choked up was I with tension and relentless misery and the constant reminders that we were a burden on my brother. Mum started having a swig or two of good brandy, saying it calmed her nerves and stopped her blood pressure rising to levels she though were fatal. Then came epileptic fits such that I thought one would surely kill her. Brandy helped then too, and glucose forced through her clenched teeth held open with a spoon. Sometimes Papa was hopeless, and scurried off to his room and newspapers; at other times he turned incredibly tender, stroked her forehead, promised in whispers that he would find work and get us our own flat. It was love, only unable to declare itself when she was conscious.

Asians all over Uganda wondered if it had been worth it, the good life built on the desolation of alienation. There were days when nothing would shift the dismal mood that settled round the table. Like mosquitoes after Flit had been sprayed in a room, all of them felt lifeless and hopeless.

6 *Paradise Bust, 1967–72*

IN OUR ISMAILI COMMUNITY children born from the late 1960s onwards seemed to bring with them tumultuous temperaments. They howled and yowled, and their tantrums appeared to come from prior, preternatural knowledge, as if they knew chaos was approaching and were afraid. More women seemed to be pregnant, including matronly grandmothers. Maybe procreation became defiance against the odds; maybe repeated sex was the only solace, the unseen future made flesh. But as the newborns multiplied, so did frightful superstitions. Rumours paced the streets. Such stories.

Births were getting more traumatic as babies clung to the womb, or so it was believed. Munira's infant, they said, had to be cut out and still wouldn't be lifted by Faten, the stout midwife with arms the size of large gas cylinders. The child won his fight to die before he was born. It took eight days to get Rumi's twins out. Faten had by then inserted a whole packet of butter into Rumi's vagina. Usually, she boasted, it only took 2 teaspoons of grease and her mighty arms. Malek's little girl never uttered a sound for weeks, and the black of her eyes dissolved to sea green (her parents were delighted with the new European colour). Then she was pronounced blind.

Faten asked families to send extra *zakat*, charity, to the mosques and orphanages. Similar tales of woe were spreading through the Sikh, Parsee and Hindu communities. Some religious pundits seeking renewed powers of intervention suggested the children were possessed or damned. The noisy babies invaded meditations, chants, prayers and hymns. Dummies sweetened with honey, songs, cuddles, bottles, even soft, comforting voices had no effect. It resounded and echoed without respite, this collective trauma of the innocents. One inventive chap started selling aspirins in mosque next to the drinking fountain. Business was brisk for a while until everyone decided it was cheaper to bring in their own.

Obote was the prototype, the stereotype writ large, of a post-independent African leader who marched his people into valleys of death all too soon after the balloons came down and the flags went up. The only difference today is that most ordinary Africans see through the beaded curtains of lies, know their thieving, callous rulers so well that they have ceased to believe things can ever get better. So they flee the continent, the cradle of civilization. How did it come to this? Those of us who woke to the early sunny days of freedom now witness the horror of African boat people perishing at sea, washing up on European shores, their corpses pleading for rights they never knew in life.

In 1968 Obote became concerned about the youth protests in Europe and the US. What if the young, educated élites in his country acted up too? So he rounded up student leaders from all across the country. Then a head prefect, I was informed that I had to represent Kololo School and be grateful for the 'unique opportunity'. We were put into a political boot camp. For three months we lodged in the army barracks next to Government House in Entebbe and were instructed on governance, patriotism, leadership, one-party government and loyalty. Obote sent us off to various ministerial departments and the army, got us to question the system, all very democratic or so we thought. Only delegates started to disappear, the vocal ones who were too curious or critical. We never saw them again, and Obote's teeth – spaced apart like prison bars – were a nightly reminder of where they now were.

This was our long vacation when we should have been jiving and picnicking on the lakeside beaches and bruising our lips with illicit kisses. What a waste. Only five inmates were Asian. At the long colonial dining table, the cruel and capricious President baited the Asians: '*Wahindi*, how much money left for England this week, eh? I like you people. I wish we could learn your dirty tricks. You must teach us.' Like all African élites, he had his own dirty tricks, his many overseas bank accounts too. Idi Amin was also present, commander of the army. I met him at the army HQ and asked him why there were no Asians recruits. He looked down at me, a malevolent laugh burned up from his belly like lava, and he spat: 'Because we do not eat *chorocco* [lentils] in the army. We are brave people, we Africans, we eat red blood meat. You are not African.'

During the key years when Obote was consolidating illegitimate power, Idi Amin had made himself indispensable, going on what were described as 'map-reading exercises' to spread fear throughout Uganda. He shed blood indiscriminately and whimsically punished entire villages, impatiently ordered mass burials (some were buried alive) and presided over them with mock solemnity. Ceremonials after killing orgies were the gilded frames around his instinctive brutality.

There was considered violence too. Political detentions increased as did torture. Key figures disappeared. Amin filled the army and secret service with Nubian soldiers. They were Muslims like him, and loyal, aliens in Uganda, speakers of strange tongues, perfect killing machines for Amin to use for, and ultimately against, any politician who tried to quell his excesses.

Obote had miscalculated. He had promoted his illiterate soldier-pleaser, convinced himself that his protégé would, for his own survival, fight off any threats to his leader's rule. The delusion was fleeting, its consequences lasting. A Shakespearean power struggle loomed.

By the end of 1969 President and commander had become irreconcilable foes. Yet they knew each other's deadliest secrets. Breaking the alliance would weaken them both, but like conjoined twins they couldn't stay stuck together for much longer. The hills of Kampala echoed with the sounds of plots, counter-plots, mutterings of double and triple agents, rumours and portentous signs. Then, on 19 December 1969, as Obote stepped out into the cool air after a party political meeting in Kampala, a shot was heard and a bullet entered his jaw, taking out two teeth but leaving him otherwise unscathed. The attempted assassination was well planned, and Amin was clearly behind it. When security guards went to question him, he fled. When they found him, he denied their allegations.

Meanwhile discrimination against Asians across the three East African states was legitimized. In 1966, Obote decreed that not all children born in Uganda had an automatic right to citizenship. Three years later, a new act required non-Ugandan citizens to deposit £5,000 in a government bank account in order to do business.

Blackenization was seen as a necessary part of development. Between 1968 and 1972, up to 9,000 families were denied the right to earn a living.[1] Asians were still too politically naive, powerless and unable to fight back except through underhand means – corrupt pay-offs, mostly, and a bigger illicit outflow of money. That only added to their negative image. In the UK, the 1968 Commonwealth Immigrants Act was passed, denying East African Asians right of entry. Quotas were established to control the numbers of Kenyan Asians with British passports who had lost the right to work and had severe conditions imposed on them by the Kenyan government. Uganda and Tanzania quickly followed suit.

The young remained untouched by these sinister developments. I should have, and didn't, pick up the messages I had been sent while at the boot camp. Rock 'n' roll parties had to keep the music down to reduce the anger of envious blacks; parents turned up early to pick up their children. Meanwhile, I attained the highest A-level arts grades in the country so was awarded a scholarship to go to university – at last a girl of independent means. The six months leading up to the exams had been intolerable at home. Nag, nag, nag all day long from everyone except Mum, whose support was unfailing. My photo appeared in the *Uganda Argus* in an Op-art black-and-white dress. Mr Raval, who had first tamed me by making me into head girl (after my *Romeo and Juliet* disgrace), handed me a pure-gold medal with little grace and much unexpected affection. His hug was tight, a father's hug I had never had.

Immediately afterwards, destiny delivered to me my own TL, in the back of a car belonging to his good friend Diamond, who was secretly going out with my then best friend, tall and gorgeous Nazira, who was promised to another. We were their cover, their alibis. I was iridescent with happiness, high on success. After Vinod I was seethingly ready for the next time. Like a ripe and ready piece of fruit, I must have exuded a powerful, beckoning aroma. My TL bit. I turned up to watch him playing his drums at a school dance and was struck down by the power of real, palpable love. From that day until 1988, there was no other for me.

By this time I had become a smooth operator; one does at that age. I pretended I was with girlfriends when I was meeting my TL at dances and parties – my face painted, in revealing borrowed clothes, my hair ironed to look like Jean Shrimpton's. I was and still am a pretty top dancer. No one could do the cha-cha, bossa nova, Twist or jive better than me. (My body moves with scandalous sensuality even now, well into my fifties. This is wantonness I was born with.) The other girls were better brought up or just not so instinctively wild. Young men, losers with no chance, would sidle up to me and whisper, 'Yaar, you are the bombshell baby of Bombay' (referring to that popular Hindi movie vamp Nadia, who drank Black Label whisky and danced in nightclubs). I preferred to think of myself as one of the *West Side Story* gals.

TL was already at Makerere University, described as the Harvard of Africa. I was headed there, away from Papa's silent retribution, my brother's volatility (so much worse now he was feeding it self-pity), his wife and my mother's endless sorrows. I could see the pain and pride in Jena's eyes as I packed, and iron determination too to help me escape. She made Japani's lemon pickle and *parathas* for me to take with me and gave me six bottles of Sanatogen tonic packed in a special-offer box. My blood, she was sure, would turn thin without her food. By this time Papa had more or less disappeared under the bedcovers, coming out only to pick up his newspapers and eat a little. Sometimes he didn't bother to bathe or shave. He looked more gaunt than before; his cheeks were hollows, his eyes moist and opaque, grey like his hair. His punishing silence never relented.

I was enchanted with TL's family, the Alibhais, whose name I still keep long after my divorce because I was so deeply a part of them once, and you can't sever such a connection without bleeding away much of what makes you who you are. There they were, fifteen of them including parents, a grandmother, siblings and grandchildren, all able to hold together in spite of ceaseless rows. Unlike us, the Damjis. Lunches there were not peaceful but always were bonding. Some complained the food was too hot so their mother, an administering angel, cooled it down; others complained it was not hot enough so it was returned to the kitchen for reheating. The father was big and spoiled, commanded absolute respect and got it. All the sons were handsome with chiselled features and gorgeous smiles. Mine also had fairish skin – a plus, plus, plus. A real family of my own at last. Or so I thought.

Next stop Makerere, the women's hall of residence, Mary Stuart Hall, a ghastly 1960s tower block, for me very heaven. It was the end of 1969, just as the country was getting calamitously close to fragmentation. The campus swept up a hill lush with grass, green as the colour of life itself. Nandi Flame trees, and others high and wide and ancient, provided shade for students reading books and debating ideas. The main building stood at the top, white and imposing with a bell tower. Shoots of new possibilities were all around us. We would retell the story of our country. Africa was neither intellectually barren nor uncivilized before the white man came. We were determined – black, brown and white Makererians – to make Uganda proud and great one day.

I joined the literature department, the most exhilarating on campus. The European canon was still faithfully taught but had to compete with compelling new voices. Paul Theroux excited us with his indefinable but extraordinary talent; we were reading James Baldwin and emerging black American writers, African dramatists and novelists such as Wole Soyinka and Chinua Achebe and V. S. Naipaul, who never returned the love we had for his books. He visited in the mid-1960s and, though a beautiful writer, had the unpleasant self-regard of a London return contemptuous of everything African. Some African tutors were systematically unfair to the Asians and possessive of the emerging nation, making up for history, I guess. But mostly it felt like we were travelling together to another country where race was irrelevant and rainbows appeared every day.

I was intellectually stimulated like never before, surrounded by friends, music, books and drama, and truly in love. I gave myself to TL one hot afternoon, in my second year there, in his room in a hall of residence. He had been remarkably patient, saintly even. The previous year, we had spent two nights in an oak-panelled cabin on a train to Mombasa (an illicit jaunt). The slow rhythmic movements invited you to make love, but I had been too afraid to let go, and so we made do with above-the-waist fumblings and exaggerated declarations of love. Till she died Mum believed I was a virtuous virgin who only did it with my husband. In fact I did it with my husband-to-be.

I shared a room with two African girls, Jane and Sophie, young women who, like me, never imagined they would, one day, be at university. Such cross-racial room-sharing was still rare; I knew I was perceived by many Asian students as a bad example.

(The *Romeo and Juliet* scandal was recycled.) I went to African bars ('*Hai, hai,*' said the good Asian girls, 'what about your reputation?').

Sophie was tall and big with a laugh to shake Kilimanjaro. Her life holds the serial tragedies of Uganda: relatives killed by Obote and, later, Amin; exile; HIV and the funeral procession that never seems to end. Jane was beautiful and distant, so irresistible to men. Messages were left for her on the message board, sometimes the whole board: 'Come and jig with me, O lady Jane.' Unfortunately, she fell for Anton, the black Californian with a tight body and mean eyes, a poseur and cheat who wore a Che beret. These black Americans were root-seeking, they said. Actually they were a pain. Anton called Jane his 'jungle bunny', and she, smitten, smiled with much pleasure. He took her money. She was delighted to provide. Sophie warned her: 'Jane, are you foolish or what? Opening your legs and purse for this man? Sister, get some sense.' One day I was wearing Jane's brown, shirt-styled dress. ('*Hai, hai,*' said the Asian lookouts, 'you will get a disease!') Anton caught me alone and tried to unbutton the dress: 'Get some thrills woman, let go, be free.' The creep.

TL had bought a handsome orange-coloured motorbike, a Honda 125. With his looks, tight bum and now this, I knew other girls would try and snatch him. But I knew they didn't have my fire. What a fast lass I was then, in high heels, wearing flagrantly short miniskirts and hot pants, riding up a storm. My father told Mum I was indeed a *vaishia*, a whore, just as predicted. She conveyed the message and apologized on his behalf.

Food was terrible at Uni – over-fried eggs, *posho* (red beans), stringy meat and *matoke*, tasteless mince and soggy rice. Precious home-made pickles made it edible. Jena sent over jar after jar of her marmalade-y mango concoction, a favourite among Asians and also among African students who had not been exposed to Asian cooking. They loved it so much they stole many of my jars.

Hot Mango Marmalade

1 lb unripe large green mangoes   1½ cup granulated sugar
4 sticks cinnamon   5 cloves
1½ tsp chilli powder   ½ tsp salt
½ pint water

- Grate the mangoes and boil in the water for about six minutes.
- Drain the fruit and return water to the pan.
- Add sugar and spices to the water, and cook until the syrup is sticky.
- Add mangoes, and carry on stirring and cooking until thick.
- Stir in chilli powder and salt; cook for a couple more minutes.
- Cool and store in sterilized airtight jars.
- Terrific with everything, especially eggs on toast.

You can call our emerging integration a small sign of unity. Away from campus, however, the mood was bleak. In his ruthlessly honest travel book about India, *An Area of Darkness* (1964), Naipaul described how middle-class Indians removed themselves from truths too awful for their fine sensibilities: 'India is a stone's throw away but in the flat it is denied; the beggars, the gutters, the starved bodies, the weeping, swollen bellied child black with flies in the filth and cow dung and human excrement of a bazaar lane, the dogs, ribby, mangy, cowed and cowardly, reserving their anger, like the humans around them, for others of their kind.'[2] This was us exactly. Some Asian undergraduates developed two personas, one obedient and yielding to family traditions and old structures, exaggeratedly so, to protect the other, which was free and liberal and in revolt against the apartheid that had served their people well before. In my second year I made a lifelong Asian friend, another oddball like me but more of a loner. Feriyal was a medical student from Dar-es-Salaam and a nonconformist Ismaili, brave woman. She was quiet and sulky and determinedly dowdy; I was loud and sparkly and fashion-mad. Unfathomable why we were drawn to each other. By this time I was so alienated from my home life that I was unable to integrate back into it; I was making my own alternative family away from home. Feriyal and I remain firm buddies – even though she is now a patriotic American doctor in Pittsburgh permanently perplexed by what I do and why. She certainly never expected this rebel to surrender to tradition just to keep a boyfriend.

By now TL's family regarded me as their daughter so I too had to grow a homely side. Outside I could be the rave queen; with them I was sweetly compliant. In return they loved me, a conditional and time-restricted love, I now know but didn't then.

Dutiful and respectful, I went to mosque every Friday. I wore saris, twisted my hair into buns (they make you look virtuous), perfected all the rituals.

In mosque, as times got harder, the low tables of food offerings were overladen. Only now the simple food had gone; the mood had swung the other way. It was time for extravagant dishes, desperate measures, hopeless hope. Sugar had gone up shockingly in price, so more atoning sweetmeats were brought in, and the *seero* – small bites of semolina given to congregations at the end of service with holy water (our wafer and wine if you like) – was cooked to a sweetness more concentrated than toffee. Dozens of ladies from the *Khushiyali* Food Committee made the most luxurious biriyanis for festivals (now marked discreetly and without *fujo* and *band-wajas*). Cooking on wood fires in enormous pots, each holding enough for sixty people, they sang laments as they cut and stirred and fried. Sometimes tears dropped into the rice.

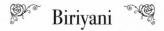

Biriyani

Serves 6–8

3 cups basmati rice

2 large onions, sliced thin

1 large onion, chopped

2 tins chopped tomatoes

1½ tbsp crushed garlic/ginger mix

1½ cup sunflower or vegetable oil

2 lb cut pieces of leg of lamb, fat shaved off

8 small parboiled potatoes

5 tbsp tomato purée

3 green chillies, chopped

1 large tsp saffron

2 cups ordinary, plain yoghourt　　　　1½ tbsp *garam masala*

3 tbsp lemon juice　　　　　　　　　　Salt to taste

Some yellow or orange food colouring

Whole *masala* made up of 8 sticks of cinnamon, 8 cloves and 8 cardamom pods

1 cup crisply fried onions (available ready-made at Asian food stores)

- You need to marinate the meat overnight, or for at least six hours, in the yoghourt, garlic, ginger, half the saffron, salt, green chillies, chopped onion, tomatoes, tomato purée and half the whole *masala*.

- Cook this in the oven in a covered pan (350°F, 180°C, gas mark 4). The meat needs to be soft. It takes about an hour and a half but may need less or more time, depending on the quality of the lamb.

- In a large frying pan, fry the sliced onions and potatoes in half the oil. Both should turn brown, not too dark though.

- Add these to the cooked meat mixture. Move the meat into a bowl (you'll need the lidded pot later).

- Add *garam masala* and lemon juice to the meat, and mix in well.

- Wash and parboil the rice in plenty of salted water, then drain.

- Heat the rest of the oil, and chuck in the remaining whole *masala*.

- Pour a third into the meat and the rest into the rice.

- Now take the lidded pot and lay down the rice, sprinkling over it the remaining saffron and food colouring dissolved in half a cup of water.

- Then top with the meat mixture and sprinkle with fried onions.

- Cover and return to the oven (350°F, 180°C, gas mark 4) for twenty minutes.

- Remove and leave covered for another ten.

- This dish is as luxurious as it gets, five-star and indulgent. During *Khushiyali* in London in July, they still make it for more than twenty thousand and serve it in the cavernous Olympia exhibition centre. The smell spreads through to the streets.

———◦———

Before love got me to surrender to convention, I liked going to mosque but only to meet mates, flirt with the boys and gaze upon the gorgeously turned-out women. How wicked I was. Jena was very religious, and it upset her, this lack of blind faith and my youthful challenges to pre-modern precepts and some of the rules. (Kassim had clearly influenced me more than either of us realized.) 'Yassi, why can't you just believe? Let me believe? Papa also asking the same unanswerable questions. Thinks he is so clever. Some things just are. I can't give you answers, I am not Allah. It gives me peace. One day you will pray as I do, you will look for that peace, wait and see when I am gone.' (She was so, so right.)

Imagine how she felt as she watched her recalcitrant daughter worshipping with TL's family while she sat by herself in mosque. Some people noticed the slight and offered comfort, which she politely shoved aside. A part of her welcomed the conversion, but I know she was also hurt. I rarely went home, but sometimes I would go back to my room at college and find a parcel of food left there by Jena, who had hitched a lift to deliver her love to my doorstep, so I would not forget or replace her. The strong smells of *dhebra* and *jugu* cake wafted off the waiting plastic boxes. Nobody else can make them like Jena could, and I feel it is sacrilege even to try. Noorbanu, a close friend of my mother, gave me these recipes.

 *Dhebra*

9 oz millet flour

1 tsp garlic/ginger-mix paste

2 tbsp fresh coriander, chopped fine

Plain, natural yoghourt to bind (not
the thick Greek variety)

Oil for frying

2 tbsp oil

2 hot green chillies, chopped fine

1 tbsp fresh fenugreek leaves,
chopped fine

1 tbsp sesame seeds

- Mix together all ingredients except the sesame seeds , yoghourt and oil for frying.

- Bind with the yoghourt to make a soft, pliable dough. Add a spoon of yoghourt at a time to make sure it doesn't become too sticky.

- Cover and leave for an hour.

- Have a bowl of warm water to one side; you will need to dip your hands in from time to time.

- Break off small pieces and pat these out in your hands into flat, round shapes the size of a small jam-jar lid.

- Coat lightly with seeds, then deep-fry in hot oil until they turn a greeny golden brown. You have to keep turning them over.

- Drain on kitchen paper, and serve with yoghourt with chopped mint, cucumber, salt and red chilli.

- *Dhebra* contains whiffy fenugreek leaves (methi), which they say purify the blood. The pong lingers on hands, the breath and sweat pores, so it's not to be eaten before going to the VIP ball or conference, certainly not before a romantic tryst unless he or she finds methi irresistible. My Englishman does, and there are times when he smells like a Bombay railway-food vendor.

Millet flour was found in Indian dhows in East Africa way back in the second century AD. It has been soul food on the subcontinent for thousands of years. *Jugu* cake, on the other hand, was created during our English period when we appropriated recipes from the white memsahib's cookbooks and localized them.

Jugu Cake

2 cups groundnuts with the skins on, roasted for five to seven minutes in the oven – 325 °F, 170 °C, gas mark 3 – until they release their aroma and change colour slightly

1 tsp vanilla essence

5 cups plain white flour

2 cups sugar

4 tsp baking powder

2 eggs

½ cup sunflower oil

½ cup milk

- Grind the groundnuts to small-chunk size – some will turn to powder, it doesn't matter at all.

- Mix the dry ingredients, then bind with oil, milk and egg.

- Grease and flour a flattish baking tin, and press dough flat into it.

- Score into the mixture, quite deep, making squares or diamond shapes.

- Bake at 350 °F, 180 °C, gas mark 4 for an hour, then test it is cooked to dry.

- Remove from tin on to a flat board and cut into pieces before it cools.

- This is so delicious, a flat cake tasting of peanuts, nothing like it. Especially with a cup of *masala* tea.

Masala Chai

Water with milk – ⅔rd to ⅓rd	Teabags, one per person
A little cinnamon, cardamom and a pinch	Sugar to taste
of clove powder or ready-made tea *masala*	
you can buy in Asian shops	

- Boil the milk and water in a saucepan, then add all other ingredients.
- Let the liquid boil up one more time.
- Serve in feminine cups, not blokey mugs; never tastes right in those.

Suddenly one day, the political villains of Uganda broke into our family home. My brother was arrested, woken up early one morning, taken off in his pyjamas to some unknown destination by Obote's secret police. No reason was given. Shocked and petrified, his wife had to cope with the family, her own terrors and the travel business he ran. Then, as if that wasn't enough, her car was stolen as she stepped out of it. Her young daughter was in the back. My sister-in-law held on to the door and was dragged for many yards. Her skin was ripped off one leg and arm. God alone knows what she must have gone through. She never said, wasn't, isn't, the sort who lets out her feelings. For the first time ever, I felt her silent suffering and admired the stoicism, her armour against excessive emoting, of which there was too much in the family into which she had married. Her child was found several hours later, wandering in some country lane. My brother, we were told, was in custody for his illegal dealings with a British diplomat whose name was Brian Lea.

Big-time Asian businessmen and industrialists always had British and Swiss bank accounts to protect their interests and ensure them against the vicissitudes of African politics. Their black friends in high places, Milton Obote included, were kept on side with a supply of nice bribes, also banked in Europe. Most Africans never had enough money for bank accounts, and ordinary Asians had no surplus cash to send out. However, the quota system and 'Africanization' were creating intolerable pressures for middle-class Asians, both professionals and small entre-preneurs. Suicides went up among the emasculated men, and those who knew time was up had to find ways to smuggle out money with more ingenuity than before. My brother was struggling in a climate of punitive regulation and intimidation. With so many mouths to feed, a British passport and little backup, he was getting desperate and reckless.

Brian Lea had a circle of Asian friends and so came to understand their despair and their increasingly hopeless situation. Usually white civil servants kept well away from the other two races – it was better for all concerned, they said. Lea had let down the side, mingled with brown *baboos*, was not careful about who his friends were. His colleagues and the other white Brits thought Lea was a man without proper race and class pride.

On 2 May 1970, Lea drove to work as usual and never came back. Frantic searches ensued, and the alarm was raised that the diplomat had been kidnapped. His wife claimed he had been taken by Ugandan dissidents. Rumours spread that he was being beaten, tortured and threatened with death, and that demands had been made by his captors. The British government under Harold Wilson offered to send security experts. Foreign Office officials in Kampala had sent a telex to London stating that they suspected foul play of another sort altogether: 'This may be a publicity stunt designed to draw attention to the plight of the Asian community and it is possible Lea will be released once his purpose has been achieved.'[4]

He turned up three days later, according to a Foreign Office report, looking 'dishevelled, dirty, haggard and unshaven with severe swellings on his left foot and left hand'.[5] The High Commission was scornful. He had been on a long picnic, they said, with his brown mates. His own lawyer, Desmond Ackner, accused Lea of 'stupidity and ineptitude'.[6] Later the 'hoax' theory was generally accepted, although Lea himself has never spoken about what happened and why. I believe there has always been more to the story than we have been allowed to know. The British in Uganda may have wanted to make an example of this chap who just wasn't one of them. Were his broken bone and swellings self-inflicted? I don't think so.

Asians were disloyal to Lea too. I interviewed two of his Asian acquaintances, who told me the man was a fool, and that his good intentions were manipulated by his 'mates'. One suggested that he was in love with an Asian woman whose brothers he was trying to please, others that he was a closet gay. He was forced to go home to Britain, obviously ordered to keep quiet and given a job in the postal service. The truth was packed away for good. An investigation by the Ugandan government described Lea's kidnap story as 'incredible' and 'bogus'.[7] I was told by insiders in Obote's circle that Lea had indeed been kidnapped by African dissidents, and that Obote wanted to distract attention away from his deepening unpopularity by denying the crime and planting it on to Asians, who would then become patsies. Getting closer to the Soviet Union, the Ugandan President also sought to humiliate the West and knock down Britain's upright imperial image; being able to point to a 'crooked' English civil servant was a good start.

After his release, more evidence emerged to show that Lea was kind yet weak and not careful in his dealings. He often bought air tickets from my brother's travel firm and deposited the money in the UK. In doing this he was trying to help a family approaching financial crisis. As they went through his private papers, the police found these pay-in receipts, proof of the illegal payments abroad. The discovery enabled Obote to produce a theatrical finale to this drama. He incarcerated my brother in a small rural police station for several weeks, hoping to intimidate him into giving evidence against Lea in court. Too wrapped up in my romance, I went to see Babu, who was emaciated and aged by fear. I gaily announced I was getting married to TL. Babu has held that against me ever since. I can completely understand why, and I am sorry for my crass indifference. But he has never for his part sought to understand how he had hurt me when I was his young dependant.

Babu went to court, did what he had to and then was driven home to his lovely flat. There a deportation order was handed to him. The entire family was to leave forthwith. By this time my father was deeply depressed and barely functioning. He chose to go to Pakistan after a fifty-year absence, to catch up with lost siblings, perhaps hear from them what had happened to his parents. The rest all flew to London. They were not allowed to take out any money and had to fall upon a gang of loving yet unpredictable relatives who behaved like they were in the land of Oz, dislocated from reality and the rules of life. One or other of them was always in the middle of a get-rich-quick scam or money laundering. Lucky for them, people's greed ensured it was easy to lure them into investment schemes promising absurd returns. Here were the precursors to Nigerian tricksters but with charm and a little more honesty. This was not an ideal stopover for my nervous, exiled family in dire need of stability and security.

Back in Uganda, the authorities were unaware that I existed, so they couldn't bundle me out. They were scary but not smart. The irony is that I was at this tense time teaching army officers who had been brought into the police force. This was a part-time job at the police-training college; I was trying to make some money for my wedding. My students could shoot down targets lurking in the bush but had never held a pencil. Five feet tall, I felt like a dwarf in a dark forest when they stood up in perfect unison to say, 'Good morning, *mwalimu.*' To them this young *mwalimu*, their teacher, was always to be respected.

In contrast, the armed soldiers who escorted my family to the airport were beastly, trigger-happy and crazed. There was no time for goodbyes, and carefully accumulated precious possessions had to be left behind. When I visited Kampala in 1996, I went back to see what had happened to the abandoned flat, the first purchased property ever in our family. The patch of green grass and flowers was no more. The avocado tree had died; its brown skeleton stood there looking arthritic and pathetic, another victim of history. Just before they were thrown out, my mum had realized that avocados weren't poisonous pears and had invented this lovely, soft, pale green dessert to tempt my young niece, a fussy eater.

 ## Avocado Cream

2 ripe avocados	3 tbsp caster sugar
½ cup whipping cream	Juice of half a lime and rind too
Very finely chopped mint	

- Mash the avocados, and mix with sugar, mint and lime juice and rind.
- Whip cream until it is fluffy and fold in.
- Cover with cling film and chill for two hours.

To find myself back at the flat was like being in a time-travel film. I remembered exactly what had been, couldn't let that go. The new reality seemed a strange hallucination. All the windows were covered with paper or sheets; I could hear much noise and Congolese music, but no one would open the door. My driver imagined it might be because they thought I had come to make a claim on their squat; by then the government of Uganda was handing back stolen properties or forcing occupiers to pay a fair price for them. Then, slowly, a sullen soldier reeking of booze, a gun slung over one shoulder, opened the door, and a host of screaming children rushed out from behind and under him, followed by several chickens, a cockerel and a lazy-looking goat. The stench of animal dung hung in the air. I explained why I was there, and he relaxed, brought out his two shy wives. He was keen for us to share a friendly drink, *waragi*, hooch. I declined. Some things you can't forgive.

A few weeks after my family was thrown out, I felt this cold realization come over me, like when the sun suddenly disappears in the tropics and the ease of the day is replaced with foreboding. Engrossed in too much pleasure and excitement, I hadn't noticed or registered the dangers. Suddenly I understood the implications of my decision to stay behind, how alone I was in a country now moving inexorably towards collapse. Sure, I had cousins there I could turn to and TL's clan, but in the end none of these folk owed me care, and if things got impossible who would save me or help me to get out? This was June 1970, a month of such arctic bleakness that I shivered all day long and spent hours in bed in the afternoon under a thick, yellow floral Swedish quilt, a present from TL. The quilt by then smelled of him and our illicit encounters.

On 10 October I received a postcard from Papa. On the front was a picture of a Lufthansa plane – a free card he must have picked up when he had travelled from Pakistan to London. All it said, in his slanting, impatient, intelligent writing, was 'From Papa'. I was both surprised and irritated at the gesture, the waste of space and possibilities.

Exactly a week later, another letter arrived, brought to me by a cousin, Amin, who had just landed from London. His brother had written to tell me that Papa was dead, suddenly, causes as yet unspecified. Having gone back to his old birthplace after so long, a lifetime really, Papa had caught some mysterious illness that left him very weak. So Babu had flown him to London, where our father had been admitted into hospital. He seemed to be getting better and then gave up on life, lasting only a week in the land he loved. Perhaps he couldn't stand it that the upright nation of the 1950s was no more. England was up to its knees in political and social chaos, peopled with purposeless loungers in halter-neck tops and bell-bottoms. Maybe he was broken by guilt. Babu wrote a tender message: 'My dearest Yassi, let us all pray that God rests his soul in peace. Please look after yourself and write to me.' I look at these words on blue paper and know that then, at that moment, my old Babu came back to me, if fleetingly.

Papa and I had never been reconciled. I was numb and had to pretend sorrow I couldn't yet feel. The mosque leaders who had excommunicated him for bad behaviour mourned properly if not with authentic feelings. Papa had never attended any funerals. Our people were, as I said before, a forgiving lot. They tried to make me cry by weeping themselves, strangers who knew Papa not at all. No tears came. They said I was probably in shock or a very brave girl. TL's parents ensured the right rituals were observed, and I did pray keenly for his soul, my eyes screwed tight until I felt release, as if the message had been received.

And then, with a ticket paid for by Amin, I flew to London for the funeral, my first-ever funeral, to bury a man who had made me but who couldn't be a father. His body was taken to Woking cemetery in Surrey, the oldest Muslim cemetery in the UK. Mosques then were makeshift, so final rites were performed in a small pavilion before the men took off the body to bury it. My cousin Alnoor (now a smartly dressed car dealer but obviously still eating strong raw onions) met me at the airport and hurried me off to catch a train to Woking. In a cab from the station to the cemetery, we discussed the troubles in Uganda and difficulties they had encountered in England. When I paid the cabbie, he looked at me, took the money and threw it at my face: 'Fuck off, Paki, we don't want you here.' I had some change in my hand which I chucked back at him, and then, afraid, I ran off down a small lane, feeling doubly bereft.

I remembered things about Papa, small things, to bring him alive in my head. How he only ever wanted one egg on toast for supper every night. How he stuffed live cigarettes into his pockets. How he had all his teeth removed at forty for 'good health'. How political he was, how unafraid to speak out. In the pocket of a tatty jacket frequently worn was that photo of me from the *Uganda Argus* announcing my A-level results. Too bloody late and pride rather than affection, I thought. Did he wave it at his friends, showing off a daughter whose voice he refused to hear?

It was a cold, rainy day. He was lying in his coffin, his face a little troubled. I took a spoon to put holy water on his blue mouth, and when the spoon touched his face it tinkled like it had touched ceramic. That sound finally brought on hot, angry tears. How dare he die before we had resolved anything? What kind of father does that?

Jena had one of her terrible fits and had to be revived before the ceremony could go ahead. I shall never forget the sight, her rolling eyes and the gurgles, the stretched body as if a demon was pulling it apart, and, a few feet away, Papa dead and still. And the skies weeping for our broken little family.

In the days after the funeral, Jena went into a delirious fantasy, claimed Papa had turned to Allah and to her, promised her all that she had craved as that child bride. Those last four days he was in hospital, she said, he was so penitent, so sincere, so affectionate, so grateful, it made up for all his failures. 'Did he say he forgave me, Mum? That he was sorry for not speaking to me for so long? For calling me a *vaishia*, his own daughter?' 'No,' she said gently. 'But he was very ill, you know. Sure he wanted to say all that, you were his favourite.' Secrets and lies.

Babu and his family and my mother had moved to a house in Ealing with Alnoor and other cousins and Maami, my mother's sister-in-law, who was gentle and generous. Although the place was crowded – fifteen living in a three-bedroom semi – and there were tensions, they were happy or at least more cheerful than they had been in Uganda in those final months. And good to me. Everyone, even my sister-in-law, seemed to warm up with this new beginning. Surrounded by her own relatives, Jena was buoyant. One day Immigration and police officers came to the door. The neighbours had got suspicious that this was a terminus for illegal immigrants – why else would the milkman deliver seventeen pints of milk and four dozen eggs every day?

Babu and my cousins didn't want me to go back to Kampala, warned me that the country was certain to implode, but, stubborn as ever, I refused to listen. I would graduate and marry TL, that was the glorious plan. The day I was flying off, we had one of those omelette breakfasts and I felt wrapped in soft, eggy warmth.

 The Omelette

6 eggs

6 spring onions, finely chopped

2 onions, very finely chopped

2 hot green chillies, chopped

½ tsp turmeric

2 tbsp chopped fresh mint

4 tbsp sunflower oil

2 tbsp chopped fresh coriander

1 tbsp chopped dill

- Beat all the ingredients together except the oil.

- Heat the oil in a large pan and pour egg mixture in.

- Let this cook slowly for five minutes.

- Slide the omelette onto a large plate cooked side down.

- Then with a smart flip turn it over and into the pan again. It may break; weep not.

- Press down and cook for another four minutes until it browns at the edges.

- You can do these scrambled too.

- Eat with bread, *paratha* or *roti*.

I had only been given one week's visa to attend the funeral. The British Immigration officer in Kampala was contemptuous: 'There are always funerals and weddings, Miss Damji. You'd be surprised how many in one family and how many times over.'

By the late 1960s, Obote was feeling unable to control tribal tensions. Less confident and more aggressive, he was not sure how to rule over his disparate nation, and couldn't curtail his own paranoia and megalomania. He saw only one way out: the army had to be placated, then used to impose order. He ignored all complaints about the behaviour of soldiers and their leaders, Amin in particular, whom he now truly feared. With the army on side, Obote felt he could treat elected MPs with contempt, and he did. Some were threatened, others silenced forever. Then came a fatal collision with legislators driving one way and Obote and Amin coming at them from the opposite direction. The President and his commander were involved with a gold-and-ivory-smuggling racket in the Congo; Ugandan politicians and legal eagles accused the two of corruption. Amin and Obote refused all calls for investigations, even though Obote's own government passed a vote of no confidence. He retaliated by grabbing power away from them. Uganda was now ruled by one man, who was taking his country towards Communism.

In his Common Man's Charter, Obote promised to create a new way of life with the means of production in the hands of the people. For a developing country the charter had noble intent and made sense. Most of the wealth was owned by non-Africans. He wanted the state to have majority shares in foreign businesses. But the West decided he had made himself a foe, and his own people had been too alienated by his actions to support any of his ideas or policies, good or bad. More dangerously for him, his relationship with Amin was beyond repair, and his commander was now plotting to remove him with the help of interested parties in other countries. The President was ignominiously deposed while in Singapore for the 1971 Commonwealth leaders' conference. The coup was clean, swift and facilitated by Israel, the US and the UK.

My niece's nanny Teresa, a replica of that big black Mammy in *Gone With the Wind*, used to say that Obote was a hyena, not a lion or buffalo, that he waited for kills and then feasted on the rotting flesh. She poured out her scorn in Swahili in between singing gently to the child: 'You see him, and you think, this man is not brave but very bad. Not like a warrior who is not afraid of anything. Obote? He is always afraid so he destroys everything, then hides in a suit. Me, I like a warrior, I like a buffalo. Uganda needs a buffalo not a hyena.'

Uganda got her buffalo. The transition was seamless and soundless. It happened one morning when there was no birdsong, or so my memory tells me, no doubt for dramatic effect. It was 25 January. I opened the yellow cotton curtain of my small room in college on Floor 6 and a baby bat fell on the floor. It was softer than I expected when I touched it, and dead. I left it there, decided it would be fun to see the reactions of the other girls. After about half an hour, students started going down for breakfast, and normal life seemed to resume as I got dressed. Then Sophie, my roommate the previous year, rushed into my room actually looking pale, her shiny skin appearing more ash grey than black: 'Yasmin, stay in, stay in. Don't go anywhere, I'm telling you. The military has taken over – Obote is out, we don't know any more. Don't go anywhere, I am telling you.'

Round and round she went around the same words, again and again, sometimes actually turning herself, not stopping so I could ask her questions, just filling me with the encircling dread she felt. Sophie had reasons to be fearful. Her father was politically involved, a lethal involvement that marked them all. They had been subjected to imprisonment and torture under Obote, and so they welcomed his fate. But they knew Amin too and were expecting even worse. Their foreboding never came near what they were eventually put through by the military dictator.

Now our tall tower residence block itself seemed to ululate; spasms and waves were felt as if the building was swaying. Loretta, a Bagandan, brilliant English under-grad and beautiful, rushed into my room with a knife in her hand. She said she

wanted to kill herself before soldiers killed her. It was a scene out of a melodrama –
Loretta hysterical, her hair literally standing up, wearing only a bra and knickers,
pushing the knife into her heart as I yelled for help. The dead bat stopped her. She
saw it where it lay and screamed like she was being murdered. This cry brought the
others in, and they took the knife off her. We threw the bat over the balcony, and it
fluttered down through the silence outside, thick as fog.

The radio played 'My Boy Lollipop' all day interspersed with horrible warnings
from military men of curfews and announcements about the new order, which would
not tolerate any troublesome opponents. The next day there was rejoicing in the
streets. The Bagandans were delirious. Obote, who had destroyed their king and
kingdom, was out, the man of the people, Idi Amin, was in. Students celebrated by
taking time off lessons and making daytime love in their rooms. Another bright
beginning; another dark ending. Asian businessmen were well pleased. That bastard
Communist Obote would no more get his hands on their assets. Some of them knew
Amin and had bribed him often. But they were nervous too. They knew the soldiers
and their ways.

Asian parents drove over and took away their girls. I couldn't go and stay with
TL's family; we weren't yet married. And my father's distant relatives, though kind,
had their own lives and worries. They would have welcomed me, but I felt unable to
ask. Only three Asian women were left behind, two who came from outside Uganda
and me. We drank lots of sweet tea made with evaporated milk to steady the nerves.
It was a test of sorts, and we didn't cope with dignity. Often, lying tight in one bed,
the three of us whimpered like lost children in dark fairy tales. Mamti the Sunni

Muslim prayed eight times a day instead of five, double prayers. Her prayer mat was always with her, and if any of us touched it, she went quite berserk. It had become her comfort blanket; my yellow quilt was mine. The African students were kind (though said that we were soft and spoiled). When lights were out and we couldn't sleep, Loretta brought in some guava cheese, and we ate it with biscuits. I had never had it before – it is a bit like very light pink quince cheese.

Guava Cheese

Ripe guavas, peeled and rubbed
   through a sieve

1 cup water to 1 cup pulp
1 tbsp sugar

- Boil the three together over low heat until the mixture shrinks away from the sides.
- Drop a bit into cold water; if it turns into a ball it is ready.
- Set in a tray and mark into squares.

Loretta was no longer suicidal but fat, very fat suddenly. She ate all the time and explained it was so soldiers would not be able to drag her off so easily. Susana, on Floor 4, was very happy. You couldn't miss her, a noisy young woman with enormous breasts she steadied with tight, bright scarves. I got to know her better in the week after the coup. She was already in Amin's circle of concubines and expected to become mother of the nation when he married her. There was only one rival she feared. Amin, she said, had his eye on the beautiful Princess Bagaya of one of the tribes. We had seen Bagaya in a Tarzan film, and she was stunning. Susana was hopeful he would tire of the arrogant royal. He loved her truly, she believed, and her 'Exeter Stew', as she called it (the recipe written down in pencil in January 1972), was a dish Amin found very pleasing.

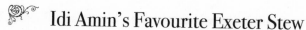 Idi Amin's Favourite Exeter Stew

2 lb mutton with bones in or goat meat
   (there had to be many bones, otherwise
   Amin threw a fit)
2 oz flour
Salt and pepper

3 onions
3 turnips
2 tbsp fat
2 tbsp vinegar

- Boil the meat in 4 pints of water with salt and vinegar.

- Fry onions in fat until brown, stir in flour, and add this to the boiling meat together with chopped turnips.

- Cook for two hours until the sauce is thick and the meat tender.

Susana died a mysterious death. We heard that Amin then added her younger sister to his collection of serving maidens. It was a rumour and, like most such rumours, understated the truth, because that would have been too much to bear. Many who knew Susana said he had had her mutilated, then thrown away in a bag, and all the while her naked sister was made to watch as he stroked her. How to verify any of this? In these states everything of substance and value, human life itself, and what actually happened, is burned away, leaving only black smoke in the air.

The dust of change had settled, and Ugandans on the whole were not at first disappointed with the new leader. Henry Kyemba, a cabinet minister in Amin's 'government', understood why they liked him:

> [His] is not a personality to be underrated. True he is nearly illiterate; he is politically naïve; he is violently unpredictable; he is utterly ruthless. Yet he is also jovial and generous and he has extraordinary talents – for practical, short-term action, for turning apparent weaknesses to his own advantage, for asserting his leadership among his gang of thugs.[8]

Amin was indeed psychologically more complex and astute then the satirists on *Private Eye* or his ex-army officers or indeed the main political parties in Britain understood. For several weeks after his enthronement, celebrations took up all the big man's time. His Excellency, Field Marshal General Idi Amin Dada, VC, DSO, MC, President for Life of Uganda, Al Hajj, Member of the Excellent Order of the Source of the Nile, (later) Conqueror of the British Empire in Africa, Last King of Scotland and Doctor of Political Science, was surrounded by enthusiastic crowds every day and everywhere, even more so after he released Obote's political pris- oners. He arranged for the Bagandan king's body to be returned to be buried with honour. The man who had blown up the king's palaces and killed so many of his people now claimed he was the Bagandans' saviour and was adored.

It was at the university that the mood first started to shift. Students soon began to sense that the festive dancing and fornicating had been foolishly premature. Makerere seemed to be full of quiet men watching us. We whispered even when with trusted friends in private spaces, and soon you didn't know whether to trust trusted friends. Metaphors were used, codes made up and changed frequently. You quickly learn how not to say the wrong thing; it becomes second nature, almost a new accent with which you speak to avoid detection.

Amin's soldiers were seen in the college bar, the canteen (run by Kanubhai, a man with one ear, always lugubrious and, after the coup, morbid) and the main hall, where we used to bop with the energy of a new nation. If they found groups of friends walking and talking, it was considered a plot. One day in May 1971, we gathered on campus to protest against the regime. Tanks suddenly appeared at the main gate. Tear gas was released, shots were heard, eight students were snatched and taken, never to return. I was there, in a checked minidress, a scarf round my head (it was a bad-hair day), knee socks and the bravery of a drunken fool who walks in front of fast cars. TL pulled me away before I got into more trouble. Two of my literacy students were among the soldiers, and they shouted at me to run away. I have a photo of us fleeing with smoke and panic all around. After that day, the process of extermination of intellectuals gathered pace. Like Pol Pot, Amin knew the country would be easier to subjugate if he could rid it of academics, lawyers, constitutionalists, writers, artists, journalists and educators. He also suffered from a pathological inferiority complex. It was payback time for those of high education who made Amin feel low.

Amin turned up at Makerere that June, for some their graduation time. Dressed in full academic gear, he insisted that he was going to conduct the entire ceremony, personally shake hands with all those who had passed their finals. TL (who had passed with First Class Honours) was graduating and had to kneel in front of the hulk and get his blessings. Students who tried to walk out of the hall were roughly pushed back in by soldiers. I was wearing the shortest silky yellow dress, sunny and bright even though we were living through the most terrible period in history.

One of TL's external examiners was the Oxford zoologist John Phillipson, who looked like a kindly Groucho Marx. He was taken with TL and offered my fiancé the chance to study for a DPhil under his supervision. My future in-laws were elated and invited Phillipson to dinner – a very rare thing that, for a white man to come into an ordinary Asian home to sup. He came and we were supplicant and flattered and absurdly grateful. Phillipson found it excessive – he was a straight guy with no imperial pretences. TL's father was so proud, his girth seemed physically to expand as the plans went forward. Then the state stepped in. TL, a Ugandan citizen, was told by his African department head (who admired Amin) that he had no right to sweep off to Britain when his own country needed science graduates. The man did have a point, but when he started to issue dark threats, we realized that TL would have to get out as soon as he could, before they took away his passport.

I barely remember what happened next, it was that clandestine and fast. I turned round and my romantic lover was at Entebbe Airport surrounded by dozens of relatives. Soldiers were sitting on the clean floor chewing *ghat*, which helped them stay high and awake. There were tears and poor jokes, fear, relief, disbelief, envy too as my fiancé stood tall and beautiful, headed for Oxford, a mythical place as wondrous as Camelot. What I do remember is our long and pressing kiss, the embrace that would not give, and the hush as all the Asians there looked at us aghast. An old Asian man spat on the floor in disgust.

TL was handed food gifts – of course – a long plastic box of fresh carrot pickle, bandaged like a broken foot, which he quietly passed to me, and a bigger container of *chevro*, a dry snack, which he kept. His mother used to make it in vats, and it took hours. On the day she gave over to *chevro*, as you turned into their street an aroma would meet you and rush you to the backyard of the house, where she orchestrated the various stages looking hot and happy. I never did get the recipe off her, but here is one that appears very similar, from a recipe book by Lella Umedaly,[9] whose daughters Nzeera and Muneera were my friends back in Uganda. You will need a bucket to mix it all up, and a little help from your friends.

Back at Makerere in my room, I ate the pickle and cried for my man, hugging and smelling the yellow quilt.

Chevro

8 oz puffed rice	**8 oz fried *sev* (thin strings of spicy**
4 oz *pawa* (flaked, beaten rice)	**gram flour; they look like noodles)**

4 oz fried *moong dhal*

4 oz fried *channa dhal*

(All the above can be bought from good Asian food stores)

5 oz potato sticks (crisps shaped like small, thin sticks)

8 oz peanuts unsalted

½ cup chopped fresh coriander leaves

1 green chilli

2 tbsp turmeric

1 tbsp (or more if you want) chilli powder

1½ tbsp sugar

2 tbsp powdered citric acid

9 oz whole almonds

6 oz cashew nuts (plain)

¼ cup sunflower oil

5 curry leaves

1 tbsp whole black mustard seeds

1 tbsp paprika

1 tbsp salt

More oil for deep frying

- Have ready a very large container or bucket, and line it with clean dishcloths.

- Heat frying oil, and very quickly flash-fry *pawa* which has been placed in a stainless-steel colander; it only takes a minute.

- Drain on kitchen paper.

- In the bucket or large pan mix the *dhals*, *pawa*, *sev*, rice puffs and potato crisps, and shake the bucket or pan about to mix.

- Flash-fry the various nuts, then drain and add to the mix.

- In a small pan, heat the fresh oil and fry the mustard seeds, coriander and sliced green chilli, then chuck the whole lot into the mix.

- Now add the dry spices and flavourings, shaking the mix to sound like maracas.

- Store in an airtight container.

 Fresh Carrot Pickle

1 lb peeled carrots, cut into the thinnest sticks you can

1 tbsp crushed mustard seeds (you can buy them ready-crushed)

A few green chillies, slashed open

½ cup white vinegar (malt will do)

¼ tsp turmeric

Salt, sugar and chilli powder to taste

- Mix the lot together with your hands.

- Adjust the taste.

- For a different version, leave out the vinegar and add a little vegetable oil, 2 tbsp tomato purée and plenty of lime juice.

Then the night raids started. Suddenly at about 3.00 we would hear heavy jackboots striding up the stairs, floor after floor. You shivered and shook when the hard steps approached; sobbing relief would follow as they faded. Rather than go out into the corridor to the toilets, we used the glass ceiling lampshades instead.

One night they took away Esther and her twin, Mary, students of agriculture, fun, always popular with the boys. Esther came back a week later, shuffling painfully and unwilling to talk. Both sisters had been taken to the nearby barracks to be gang-raped until the soldiers grew bored. Mary was in hospital with a severely ruptured anus and bleeding, infected nipples. They both went back home without graduating. They would have been the first young women in their extended family to get to this level of education, but it was not to be. All that money saved and donated by their village and relatives came to nothing.

There was worse to come. Doors were kicked down every night and the screams ricocheted. Soon it became clear that they were carefully selecting the Bagandan and Langi females and, most of all, Acholi women from Obote's tribe. One of Amin's favourite killers, Lt Malyamungu, reputedly good at disembowelling live victims slowly and with relish, was seen in the corridors. Names were on the doors so tribes were easily identified. Some of the women the soldiers came looking for hid in the rooms of the Asian students because, strangely enough, the soldiers never touched us during this orgy. It was as if we still had round us an aura, a circle into which they didn't dare step, men with guns and nothing to lose.

A handsome student who was a part-time newsreader on TV was escorted every night to the studios by soldiers, for by that time we were living under an interminable series of curfews. 'Rocky' was his nickname, and he played the trumpet like no other. There was this evening when, lonely and afraid, I had jived with him in the hall, and then, as he escorted me back, he took my hand and kissed it, asked gently if I wanted him to come up. Rocky was gorgeous. But I was engaged, and he was black. Memories rushed in shouting and banging, ordering me to step away, to remember that night of *Romeo and Juliet*, the lessons beaten into me. I stepped away as if I had been burned. One night a few weeks on, Rocky's protectors said they wanted to shoot a part of him. He was free to decide which bit. Before fear turned his words to gibberish, he chose his left foot. They shot it and, laughing all the way, drove him to hospital. He too left Makerere and vanished into the vast countryside.

My friend Joyous and I were stopped as we made our way to a lecture on *The Insect Play* by the brothers Capek. A tall Nubian soldier twirled Joyous around, lifted her skirt with his gun, sat down, then pulled down her knickers and jammed his hand up her vagina. She was tall and serene with gazelle eyes. Didn't say a thing, didn't move a muscle in her face, and he withdrew feeling a little ashamed, I thought. Meanwhile I had wet myself. They couldn't see because I was wearing a long cheese-cloth skirt. I wasn't touched, though he did say one day it would be our turn too. Joyous came to class and worked hard on the text we were studying. It was awesome, her courage. She never talked about what happened. That would have been further violation.

The British, American and Israeli planners who had successfully planted their man didn't intervene when Amin showed his true colours. It was the geopolitical game, and there were winners and losers. Declassified documents reveal the level of informal collusion by the British government. Eleven days before the Amin coup, Richard Slater, the British High Commissioner, sent home an assessment of Obote. Anglo-Ugandan relations, he concluded, were in a 'deplorable state', and Obote's nationalization policies were a threat to British interests. Obote was also starting to incite other African leaders against British arms sales to apartheid South Africa.[10] And both he and Nyerere were enabling the Soviet Union and China to extend the Communist spheres of influence in East Africa. High Commissioner Slater was very satisfied with the new political arrangements: 'At long last we have a chance of placing our relations with Uganda on a friendly footing... [Amin] was deeply grateful for the promptness with which Her Majesty's Government recognised his regime.'[11] Two days after the coup, Harold Smedley, a top diplomat, concluded: 'There is something of the villain about him and he may well be quite unscrupulous and indeed ruthless.'[12] As the historian Mark Curtis concluded, 'Britain thus welcomed the violent overthrow of a government recognised by British officials to be in the best interests of Ugandans. British support also came in full knowledge of why Amin had acted in the first place.'[13] In gratitude Amin removed the threat to nationalize foreign companies. To reward him, the three allied nations agreed to supply him with arms.

Amin was honoured by a state visit to Britain in July 1971; the *Telegraph* called him a 'staunch friend of Britain'. He met the Queen and later offered to marry Princess Anne; the *Financial Times* praised him fulsomely. In November 1971, however, the Foreign Office noted that measures instituted by him were getting more repressive, and by early 1972, the British government had detailed information of mass killings on his orders. The Israelis were unconcerned. Col. Bar Lev was a close ally of Amin; Moshe Dayan went to Uganda on a much-publicized visit. In May 1972, someone I knew and who was widely respected, the Ugandan Asian Anil Clerk, a lawyer and ex-MP, was disappeared. High Commissioner Slater acknowledged that the world were dealing with a Jekyll-and-Hyde leader but added, 'We do not have a choice. We cannot tell him to stop murdering people and my plea is business as usual.'[14]

Amin had been to Libya and met Col. Gaddafi. He came back a liberationist and adopted the Arab cause, denouncing 'Zionist imperialism'.[15] In June 1972, British officials started to talk of withdrawing military and financial support, and in August Amin retaliated with an order expelling Asian British passport-holders, followed by another which dispossessed Ugandan Asians of their citizenship and residence rights. Asians were lucky that only a dozen or so were murdered by the Ugandan military. More than 700,000 Africans lost their lives.

Meanwhile the townsfolk, like us students, were being made to understand what this new Uganda really meant. Servants were too afraid to go home and slept on kitchen and bathroom floors. Citizens bowed their heads as if they were walking against a bitter wind, and everyone – black, brown and white – prayed they would remain unnoticed by the roaming soldiers. My friend Nazira was getting married, having surprised us all by falling for a man much older than her. Their unexpected relationship was taking off in choppy waters. The wedding was hastily arranged around the curfew, and an existential fear loomed as henna was painted on hands and feet, wedding songs were sung like dirges, the bride was dressed and blessed, and prayers were prayed. Laughter and sobs burst out, and they sounded the same. Going back to college before the curfew, we were stopped by soldiers, and a few of us had molesting hands crawl over our breasts and faces: 'Looking to see if you Indian ladies are having bosoms, too small, not like our African women. But never mind, quite nice.' They took our purses and watches.

Amin was still good at making Ugandans laugh with his antics – jumping on to traffic islands to direct the traffic, joining the people gathering grasshoppers when the swarms arrived twice a year, like all politicians kissing babies and throwing them in the air – in his case too fast and too far up, and nobody dared to object. There is this story that speaks for that era, what folk do when they panic in failed states. A baby boy was found abandoned on a doorstep next to a nightclub where a number of prostitutes served Amin. Crowds raised a cry that the child belonged to him, and the tiny infant was stamped to death. The story as it appeared in the state-controlled newspaper said the child was thought to be possessed. The media were not able to report the real reason for this infanticide.

Victor Hugo wrote in *Les Misérables*, 'Liberation is not deliverance.' Ugandans by this time knew exactly what that meant. Independence had given them two dictators and full and fast rivers of blood.

7 The Nation of Shopkeepers, 1972–77

IN APRIL 1972 I got my results: First Class Honours, one of the best they had ever had in the literature department at Makerere. There was no one to celebrate with. Uganda was a graveyard filling up with the dead and bereaved. Those still mercifully untouched by the killings gave off a whiff of primeval fear. The streets and marketplaces reeked of danger. You heard no loud laughter, and music seemed to shake and tremble as the volume was kept low on small radio sets.

As the day of my departure approached, I believed I would come back and teach one day at Makerere and that Amin's reign of terror would soon self-destruct. Things were so bad, they could only get better. Surely. TL had always said he wanted the same, to return and work as a zoologist in the profuse, untamed expanses of East Africa. It was not to be. In those final weeks before I was due to fly off, though, I had not even the slightest sense that this was a final parting from who I was and the history that had made me. I was going on a once-in-a-lifetime trip, a thrilling sojourn before real life back home. I left my records and the kitsch stuff of a 1960s young one in storage at the university and entrusted a good mate with old photographs, letters, my school reports and all those precious things girls collect and never want to lose.

I went to visit Mama Kuba to say goodbye. She was by then small and weak, curled up on a bed in her living room. She was pining for all that was now gone, her power and Uganda as it once had been. The Big Mother who had scared snarling dogs and black police chiefs had submitted to Amin's rule and the watchful, cold new daughter-in-law brought in for her second son, whose first wife was barren. Maybe, I thought, Mama Kuba was being poisoned. With hands dry and bony like a chicken's foot she clawed at my face as if she wanted to scratch off a piece of it to keep and kiss. Her ring with a diamond the size of a Smartie now blazed on the new wife's hand with nails long and polished red. Mama Kuba had always told me the ring would one day be mine if I was really good: 'See this, Yassi? For you I am leaving it when I go to Allah. Only girl here with brain. Second husband gave it to me, no good man but enough money. Find a man with money. Only thing they are good for, the bastards. That's the mistake your mother made marrying that useless man. Your father will give you nothing. So this ring I am keeping for you.' Now the greedy bitch had it. I seemed the only one who had no outstanding emotional debts to settle with Mama Kuba. She died soon after I left Kampala, and I was happy for her. I wouldn't have to imagine her cowering on that bed. She was buried fast and remembered by few. I, though, remember everything she'd told me about her early days in Africa. Her life was the story of our tribe, disgorged by the subcontinent, strangers on African shores and in dark hinterlands who hacked through the wilderness to make homesteads and then were no more.

The night before I boarded my flight, there was what turned out to be the last supper in paradise with my best friends, more precious than family. We met at

Nazira's house. Her mother, Moss, brought on dish after dish. Her dad was nick-named 'Poss'. Both were living embodiments of goodness and Islamic charity, *and* they were fun. They had paid my school fees when times were hard, bought me clothes, given me refuge – an escape from the frequent bouts of brutal misery at home – loved me for years, and on this day gave me some gold jewellery for my wedding, knowing I had little of my own: '*Aree*, we would give you so much more than this if we could, but it will help. At least your in-laws won't look down on you, won't say you came with nothing. Tell your mother we are your other parents. Remember us, Joan of Arc.' (They called me that because of my austere fringe and mad, messianic eyes.) We remembered the years gone by and wept as if there was no tomorrow.

So what did we eat that bittersweet night? Biriyani, obviously, but also coconut cassava, fried green tilapia, East African fruit salad and much more.

 The Last Supper

Fried Green Tilapia

Serves 6

3 lb tilapia fillets
Juice of 2 fat limes
1 small bunch fresh dill

Salt
1 large bunch fresh coriander
10 fresh mint leaves

2 green chillies	1 tsp turmeric
White flour seasoned with salt	Sunflower oil about 2 in. high in a deep frying pan

- Rub salt and turmeric over the tilapia and refrigerate (covered) for a couple of hours.

- Whiz the herbs, chillies and lime juice, and stick paste over the fish. Return covered to the fridge for at least another two hours.

- Take the slices from the marinade, let excess liquid drip off, then coat well with flour.

- Heat oil until a small piece of bread rises when you throw it in.

- Fry the fish, turning over after three to four minutes on each side.

- Drain excess oil off on kitchen paper and serve with salad or chips.

- You can make this with fish batter too; that requires deep-frying.

Batter

4 oz plain flour	2 tsp malt vinegar
1 tsp oil	Salt
1 tsp baking powder	

- Mix into a thickish batter – a bit like wall paint – and leave to stand for twenty minutes.

- Dip marinated fish in the batter and fry until golden brown on both sides.

Coconut Cassava

Serves 4

1 packet cassava (frozen) (but then it was fresh and smelled of newly turned earth)	2 tsp garlic/ginger mix
	2 hot green chillies, chopped
Some fresh coriander	1 lb leg of lamb cut into small pieces

3 cups coconut cream (made with fresh coconut on that grater I brought with me, though now we use the tins and packets and powders)

Salt and lemon juice to taste

- Boil the lamb in just enough water to cover it with ginger/garlic and chillies added. It should be well cooked.

- Boil the cassava separately until cooked. Drain and cut into small pieces.

- Add the coconut cream (tinned or mixed as instructed on the packet) to the meat.

- Then add the cassava, and cook over low heat for ten minutes until it combines to a thick consistency.

- Add lemon juice and salt to taste.

- Finally sprinkle over the coriander leaves.

Fruit Pudding East African Style

Serves 6

2 ripe mangoes

3 passion fruits

4 slices very sweet fresh pineapple

Icing sugar to taste

1 medium-sized ripe papaya

3 bananas

½ can evaporated milk

- Peel, chop and mix in a bowl all the fruits except the passion fruit, which needs to be scooped out.

- Stir the sugar into the milk, then add to the fruit salad.

- Refrigerate and serve.

Moss's gold and my few bits of jewellery were hidden in a secret compartment in a handbag specially crafted by my future father-in-law, a shoemaker by trade. The bag itself was gold and brash – would do for the wedding too, he told me, proud of his handiwork. Luckily there were no roadblocks on the 20-mile stretch between Kampala and Entebbe Airport. TL's family and Feriyal waved me away cheerily.

And so I arrived in London. In the days that followed the ecstatic reunion with TL, I came down to earth, was pulled down to earth. My encounter with the Immigration officer was the first sign that maybe all was not well. People had turned disagreeable; the country was smaller, meaner and colder than I ever imagined it would be. The strawberries were sour, even in June. Britain wasn't the country we had been led to believe. She had lied to us, so many lies, big and small. Prime Minister Edward Heath, portly and florid, was losing his hold on the nation. Dismay was trapped in his small eyes; his shoulders seemed frozen with tension as the people turned on him, held him responsible for the country's galloping inflation, fuel shortages, shocking rates of unemployment, and immigration of course, always blamed for all other ills. Bitter industrial unrest had resulted in a three-day week and power cuts. Power cuts in Great Britannia? How could that be? The media pumped out relentless outrage, and the nation seemed to be looking for trouble. Everybody was angry. On TV I heard some men attacking Heath with such intemperance I broke into a cold sweat. Surely they would surely be taken from the studio to a torture prison.

Enoch Powell was the hero of the white working classes – like he really cared for them, this toff who never got over his thwarted ambition to become an Indian viceroy. Oh, he would have been just the man, the vain white supremacist who felt entitled to the pomp and glory, to lord it over 'inferior' colonial subjects. Denied that privilege, he became acrid and spiteful, incited racist attitudes and populist xenophobia. I detested him, and his followers adored him, which may explain why I have never since been quite as inclined as others to hold a romantic view of the solid British working classes. Once upon a time, during the Empire, many from this class offered internationalist solidarity to the oppressed in subjugated nations. When he came to Britain, Gandhi was despised by the upper classes and mobbed by the poorest and exploited, even when their factory jobs were affected by his boycott of British goods. All that started to change when 'coloureds' came over, beginning with *Windrush* in the late 1940s. As more of Britain's overseas chickens came home to roost, politicians used race as a political weapon. The result was appalling hostility. The cabbie who abused me on the way to my father's funeral was only expressing what millions felt and said then.

The Conservative post-war government was oddly both sanguine and anxious about non-white immigration. In private the leadership had expressed worries and its own prejudices. Winston Churchill told Sir Hugh Foot, then governor of Jamaica, 'We would have a magpie society; that would never do.'[1] Through the 1950s, questions had been raised in Parliament about 'coloured' immigrants and the need for controls, as they would create housing shortages, unemployment and crime, and provoke racism against them. Irish immigration at sixty thousand per year was not regarded as a serious problem for they were white.

Yet labour shortages in the private sector and public services made immigration from the old colonies unstoppable and essential. Politicians and the private sector understood that but did not use their influence to reassure or educate the British public about the push-and-pull factors that were involved. Although the arrivals encountered overt and at times violent racism, most white and black people managed to rub along with less aggravation than the political and social élite feared.

In the 1960s decolonization had speeded up. Across Britain, resentment over the loss of world supremacy had mixed with xenophobia and white nationalism. The amalgam was caustic. In the general election of 1964, candidates who stood against black and Asian immigration did unexpectedly well, and this struck fear into the hearts of many Labour politicians, who were worried that the electorate was deeply prejudiced. The 1968 Immigration Act came out of this fear: 'This was when the British Government decided, on grounds which were quite openly those of expediency rather than principle, that it could no longer accept responsibility for certain of its citizens because of the colour of their skins.'[2]

It was to get worse. In the early 1970s, attacks on 'coloureds' rose sharply; abuse was rife. As Zig Layton-Henry wrote,

In the sixties there were sporadic, unprovoked attacks, particularly on Asians usually by white youths. 'Paki-bashing' occurred widely across the country, but appeared to be unorganized and unsystematic. However in the 1970s... the incidence and level of racist attacks grew significantly and appeared to become more organized and systematic. The continuing campaigns against immigration and increased publicity and activity of the National Front [formed in 1966] created a climate of hostility towards black immigrants and immigration. In particular the speeches of Enoch Powell may have legitimized anti-immigrant violence by implying that black people were 'attacking' the white English...[3]

Powell's warnings of 'unparalleled invasion', 'aliens' and 'rivers of blood' had aroused the indigenous British.[4]

Meanwhile, 1960s culture had largely lost its innocence and charm. In 1972, the fag end of the lovely revolution, you felt it was the morning after a crazy party, and everyone was hung over, depressed or simply exhausted. Taken for drives in the evenings around London by my cousins and TL, I saw with disbelief young people slumped on benches while others, unwashed and unruly, roamed the streets aimlessly, many of them stoned. Couples were in parks, their legs akimbo and in states of undress we wouldn't allow ourselves in the dark intimacy of a bedroom, and nobody stared, *nobody even looked up*, as if lifting the eyes was too much trouble. One evening as we parked in Carlton House Terrace, I saw a teenage girl in a micro-skirt defecating under the Duke of York memorial. She wiped herself with an orange ice-lolly wrapper and casually threw it away.

Mixed feelings assailed me as I adjusted to the Britain I never could have imagined.

This was deserved comeuppance for a haughty power, a part of me thought. Yet the sights were distressing because deep down we cared what happened to our erstwhile rulers. Their cause had shaped our fate, and we had a co-dependency going, an S-and-M relationship even. Witnessing an imperious nation letting go of itself to a piteous extent was unbearable.

Yet there were times when the bacchanalia felt reassuring. The country no longer felt the need to be uptight. Corsets were off, stiff upper lips had turned to blubber. Nobody wore hats any more except on TV comedy shows. They were sweeping away Victorian Britain and returning to the raucous excesses of the eighteenth century. What would stern Queen Victoria have said, I wondered, as I sat under the gaze of the watchful Albert enthroned in Hyde Park. A KFC box was blowing around on the grass. I had with me George Eliot's *Middlemarch* to read; I'd chosen to study that era at Oxford. I opened a box with *khari puri* – a crisp savoury snack – and some sweet pickle. Nearby a man with long, unkempt hair was smoking pot quietly, and loud transistor radios were blasting the peace. A policeman riding his bike smiled indulgently and didn't bother anyone. The hippy asked where I was from and how come I was reading such a fat English book. He had a jeans stall in Kensington Market, he said, and never read books. I offered him the *puris* and told him a bit about Uganda He looked at me blankly: 'Is it sunny then? Is it in Rhodesia?' Eventually, he drifted away at peace and in love with his simple self. Later I found that my precious camera had gone.

Khari Puri

10 oz plain flour	½ cup gram flour
½ cup warm oil	1 tbsp cumin seeds
½ tsp salt and coarsely ground black pepper	Oil for deep-frying

- Mix flours, cumin, salt and pepper.

- Add the warm oil, and mix that in with your fingers.

- Then bind into a stiff dough with cold water, adding a little at a time. There is no exact measurement for the water.

- Roll out (using flour to keep the dough from sticking) until as thick as a coat button.

- Cut out into rounds using a small lid, then prick with a fork.

- Repeat until you have used up the dough.

- Fry in hot oil. They will turn golden. Turn them over a couple of times.

- Eat with fresh carrot pickle or preserved pickles.

In June I married TL. We both wanted this confirmation, the stamp of recognition of extraordinary emotions neither of us knew how to name or handle. It was love for sure, and much more. We were swept along on social and political rapids, surging and bursting through the banks that had kept the old folks steady and sensible. We were not sensible, that was plain to see. Both families agreed it was for the best. The perils were obvious if we were together in Oxford and unwed. What if I got pregnant? Another scandal, thought my lot, always mindful of my poor sister and her child. TL's parents believed their son needed a stable wife so far away from them. Jena was thrilled that I was marrying in and had ended up such a very good Ismaili. Her prayers had not been in vain. I was only twenty-two, TL twenty-three. Plenty grown up already, said the elders; too early, I now think, and much too much to take on back then.

The wedding plans were simple, but incessant quarrels went on and on and on, raising Jena's blood pressure alarmingly. It was mainly the cost. Even the cheapest wedding was beyond our means. To save face, my brother would have to ensure he didn't appear mean or stretched. Imagine the gossip if the show was poor. The fatherless girl was married off without a bean, they would say, and tut-tut for months, perhaps years. Social death – the ultimate horror in all Eastern families – is feared more than real death at times. My family had quite enough to deal with already, and this was a pain and drain. They let me know it too. Glasses and cups flew; mirrors were broken, foretelling bad luck. The neighbours banged on the walls.

As the wedding approached, I did try especially hard to be nice and good and appreciative. TL's parents came over, full of more terrible stories about Uganda's descent into chaos. They were badly hit by inflation and blackenization. Every night, they said, *kondos* – armed robbers – were attacking Asian shops and homes, taking what they wanted while the police watched and laughed. It was their country and Asians had no rights to basic protection from the state. TL's father was apoplectic: 'These *shenzis*, and monkeys, now I have to bow to them? Do they know who I am?

Who my father was? All these years we gave the blacks, made the country – Mombasa was a latrine before Asians came – today they are pushing our faces into the latrine. They will have to kill me before I leave my country. Better to die than let them win.' It was empty bravado. He was a frightened little man inside a pompous big man, and he left meekly in the end, walked between lines of soldiers who shoved and prodded him.

My in-laws shared Jena's bedroom. Courtesy is always kept up with guests and was then, but beneath the skin of politeness resentment was swelling, and silent rancour was exhaled through the small, crowded house. The sister-in-law drove her car off with excessive sound and fury, and disappeared into her room for hours, wordless protests we all understood. It was perfectly understandable. We had been a drag on her since the day she married, and it was too, too much. From the age of eighteen my brother had been obliged to support us, and we had never been as he wanted us to be. There is always a deficit of gratitude in these situations. My wedding made him feel extra-beneficent and bitterly undervalued, a martyr.

I had tried to do my bit by contributing the money I'd earned teaching literacy to the soldier-policemen. Jena claimed she had saved a thousand pounds (in bra boxes) and had donated that to the wedding fund. This was hotly disputed by Babu, who said her money had got absorbed into all the other expenses incurred as they tried to make new lives in London. There had to be gold, 24-carat, burnished orange gold, not the rubbish, palely cheap alloys used by British jewellers. From the poorest peasants to modern urbanites, the most tangentially subcontinental Asians have to be able to give their girls gold. We got together enough to stave off shame. Babu and my cousins, bless them, gave me a heavy chain and gorgeous earrings; Jena parted with some of her precious few bangles; I had Moss's bits, and TL's mum gave me diamond studs and a ring. Before leaving, my friends had contributed towards a pearl necklace and bracelet. The gold and pearls were displayed – as was required – in cellophane and in boxes, together with the trousseau. Guests had to see for themselves that there had been no skimping. It was both grown up and odd that I should be conforming to these absurd requirements.

On 17 June 1972 it was a grey day; the clouds were heavy and just holding back a downpour. I woke up at 5.00. My mum was in the kitchen in her green-checked cotton housecoat. She was crying softly and making *nan katai* for the reception, padding around, trying to make as little noise as possible. My sister-in-law, pregnant and exhausted, came in to complain we were disturbing her and banged the kitchen door. Jena's quiet tears broke into a noisy sob. She told me I was hers no more. I would henceforth belong to my husband and his family. I too cried, nervous I would fail to be the perfect wife, and feeling guilty that I was leaving Jena where she couldn't be herself, and where subordination was killing her pride and freezing her soul. What she wanted was freedom from obligation: 'I have nothing, Yassi, and this country will give me money and a flat. I don't mind doing that, it will be mine. Your brother says it will give them a bad name. I say who cares about a bad name? We can all be happy if I move. He and his wife should have their own life. Your father gave me nothing but I never felt like this then. I had courage. Not any more.'

 *Nan Katai*

6 oz melted butter	4 oz caster sugar
1 very large egg	1 tsp baking powder
1 tsp vanilla extract	½ tsp cardamom powder
7 oz plain flour	2 oz semolina

Some strands of best saffron, infused in 2 tbsp hot water

- Beat the sugar into the melted butter, then add the egg and vanilla.

- Beat in the flour, semolina, baking powder and cardamom, then, using your hands, knead the dough. It should be soft but not sticky.

- Grease a flat baking tray.

- Break off small pieces and roll them into balls.

- Flatten the top, then indent it with a finger like a dimple.

- Place them on the tray, not too close.

- Now colour the indentation with the saffron water, an orange spot in the middle, like a *tikka* on a married Hindu woman's forehead (I am sure that is what inspired this strange ritual).

- Bake at a medium temperature (350°F, 180°C, gas mark 4) until they are still pale but cooked, the colour of shortbread.

———

At around 6.30 I crept into the garden of the next-door neighbours, the Whartons, to steal some roses for a small bouquet (I wanted it all to be just right). One of the Whartons saw me from the kitchen window. They came round some minutes later, Mr and Mrs Wharton and three boys who all worked for the London Underground and had never once smiled or said hello. She had curlers in her hair and a cigarette in her mouth. They screamed racial abuse with thick voices and threw stones at the car parked outside. 'Nice gift, guys,' I wanted to shout and didn't. 'I am not a "Paki".' Instead we cowered, and the whole house began to stir. Then, suddenly, Jena piled a plate with hot *nan katai* and went out the front door, covered in flour, her hands shaking: 'Here, taste, very special. My daughter today wedding, you know, lucky food, have, give her your blessings. Big day, no? Want one more?' They were so surprised they took one each and went away, remembering to say thank you. Jena came back in, and suddenly all seemed well with the world. After that, she said, they became her friends.

My cousin Marunisa was my *jedel*, the knowing bridesmaid who was chosen to dress me and brief me on the deflowering. As she slapped make-up on my face and washed my long hair, she stuffed nuts and sultanas into my gold handbag (with the secret compartments) to help with the high-energy requirements for the wedding night. We had no money for a honeymoon, so she paid for a night in the local big hotel. Marunisa always had money, even though her official job as a secretary paid little. While I burned under an old beehive hairdryer (hers), she shouted out the rules of married copulation. I was to let him take charge; good girls were not eager on the first night. 'Smile, but don't laugh too much before he starts. Don't look at his thing. If it hurts don't cry or complain. Husbands hate that. I have a nightie for you in the suitcase – with buttons in the front so will be easier. Don't worry – soon it will be as easy as having a bath. Never say no if he wants to do it and you will have a long marriage.' I listened to her with convincing innocence, pretended fear and timidity. Something in her eyes told me she knew I was already eagerly enjoying my lover in bed. And that she did too, the young, merry widow. We all knew she went out at night and came back in through an open window before dawn. Geoffrey, the local bank manager, had fallen under Marunisa's spell and could never refuse her a loan. She smoked and was brazen; her long hair had been dyed flaming red. I knew she would be the one they all looked at, especially as she had decided to also wear a white-and-gold sari for the religious wedding, the same as me. I would have preferred an ugly *jedel* or one less compulsively competitive. But I always admired Marunisa's spirit and the wayward life she chose to lead in spite of the gossip.

First there was the civil ceremony in a dull office off the main street, opposite Debenham's department store in Harrow-on-the-Hill. I wore a white mini-smock with a daring swing and kinky boots. The gear, bought in Carnaby Street, made me feel like Sandie Shaw, only more risqué. The stolen roses made a thorny bouquet. I was free with TL, kissed and hugged him as if he was already mine. He wasn't, not until the real marriage vows at the mosque. People talked. I didn't care. Heck, we were in England now, not backward Kampala. TL and his friends in Oxford were oh so cool, and I was soon going to be one of them.

Maami sat me down that night, peeled and sliced oranges, and gave me some loving advice on how a decent woman behaves. 'We are not like the English, *beti*. Today you forgot that. Marriage is different for us, it's about duty and *izzat*. Spoil your name and you can never buy it back. Please for my sake, no more these short frocks and low-class things. Did you know your *chuddi* was showing?' As the slices were popped into my mouth by this lady of grace and wisdom, I saw Sandie Shaw running away and hiding in shame.

The religious ceremony had me draped in my white embroidered sari and adorned in gold. The necklace and bracelet boasted several mock guineas. Don't ask me why I thought them lovely. They were in fashion then, and for many more years the ultimate symbols of success for *dukanwallahs*, mini mayoral chains honouring coinage. My head was covered and my eyes lowered virginally. I exuded piety. When the time came, I got right down to touch the feet of my father-in-law and in that scene turned myself into the perfect Hindi movie wifey. This wedding had split one bride into two – the immigrant's dilemma personified. Back in Uganda, the various cultural parts of us held together and melded more easily into a manageable whole. Our communities there were grounded in immutable strength and enduring conventions. We knew and understood ourselves. It would take a long time to get that confidence and solidity in the UK, if ever we did. In the meantime there was the traditional Miss me and the modern Miss me, and the skill was to keep them apart successfully.

Clay plates containing a coin, rice, sweets and saffron were tied together and placed on the floor, one for the bride and one for the groom. We had to smash them with our feet. The first to do the most damage would rule the roost. They represented fertility, money, sweetness and good fortune. My heel broke before the plate, a bad omen I was told. TL wore one of those brassy purple suits so popular in the early 1970s (why, oh why?), and his Carlos Santana moustache was luxuriant. At the reception in a despondent Harrow school hall with graffiti on the walls and stinky toilets, a hundred people gathered to wish us well. I had known many of them since my insalubrious birth. The tables were covered with orange candlewick bedspreads – didn't matter at all. The biriyani and *ladoos* were excellent.

My brother and his wife and all my cousins had given us a memorable wedding. Crooked relatives got to cheat a few more clients; rich uncles turned up for the shortest time possible and left behind the cheapest gifts but sulked and had tantrums: 'Is this the way? You show me respect like this? Putting me next to a tool maker? No. I will be leaving now, don't need your biriyani.' My family managed to smile for the photographer, who was never paid and pursued me for years. He would have got his money, but Alnoor, who was given the cash to pass on, bought a new Terylene safari suit for himself instead.

Malek, my dearest cousin on my mother's side, gave me the most lovely thing I then possessed: a Kashmiri cape embroidered with deep pink and red flowers. I put it on as TL and I quietly left the hall and were about to head for the hotel in a cab when Marunisa appeared to wave us down. The hotel room had fallen through, she informed us, genuinely distressed. One of her dodgy deals had failed. So that night there was no nut fest, no easy-to-open nightdress or virgin. We had a sleepover in the overcrowded Harrow house, downstairs in the living room, unable to touch at all.

So I felt like a princess when Prince Charming took me off to a small attic student flat in Oxford the next day in his old Citroën 2CV. His parents came along too, unwilling to stay on in Babu's house although they were warmly invited to do so. Late into the night I drank Woodpecker cider, TL got high on Coca-Cola, we munched Cadbury's whole-nut chocolate (full-cream milk and nuts for energy) and made love on a mattress. As I lifted myself up to go to the bathroom I actually fainted briefly, as if spent to oblivion. Or maybe it was the combination of released frustration and impossible self-control – we had to be quiet because his parents were in the only bedroom, snoring in unison. The night was long and fulfilled honeyed promises. I wanted nothing more on earth. Uganda became an old postcard, far away in time, a funny old place.

I could please TL in bed all right but couldn't cook. That, for an Asian bride, is an invitation to a beating or a kick back to her parents. Neither came about. In the first weeks I made some revolting grub which left a layer of grease on the tongue: pineapple-hamburger patties, spaghetti with tinned mushroom soup, rice with mashed sardines and ketchup. TL was kind and patient, and never complained. But I feared he would run off with the first lovely young woman who could make him lasagne from scratch. Some of the other wives were already competent cooks, and one, a gorgeous Italian, made food that gave TL an erotic charge. I blamed Jena for sending me off without adequate culinary training and set about learning the basics from her over the phone. She taught me patiently to make good food quickly out of the cheapest and past-their-best ingredients.

I have it still, my red hardback notebook with the first simple dhal recipes and a dozen ways to make spicy potatoes. Here are three of them.

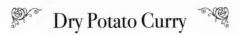

Dry Potato Curry

Serves 4

1 cup diced boiled, peeled potatoes

2 tsp cumin seeds

2 cloves garlic, chopped into slices

2 tbsp desiccated coconut

1 tbsp sunflower oil

1 tbsp sesame seeds

1 dried chilli

1 tsp turmeric

A little sugar, salt and citric acid

- Heat the oil and throw in the seeds, chilli, turmeric and garlic.

- Cook for a couple of minutes, then stir in the potatoes.

- Stir-fry over low heat, then add the sugar, salt, coconut and citric acid.

- Stuff into pita bread, adding a little yoghourt and a few slices of cucumber.

Wet Potato Curry

Serves 4

2 cups chopped boiled, peeled potatoes

½ tsp garlic paste

2 tbsp tamarind juice (pour boiling water
over dried tamarind and leave until cool,
then crush with your hands and strain)

1 tsp turmeric

2 onions, finely chopped

1 tin chopped tomatoes

2 tsp *jeera* powder

1 tsp *dhania* powder

1 tsp fennel powder

Chilli powder to taste

½ tsp mango powder

1 tsp sugar

2 tbsp vegetable oil

Pinch asafoetida

Salt to taste

- Heat the oil and fry the onions slowly until they turn brown at the edges.

- Add all the other ingredients except for the potatoes, and cook over a low heat for eight minutes.

- Stir in the potatoes, then cook for a couple more minutes.

- Serve with rice and yoghourt. You can add peas to this dish or green beans or even parboiled carrots.

Roast Red Spicy Spuds

Serves 4

2 lb boiled potatoes cut into wedges

Salt and chilli powder to taste

A squeeze of garlic purée

1 tsp *jeera* powder

1 tbsp oil

2 tbsp tomato purée

1 tsp paprika

- Mix all the ingredients together except for the potatoes.

- With your hands, smear potato wedges with the paste.

- Line a roasting tin with tin foil, and cook in the oven (350 °F, 180 °C, gas mark 4) until the wedges are brownish and a little crisp on the outside.

- These are great eaten with white bread or with fried eggs, which you can serve over the top.

Jena was still miserable, but her spirit didn't completely cave in because she found herself a role nurturing Babu's two children, a girl and a boy. The third child, Zarah, born a month after my wedding, gave Jena a new purpose of life. The baby was underweight, weak and vulnerable to illness. Stress, I was told, caused in part by the wedding. It must have been. Jena fell in love with the child the minute she saw her, and until the end of her life that bond was deeper and stronger than any other she had ever had. Her God gave her this solace, pure and complete joy just when she most needed it. Zarah loved Jena back with the same intensity, and together they weathered many vicissitudes and domestic dramas.

The land I had left behind imploded within three months. On 5 August Idi Amin announced that he had decided to banish British Asians from his country and take over their businesses, lands and possessions. Nobody believed he was serious. He gave them ninety days to pack up and go. The redeemer had turned. His Asian suppliers of illegal cash and hooch and various bribes in kind (cars in particular) were shaken and furious. Five days later he spoke again on the matter: 'Asians have kept themselves to themselves and as a community have refused to integrate with Africans. Their main interest has been to exploit the economy. They have been milking the economy for years and now I say to them all – Go.'[5] Black

Ugandans cheered. As before he knew how to win popular support even though he had betrayed every previous over-enthusiastic collective of fans.

Trevor Grundy, a journalist in Uganda then, remembered the panic:

Almost overnight Kampala became a city of queues – for injections, for passports, for the tiny amounts of currency they were allowed to take with them: less than £50 per family... no family could take more than two suitcases of possessions... by the end of October more than thirty flights a week were leaving Kampala for London... More than once Amin turned up at the airport, his massively decorated chest puffed up, laughing at the Indians who had once seen him their protector. 'This is wonderful,' he told his cronies. 'Wonderful'.[6]

One old man, Virendra, who had a small shop in a transit town, described to me the way Asians were treated by black soldiers and the British at the High Commission: 'They took our thermos flasks – these soldiers and poured the tea on the grass, sometimes at us. They pulled up the clothes of the ladies and started to feel their breasts and we men could do nothing but watch. Imagine that, *beti* – a man having to see this and not protect the womenfolk. If they cried they were slapped. This was outside the High Commission. The English took coffee breaks, never thought anything was urgent and our lives were in danger. Without the right stamp we were stateless. It was all over for us.' Mahmood Mamdani, an academic at Makerere, recorded the same British attitude: 'The High Commission's view of the world was particularly conspiratorial. To them as we had ample opportunities to witness, every affidavit was false, every statement was a lie and every Asian an inscrutable oriental.'[7] Her Majesty's devoted servants were as hard as the Rock of Gibraltar, even at this tumultuous time.

In June 1972 the British had finally decided to withhold military and moral support from Idi Amin. The U-turn was the result of new concerns – not about human rights but about speeches the dictator had been making attacking 'imperialists everywhere'. A British military-training team due for Uganda was quietly retired, and the FCO internally accepted the fact that the undisciplined Ugandan army no longer had the support of the population.

In a series of speeches in July of the same year, Amin slammed both the British government and Asians he described as 'parasites', who, he claimed, had been bleeding his country dry for too many years. There was some truth in his accusations. Insecurity and greed had made many East African Asians careless and dishonest, and they had invited antipathy by not opening up to Africans socially or economically. The British government at first didn't believe their chosen man meant to expel Asians; after all, they were the mainstay of Uganda's economy. As Amin's deadline approached, he threatened to herd Asians into concentration camps. Heath tried to placate him: 'The British government have gone out of their way to try and be friendly and cooperate with Uganda ever since your administration took over. We were and are very anxious to help you in all the economic and security problems which face your country. I have hoped that our personal relationship could be close.'[8] When this had no effect, Heath, even more abjectly, attempted to persuade other nations to 'share the load'. India, Pakistan, Sweden, the US and Australia reluctantly agreed to take a few exiles. It was not a fine hour. Even at this point, wrote Mark Curtis, there were British officials who wanted to carry on with military support for Amin.[9]

By the autumn of 1972, Asians started leaving, British citizens first, followed by the rest, Ugandan citizens declared stateless by the Amin regime. They were allowed to take some clothes, but money, jewels, land, homes and businesses were confiscated. Canada acted with admirable humanity, airlifting all those not eligible to enter Britain, the government under Pierre Trudeau welcoming the arrivals with enthusiasm and providing substantial resources for integration, education and self-start schemes. There was little sign of public hostility to the influx. In Britain, although Heath eventually emerged an honourable leader who felt the country had an obligation to the ejected overseas UK citizens, the popular mood was hostile. The decision boosted anti-immigrant political parties and Enoch Powell's heroic status. While honourable people in the Conservative Party agreed with Heath, and their liberal voice won the day, local authorities like Leicester and Ealing placed full-page adverts in the national press asking the arrivals not to move into their localities. The Uganda Resettlement Board, a quango set up to manage the inflow, provided accommodation in old army camps and unused schools. Volunteers signed up. There was a failed attempt at dispersal to areas without 'too many Asians'. The government did not provide retraining, or arrange for loans and the recognition of qualifications, or arrange suitable housing.[10] Those who had no resources, however, did get respite, food and accommodation for a limited period. Bankers, teachers, social workers and entrepreneurs all gave some assistance to the bewildered exiles.

In Uganda the stolen assets brought in a temporary boom and only for some. Committees of the corrupt took what they could and gave the rest to cronies, wrote Henry Kyemba:

Thus people with no education and no knowledge of business were given big firms like the furnishing store Fazal Abdullah on Kampala Road, or General Motors on Bombo Road, the main importers of Peugeots. Some army officers became fabulously wealthy... Many neglected their duties to manage their new businesses... [They] were completely at a loss. They did not know the prices of items in their shops.'[11]

Ugandan Asians never protested, never rioted, meekly accepted their lot. Long before Idi Amin Dada boxed his way to the command post, we brown Ugandans were accustomed to being kicked about and humiliated. For the powerless, pride is a luxury. Bahdur Tejani, whose siblings were my friends for many years, captured our surrender to fate: 'We had become used to being treated as the outcasts. We were not a tribe, we were Asians, a vast amorphous group lumped together for national convenience, owing loyalty (and hostility) to no one but ourselves... The day Amin declared that all Asians had to quit the country, my father said: "we came here with empty hands, and leave with empty hearts".'[12]

Some of those who had to flee were filled with renewed racism against blacks;

others were broken-hearted and overcome with self-pity. For a small number, fear and pain brought on an awakening, a reckoning with history, quasi-religious contrition. During their last days in Uganda, they invited their servants to eat and drink with them at their tables. Never happened before. They cleared and washed up together. Departing Asians gave their Janes and Johnnies clothes, cars, furniture and cash; their Janes and Johnnies, in turn, begged the masters and mistresses to stay on. The shelters over their own heads were being blown away. Where were the replacement jobs to be found? What would happen to Kampala? Browns and blacks apologized to each other, one side for years of racial exploitation, the other for Amin's ethnic cleansing. They cried. It was too late.

As TL's family prepared to leave, we were terrified Amin would incite the massacre of Asians. Mob violence is an effective tool used by African dictators. The worst that happened was never as bad as anything we feared. But we were in Oxford, far away from the daily invective and the low-level violence. Imagine the shock and numbness as they stood stripped of everything, nowhere people without an identity, rights or respect, turfed out with contempt by co-citizens motivated by grubby greed and shoddy revenge. From a distance it was both harder and easier to bear. What storms must have raged in their heads and hearts, how they must have strangled their voices as they handed over land, businesses and houses to bullies with guns.

In the final weeks, Asian girls and women kept off the streets. Small groups of African men were roaming, looking to violate them, as if they were now entitled. Amin had made incendiary speeches about Asians not giving their girls to African men, and there is some evidence that he was this angry with Asians because the beautiful widow of a millionaire industrialist had spurned his offer to marry her and then, worse, left the country the night after the proposal. The sister of a Sikh school mate, only fourteen, was raped by their *askari*, a man who had been their guard for thirty years. All her life she had sat on a stone next to him playing and talking. Her family never revealed the assault – the shame, the shame – and she ended up a mental patient in Birmingham. I met her by chance much later; she was silent and obese.

The arrival of unwanted Ugandan Asians hastened Heath's decline and the general national disintegration. At the airports, Asians clutching their children and a few belongings were welcomed by lines of 'patriots' with obscene placards. The objectors included mothers with buggies, East End butchers, miners, the National Front and local councillors. Contrary to popular myth, we were never 'refugees' received in with British generosity but people conned by the state into opting for passports that were rendered worthless. I have a press photograph of a girl, Cuckoo Inderjit, only twelve, one of the expelled. In one arm she holds a huge white doll and in the other an equally big carving of a black warrior in wood. The two forces on either side seem to press in on her, controlling her destiny. What happened to her, I often wonder.

As a journalist I met and interviewed Heath a number of times in the years after the exodus. In 1982 he told me, 'Few other countries helped us with this problem so we had to take them. The British people have a reputation for looking after people. We were very careful to get them to a wide variety of places so they would be spread out.' At the time this self-regarding, duplicitous, very British chap made me livid. Heath's dealings with Amin were immoral, and both Asians and Africans paid for his Cold War machinations. Today I think of Heath as one of the more honourable British prime ministers. He let us in in our time of need. (In contrast, Blair's government has ignored Iraqis made refugees by our war.) There are Ugandan Asians all across Britain who have framed pictures of Heath. Some have pictures of Idi Amin too. Garlands of false marigolds adorn them both – together they delivered Ugandan Asians to richer pastures. These days Ugandan Asians are as likely as their indigenous compatriots to show total disregard for others who have had to flee their countries. They forget what they felt like then.

Around half the fleeing Asians had some money in European banks, the others were genuinely destitute. The bigotry pushing itself into their faces was possible to bear because thousands of other Britons were caring and generous. Others before us who arrived here to find the same pattern of xenophobia and hysteria have their own stories of welcome. For years I hung on to an old coat – brown with a velvet collar – given to me by a dear old neighbour in Oxford after I moved there. I had no money, and she had a big heart. We owe these kindly souls, those who tend the ever-increasing mass of human flotsam and jetsam. As Thomas Carlyle accurately observed, 'One may mark the years and epochs by the successive kinds of exiles that walk the London streets and, in grim, silent manner, demand pity from us and reflections from us.'[13]

In reception centres visitors brought solace, winter coats, nappies, shoes, sanitary towels, bus maps, story books for bewildered children. The ex-Liberal leader Jeremy Thorpe and Conservative MPs Peter and Virginia Bottomley were exceptionally generous to needy families. There was a camp in Oxfordshire where I went to help. Brisk WI-type women were always there, doing their bit without a hint of sentimentality. Some of them reminded us of those types back home, do-gooders wanting to bring on the natives. One old woman, a Hindu widow, unlucky she told me to have produced only daughters, wanted to know how much a replacement set of false teeth would cost. The soldiers had made her spit hers out at the airport for fun. You should have seen her face when I told her that dental treatment was free in the UK. Mamdani, who found himself in a camp in Kensington in London, was less thrilled. He remembers an administrator barking:

'I don't want to see anyone but camp residents eating here. For each guest you must pay 5 pence and remember only I can grant permission.' The staff had successfully turned the camp into a total institution like a prison or insane asylum with the distinction between private and public life obliterated with all those living there subject to controls and reduced to dependency... it was my first experience of what it would be like to live under a totalitarian system.[14]

The women shed tears, sang sad Hindi songs and cooked. I remember Mithi (meaning 'sweet', a name her husband, Ali, gave her on their wedding night), who was inconsolable. She was forty and had had to part from her beloved Ali because she had British nationality and he was a Ugandan citizen so sought refuge in India. She wanted desperately to prepare a feast for seven virgins, a last-ditch ritual used by Shia Muslims with mounting troubles. Seven pubescent girls had to be found in the campsite, to be fed *sev* – sweet vermicelli with plump sultanas – saffron mutton rice, and sweetened milk with crushed pistachios. White handkerchiefs perfumed with rose water would be given to each innocent child, and prayers would be said.

Mithi's magnificent breasts trembled appealingly when she was distressed. She caught the eye of Mr Eric Morris, a volunteer in the camp, once an Anglican priest in a rural church in Uganda. He brought in a collection from his parish, and seven virgins were duly indulged but not as they would have been back home. Mithi had to make do with the supplies brought in by dearest Mr Morris, using spaghetti instead of vermicelli and substituting crushed almonds for the pistachios. It was to be fifteen years before Ali and Mithi met up again. By that time her vitality had drained away, and her breasts were small and still.

Sev

Serves 6

1 cup broken fine vermicelli	½ cup sugar
½ tsp cardamom seeds	2 tbsp sultanas
2 tbsp almond slivers	2 tbsp chopped pistachios

3 oz butter   1 cup water

½ cup full-cream milk

- ◎   Mix water and sugar and boil, then simmer until it turns to a thickish syrup.

- ◎   Fry the vermicelli in butter on low heat, add the syrup and sultanas, then mix
    thoroughly.

- ◎   Put into an ovenproof glass dish, cover with foil and cook in an oven (350°F,
    180°C, gas mark 4) for fifteen minutes.

- ◎   Remove, mix in milk and cardamom seeds, and return to the oven for ten minutes.

- ◎   Garnish with almonds and pistachios.

The men in the camp were down and depressed on some days, upbeat most of the time. They already saw infinite possibilities: '*Aree*, you know they shut down at five o'clock – we will be OK here. We will be rich.' 'Feeling very hopeful. We shopkeepers have joined a nation of shopkeepers, nothing to worry.' 'We came, saw and opened all-day food shops, that is what they will say one day. Our *dukans* in the hard jungle didn't frighten us. Do you think this place will? Business is in the blood. We will make it big again. Africa's loss their gain.' The busy bees remade their honeycombs.

And the ones who could not forget never forgave. They looked across at their old homeland with treacherous disdain, scorning the people and the land. You still hear them from London to Vancouver, Leicester to Texas, claiming all credit for progress in East Africa and none of the responsibility for the subsequent ruin: 'See what happened when we left? The *junglees*, see how they made a mess of paradise, heaven on earth.' 'We tried so hard to teach them correct things, good business ways, but no, telling you easier to teach the monkeys than the blacks.' Later, when news arrived of Ugandans being massacred and tortured, there was little pity they could spare. Only *junglees* killing each other, what's to say? They claimed they had no more thoughts of back home. They lied.

TL's family, who had faithfully opted for Ugandan passports, were taken to Canada. Half of those folk, including Nazira, went to Vancouver, the rest to Toronto. Moss and Poss went to some hick town in South Carolina and for some years broke their backs doing dirt labour in an industrial bakery. Feriyal took off for Pittsburgh to marry Barry, an American she had met back in Kampala. There are people who were dispersed then whom I have never found. Some of Jena's oldest friends are among them.

The loss of our homeland, empty longings linger on and on. Sometimes seem to be getting worse. We got the houses and cars and businesses and gold – bigger and better than most ever had in Africa. But how to remake the inner landscapes of beauty, the pictures imbibed as a child? The only time I have returned to Uganda, I rushed back to London after four days. I was acutely distressed. My country was gone, burned away in the violent years.

In Ealing, where my family lived, a small mosque was opened up in a back street. In other places converted sheds and garages were turned into temples and mosques. During those early years these were packed out. Immigrants call upon much divine goodwill as they struggle to make it. Windows had to be shut and double-locked and the broken panes covered with paper. The airless, miasmic atmosphere brought out the best and worst in worshippers. Sometimes they called on each other when they couldn't manage, and, just like my mum had found back in Kampala, someone always provided. But under pressure people turned bitchy too, and envious. Sometimes unseemly rows broke out on the women's side, and the men were embarrassed. I witnessed one of these on the evening we all went to pray for a relative who had died in Canada. A woman sitting next to me hissed across to another sitting in the row in front, 'Your son is living with his girlfriend in Earls Court, unmarried and she is black, Khusabai, so don't tell me about sin.' 'You have no shame, stupid girl? *Besharam*, wearing so many *tasbis* and talking back? To me? You are talking to an elder like that? Making black stories about my son, when look at you, burnt matchstick, jealous of everyone. Not even a *kala* houseboy would marry you?' Khusabai swept herself up from the mat, discharged the *elaichi* she had been chewing on throughout the evening. The spitty cardamom pod landed in her adversary's hair, though she only found it later, lodged in her spindly plait.

Inside the mosque they tried to keep the singing soft and the prayers short. They tried not to take up seats on buses taking them there. They staggered arrival and departure times, but still they were abused and mocked, pushed around and sometimes slapped by the natives. In shops and bars (too soon to know they were called pubs), sullen service was the norm, unspoken hatred that took time to hit and then hurt longer than straightforward invective. Or jokes. Sundays were the hardest. How come the streets were empty on this day of fun? Why were there no crowds walking up and down or driving round and round to greet, meet and be jolly? It was death in life, the English Sunday, they moaned, turning to the mosque to give them a couple of hours of crowd warmth.

Bit by bit, TL and I withdrew from these people, no longer our people, the huddled masses. So many were struggling – in small rooms with no heating, bathing every other day using bowls and cups. The old and the young both had to learn humility. Most realized for the first time that for white Britain they were black and here on sufferance. Sure, we pitied the expelled, but what good was that kind of pity without connection? I remember being embarrassed when my mother visited and the times when I enjoyed demeaning programmes like *Mind your Language*.

In Oxford, supremely detached from all reality, we believed we could drop our past identities, dump them as we did our old clothes from back home, home-made and embarrassing. The college house we shared with other students could have been an eccentric director's film set. Takashi, a Japanese economist, cooked wearing a cotton headscarf and stir-boiled tea towels to destruction. There were various young women. Earnestly Christian Susan's ship came in the day I took her to a resettlement camp, where she prayed on her knees and handed out sweets to the brown babies. Amanda was a bulimic who stole food and resembled members of the Addams family – lanky black hair, pale face. With incense sticks in her hand she traversed the corridors and stairs. Linda was a short American with good teeth who memorized pages from the *Shorter Oxford Dictionary* with her tall fiancé. They just adored the old university and the English. And I adored them, so untainted by history. Then there was blonde and vivacious Kathy, my first proper English friend. She had an innocence about her. Later she married a TV mogul and became very grand.

All these women were mad about TL, and his vanity was daily warmed by their hot girlie breath. It took him ages to climb up the three floors to our door – there were always plugs, broken heels and hairdryers to fix, or Amanda to rescue from herself.

Superior exotics were sought after in Oxford. Benazir Bhutto and Tariq Ali and spoiled children of pampered, erstwhile maharajahs were A-list. But we too were different enough to appeal to a generation seeking new cultural thrills. For us, tri-cultural Britons, it was and always is a matter of precise calculation which identity is most useful when. Laura Ashley Victorian gowns and straw hats with plastic strawberries were for times when I wanted to erase any ethnicity (as if that is so easily done), saris came out for those occasions when white people lusted for Eastern promise and mystique, and my few African patterned tops featuring ferocious masks were good for hanging out with hippy freeloaders and dopeheads. Food too had meaning and purpose. At summer parties and punting picnics it was best not to mention samosas. That was the time to impress your friends with the perfect Victoria sponge and scones. But invite people in for some Indian, and it was all incense sticks and Ravi Shankar.

I was fooling myself. In the English department they barely tolerated me. The arts faculties weren't yet prepared for foreign sorts. Science, economics and the law had always had students and experts from around the world; the English department was very much for the English-speaking first world. At my entry interview, I had said I was keen on V. S. Naipaul. They looked askance, and one said patronizingly, 'For that sort of thing, you should have applied to Leeds or somewhere like that. I believe they do African stuff up there.' And then in a dozen different ways they enquired why someone like me would be interested in Victorian studies.

It is extraordinary how much hurt you can feel when you are the only postgrad student never offered a sherry in the tutor's den, never invited to Sunday lunch by men and women paid to provide pastoral care. Most of the other postgrads on my course spoke like they were masters of the universe, and I could barely get to form a tentative opinion. Tutorials were purgatory. Maybe I really am no good, I soon thought. Just as they thought. There were friends – Scots, American and Irish – who were managing well in this airless world. I wasn't. Lectures were less oppressive because I could be anonymous, but they were mostly a waste of time and enthusiasm. The temple of scholars turned out to be shambolic and indifferent, clung to rites and status like fading aristocratic families. Most of the lecturers were fumblers who would not, could not, communicate. Students to them were a nuisance, postgrads more so because some were a threat. Oxford academics always had better things to do – concentrate on the tome or the perfect poem that had already taken six years, drink with their own sort, tend rose gardens and dine heartily in colleges, rounding off with the best port in the world. (Is it passed from left to right or the other way?)

A few in the faculty were brilliant, no question, and knew it too. There was the trendy lefty Terry Eagleton, whose radical literary criticism made my pulse race. Hungry, sexy young females were always at his feet in the King's Arms, and I didn't dare approach. But there was one, only one – John Carey – who was inspirational, like my favourite lecturers in Uganda. With sharp, glinting eyes and beautifully modulated language, Carey saved my intellectual life, kept the flame burning. My gratitude to him is immense and forever.

In the Bodleian Library, for hours on end, I withdrew and read. I discovered Anthony Trollope and went through all his novels in a few weeks. They took me into a provincial, petty, heathery England that kept to itself. Still does. Carey inspired me to revisit Dickens, and I found the courage to read Wordsworth. When I finally got 'Tintern Abbey', it was like the most pleasurable orgasm. My micro suede skirts gave similar pleasure to the men who lived and probably died in the same library seats, speaking only to old leather-bound books.

The college, Linacre, was different, new, internationalist and unpretentious, very 1970s. One woman arrived chaste as a nun and was ravished by an American with the beautiful physique of a horse. She fast made up for lost time. A gorgeous Welshman with a deep valley voice seduced all who were willing, and many were. A Muslim imam and a Catholic priest were brought down by the same Syrian vixen with hot red lips.

Linacre had a croquet lawn, and TL was a natural when it came to physical sport. His squash was fast and furious, his tennis beautifully pacey, his legs were like Ilie Năstase's, and by this time he played croquet like he was born to it. One scene comes to mind. He is out there knocking about with three men. One, let's call him Charles, struts, smokes disdainfully and has that look of ennui only old money can buy. He asks the two white guys if they want a drink and ignores TL, who is beating them all. Again. The Empire strikes back on the playing fields. TL asks anyway: 'A Coke please.' Charles ignores the request, and so I rush up and call him a rude bastard.

He laughs, grabs my hair and kisses my lips as if he owns me, as if I am some milk-maid on his estate. I feign outrage but am flattered and excited – a thoroughbred Englishman's kiss, my first ever.

So here we were, a married Asian couple surrounded by wild sex, drugs and rock 'n' roll, the real thing, not the tame copycat stuff back home. What made it so electrifying was that there was no guilt, no shame, no censure. Couples passed partners faster than a Scottish reel, and a dalliance was already too long. We declined the drugs and excessive drink (TL was a proper Muslim then, refusing even liquid food supplements with traces of alcohol; I always drank wine), but the wild times did catch up with us, and we lost our bearings then. I flirted but could never abandon myself enough to betray the vows I had made. Barely a year after our marriage, TL confessed that he had been spending an awful lot of time on a filthy mattress with a sexy woman with long hair who wore calico, didn't wash that much and lived in a squat. Her feral sex consumed him for a while. I can't blame him. We had no compass. The past was not even another country; it had been dissipated, and we were in a place without restraint. Values drummed into us in East Africa would once again be reconfigured and formulated but at this time were scraps flying in the wind. By the time I recovered direction and constraint, years later, TL was gone. Sex gave migrants one way to belong. Food was the other.

By then I had mastered ten recipes, and new chums were filling our North Oxford flat to eat with their plates on their laps. The kitchen had a small, old electric cooker and a little fridge. It was easy to impress then – nobody knew much about Eastern food, and they couldn't tell I was no expert. It was just a damn sight better than spag bol. And even though we were always struggling to pay the bills, these cheap feasts made us feel like somebodies. We were artless and eager to please our new best friends. Most have since vanished, and I miss them. For exiles those first bonds in the unexpected afterlife mean so much more than they do to those who ever so kindly befriend them.

Carrot *halva* was much appreciated by our skint guests, cheap, buttery and wickedly sweet. Advanced cannabis users always requested some to take back. Anne, our beloved Scottish friend, taken too young by cancer, used to eat it spread thin on brown toast to slow the sugar rush.

Carrot *Halva*

Serves 8

2 lb peeled and grated carrots
1 pint full-cream fresh milk
6 oz butter
3 tbsp sultanas

1 mug powdered full-cream milk
10 oz granulated sugar
A few cardamom pods

- Heat the butter at a low temperature in a heavy-bottomed pan with a lid you can put in the oven. Throw in the pods.

- When they start to cook, add the carrots and stir, cooking slowly for five minutes, then add the fresh milk, cover (leave a slight opening) and cook over very gentle heat for ten minutes.

- Check and stir often.

- Add sugar and milk powder, and cook a little longer.
- Cover and cook in a low oven (325°F, 170°C, gas mark 3) for half an hour.
- Finally, add many golden plump sultanas and serve hot.

The college offered accommodation only for the first year. The following year, we were lucky enough to be given an almost rent-free flat by a German Jewish scientist and his Quaker wife, Hugh and Mary Blaschko, who lived downstairs in the rest of the house. It was in Parktown, a lovely crescent in North Oxford, close to the river. Hugh loved my *halva*, and Mary scolded him because he ate more than was wise. He had humanity, curiosity, intellect and passion; she filled our lives with affection and put up with dozens of people traipsing through their home. He was seventy-three when we moved in, and when he died twenty-one years later I felt the grief of an adopted daughter. I had finally found unconditional paternal affection – in a stranger. This man had lost most of his family in the Holocaust – he would point out the dead in a beautiful painting that hung above the piano – yet always said displacement was a privilege, the best alternative to nationalism. Israel, he said, would bring out the worst in his people; the Diaspora had brought out the best.

Back in Uganda, Amin's troops were intimidating and killing on an unprecedented scale. Kyemba, an eyewitness to some of the horrors, reported:

[They were] no longer killing people by the score but the hundreds. It was impossible to dispose of the bodies in graves. Instead truckloads of corpses were taken and dumped in the Nile. Three sites were used – one just above the Owen Falls Dam at Jinja, another at Bujagali Falls near the army shooting range and a third near Karuma Falls near Murchison Falls[15]

– this last being the most beautiful nature reserve in Uganda. The intention was for the crocodiles to feast on the bodies. They didn't oblige, and the bloated corpses twirled around in the waters. Amin still had good friends abroad. An American fighter pilot, Tom Friedrich, told an interviewer in 2007 that he personally took charge of a delivery to Amin of a consignment of military planes. He stayed for three years training Amin's henchmen to fly: 'At times I would see Amin several times a week, and when my children came over for the summer, they taught Amin and his children to swim... He was an extraordinary man, a natural leader. Not too bright, but with amazing authority.'[16]

Three years after we were expelled, Amin shook hands with a long line of smiling leaders: Jim Callaghan, Jomo Kenyatta, Yasser Arafat, President Mobuto (a kindred spirit), Fidel Castro, the Pope, Kurt Waldheim (who as UN Secretary General had refused to intervene when the Asians were thrown out), the British ambassador to the UN, Ivor Richard, and his smiling wife. Bad history is a gallery of cordial handshakes.

During these years, Amin's loyal soldiers rounded up villagers and built efficient torture and execution rooms, always windowless. Jinja was the control centre.

Countless people – literally, for the numbers will never be known – were maimed, raped and murdered. Daniel, my friend from near there, says the folk left over can hear the banana trees wail at night, and the fat, small fruits pile up untouched, rotting gently back into the ground to placate the restless banshees. The skies are still as blue as I remember, he tells me, and that time still comes in the afternoon when a burst of cool rain washes the land and raises a scent fresh and yet musky.

In 1973, I got pregnant and we decided on an abortion. We had no money to raise a child, and we were both changing so rapidly we barely knew ourselves, even though love held us together and mutual desire was strong. Thanks to the girl who smelled, and my man who didn't resist her, that year I regretted the marriage and the extent to which I had conformed to family expectations. Turned upside down and inside out, we felt out of place and time, as did the sombre commitment we had made only a year previously. He took off his ring; I didn't show him I minded. I didn't mind all that much anyway. I worked all hours, passed the MPhil exams, showed the super-cilious dons who had so little faith in me. But their civilized malice had snapped my confidence and sapped my passion for literature. It felt like a worthless prize, prob-ably, I thought, given as an act of sympathy.

The extended family turned up for the graduation in 1975. They were elated, didn't know I felt pathologically unsure, patronized by the handshake and rolled

certificate. Around the Sheldonian Theatre, cousins took pictures and hugged innocent passers-by; their voices and laughter – loud and uncouth – echoed and bounced
off the hallowed walls: 'First class, *beti*, made us so proud really. Here, have twenty
pounds.' 'Yassi, wish Papa was here. Like him you are, too clever.' 'Look at her,
Alnoor, feel ashamed. Didn't get one O-level even.' Alnoor grabbed me and danced,
singing 'Bombshell Baby of Oxford'. Maami took out her *tasbi* and thanked Prophet
Mohammed and Imam Ali. Other students and their relatives in Jaeger were not
amused by this alien invasion. Nor was TL, who was by then pleased to be mistaken
for a Brazilian or Italian.

The happiness radiating from Jena's face made me believe I was worth it. My
clan was proud of me; the bitter disappointments and battles of the past were swept
away, and I was rehabilitated. But like TL I wanted them gone fast. Mary Blaschko
threw a canapé party for my family, who thought real dinner would arrive after the
titbits and hung around so long that poor Hugh fell asleep in his chair. Jena
fulsomely praised the spinach dip to be eaten with salty Ritz crackers: 'No more,
Mrs Mary, will not be able to eat the next food.' There was no next food. We retired
to our flat and watched *Rising Damp* on TV. Rigsby putting down Philip – black,
polished and superior – was very funny. Then.

TL's research on voles went on and on and on. It took him years to get his DPhil,
possibly because of non-zoological distractions. With no confidence at all that I
could do something with the MPhil, I went for a job teaching English to foreign
students. In some ways it was the easiest way to earn a living. We teachers, like back
home in Uganda, were revered. Young men and women from around the world were

eager to learn the language they needed to fulfil their dreams. Some were spoiled sprogs of rich dynasties; others had been sent away by anxious parents living under horrendous regimes. As always the history of the world was found walking the streets of England.

This was when South American nations were owned by ruthless juntas and perpetually at war with 'terrorists' – folk heroes of the left and their supporters. So Chilean, Argentinian and Brazilian youngsters found themselves in Oxford. The war in the Lebanon broke out, and the language schools received kids from there, children of enemies – Christian Druze, Shia Muslims, Syrians, Jordanians – all learning together, always impeccably polite, then fighting with fury on the street outside.

In 1976, I got pregnant again, another slip-up and another abortion, only this time an incompetent doctor made arrangements almost too late. Abortions didn't worry us then. At night, though, for weeks afterwards, Fleetwood Mac's 'Rhiannon' played repeatedly in my dreams. I saw a child of about eight in a black-lace Victorian dress, with curly, long black hair tied with a red ribbon, smiling and disappearing straight down into a perfectly square lake, waving until her ringed fingers were no more. Sleeping tablets only made the images crazier, the song louder. I told TL we would one day have a daughter and would have to call her Rhiannon.

8 *Rhiannon was a Blonde, 1976–86*

THE NOVELIST NICK HORNBY remembers England in 1976 as a 'dark shade of grey'. It was. 'People ate Wimpys, watched *On the Buses*, and hurried to the shops before they shut at five.'[1] Then in December, live on Thames TV's *Today* programme, the Sex Pistols said 'fuckin'', 'fucking', 'You dirty bastard' and 'What a fucking rotter' during an interview that lasted but a few minutes. You felt the jolt, worse than an electric shock, more alarming than if every TV set in the land had gone up in smoke. Like millions of others, Uncle Hussain (not a blood relative, just one of the many you pick up on the journey of life) was furious. He wrote a prissy letter of complaint to the interviewer, Bill Grundy, who was briefly suspended. A line had been crossed, said this uncle, a schoolteacher back in Kampala; it was more shocking than witnessing 'a man defecating in daylight in Pall Mall. What difference now between the *junglee* blacks and the great Britons?' Four years on and Ugandan Asians were still trying to come to terms with post-1960s Britannia, who seemed to them to have sunk low, her hair dishevelled, holding a joint (not the trident) in her unwashed hand.

I was ready to leave Oxford. It was too small and precious to hold my interest much longer. Besides, all our friends had gone, and we felt like leftovers at the bottom of the bowl.

At long, long last, in the summer of 1977, TL's voles of Wytham Woods could move on to the next bespectacled, hirsute DPhil student. TL put his head down and wrote, day and night. We kept a thick blanket in the smelly lab for conjugal requirements, and when we lay down on the hard floor, I thought I could hear the chatter of dirty little voyeur voles all around us. The tome emerged, hundreds of pages and thousands of figures on their progenitive behaviour. It would never change the world, but a DPhil in Zoology from Oxford was an extraordinary achievement for a young man born in a nondescript African town to lower-middle-class parents. The people in mosque blinked a lot and looked baffled when we tried to explain what TL had done and why he was going to be a doctor but not really: 'What kind of doctor is this? Are you joking with me? Never heard this before. After all this time, he knows nothing about medicine? Wasting the life. So much money to be made in pharmacies, more money than even doctors could make.' We of course knew better, or so we thought, having freed ourselves from those petty-bourgeois imperatives.

TL's thesis was dedicated to me and to his small mammals. We deserved the honour. Together we had given him many of the best years of our lives. The bound and beautiful volume was delivered to old Oxbridge examiners – wizened, often vengeful arbiters – who would take weeks to pore over the contents and then preside over the daunting viva. Perhaps pharmacy would have been better after all, or accountancy, which allowed you to repeat failed exams for years. Most old school friends had, by then, settled down into jobs and shops which stayed open long after 5.00 p.m. Within a short decade, some would appear, grey-haired or bald and smiling, on fawning lists of self-made millionaires. A couple would also end up in Her Majesty's prisons too soon after going into Buckingham Palace to pick up imperial medals for services to business.

TL started looking for work. There was no opening in the academic field for an expert on vole propagation. We were broke. To show him I loved him more than money, I made him a dressing gown from an old candlewick bedspread. It was lemon yellow, short and cute, and the big pocket on the front had a smiley face. This time of waiting for the viva, the unknowable future, brought up unspoken biological cravings for me. I realized I could no longer put off motherhood. I had played at it long enough, borrowing my brother's children and the young ones in TL's family. What songs I had sung to them, the games we had invented, the poems and books I had read with them. Most popular of all were my quirky cakes – Goldilocks's cottage, ladybirds, butterflies, fairies, dolls, cars, military tanks, guns, ducks, hats, cradles, goldfish, clowns, mermaids, teddy bears – all sculpted out of perfectly baked sponges. That year saw Snoopy with chocolate ears and a fabulous Humpty Dumpty cake which had the toddler guests laughing and crying noisily. Some mums said they would pay me to make the same for their kids. I refused even though we sorely needed extra money. These were labours of love, not for sale. I think I was expressing my maternal urges and surges through cake.

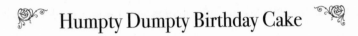 Humpty Dumpty Birthday Cake

You need a lot of cake for this, and much will end up as scrap – good to eat
with sips of tea for an awfully long time. Still the thing itself is a work
of naive art.

24 oz self-raising flour

24 oz soft margarine or butter

3 tbsp hot water

A pudding basin (for Humpty)

Two shallow sandwich-cake tins

24 oz caster sugar

12 eggs

A square cake tin, deep and large
(for the wall)

To decorate the cake

Plenty of Smarties, like 15 tubes

Some decorative sugar flowers

Sweets shaped like eyes and a mouth –
available in my local sweet shop so
should be anywhere else really

2 pretty ribbons

Butter icing made by beating together
1 lb 8 oz soft butter, 1 lb 8 oz icing
sugar and juice of half a lemon

2 cups desiccated coconut

Colourings (green and red)

Cocoa powder

- ☉ Grease and flour well the tins and basin, particularly the latter as the shape needs
  to be intact when you take the cake out.

- ☉ With a small electric beater, beat all the cake ingredients until they are well mixed.
  When the mixture is the right consistency, it should drop down slowly from a
  spoon.

- ☉ Pour into the tins and basin and bake at 375°F, 190°C, gas mark 5 for thirty
  minutes.

- ☉ Check with a skewer. If it comes out wet, return to the oven to bake but reduce
  the temperature. You may need to place a sheet of foil over the top if it is turning
  too brown.

- When baked, slide a knife round the edges and turn out the cakes carefully. Let them cool.

- Using the same beater, mix the icing ingredients until smooth.

- Divide the icing into four parts, one larger than the other three combined. Put them into separate bowls.

- Into the largest portion, beat in the cocoa. Leave one portion as it is.

- Carefully colour the third portion green using tiny drops of colour and building up the shade.

- For the fourth portion add drops of the red colouring to make pink icing.

- Separate out the different-coloured Smarties (get kids to do this).

- Cut the square cake in two, then place one piece on top of the other to make a wide wall.

- Slap on the brown icing, and carefully etch in rough brick shapes with a skewer.

- Using an icing set, squeeze some creepers over the wall, willy-nilly, with the green icing, then have fun beautifully arranging the flowers around these.

- Cover Humpty with white icing and roll in desiccated coconut. Place the two eyes (or brown Smarties) and a mouth (or a line of red Smarties to make a smile) on to the face.

- Place the egghead on top of the wall.

- Using the spare cake, cut some legs and stick them in front of the wall. Cover in pink icing and pink Smarties – the trousers.

- Take one round cake and cover with green icing.

- Round the outside rim, carefully arrange Smarties in two alternate colours.

- You need to cut out a smaller circle with the other round cake, using a bowl to mark it out.

- Cover this in green too, and place in the middle of the larger circle. It is the hat to place on top of Humpty's head, which you will need to flatten by cutting a slice off the rounded top.

- A ribbon around the hat and a bow tied round the neck complete the cake.
- Add candles on top of the hat.

⌒

We agreed it was time for a baby and went for it. All too soon we started to get anxious, as you do, even though from the earlier pregnancies it was clear we were both fertile. This time, dammit, when we were ready, the tot-to-be wasn't. Six months on, and still his seed and my egg couldn't get it together, in spite of our energetic attempts to make it happen, night and day. I came home around 4.00 most days and we jumped straight into bed for another round, and another. Mary Blaschko, innocent as milk, often asked why the floor creaked quite so much and if the planks had come loose. If so, old Mr Somerset, the carpenter, would come in and fix them. Sometimes, at peak moments, her kind voice called out on the landing just outside the bedroom, 'Is anyone in? Hugh and I are going for a walk by the river. Want to come along? I can make extra sandwiches. I have some fish paste left over and elderflower water...' Sounding as false as thieves, we would mumble excuses – colds, coughs, late nights...

The weeks went by without fruition; I got weepy and felt guilty about casually ridding myself of the previous two children I might have had. Every month as the blood came, dark and malevolent, I cried in the small, windy attic bathroom with its dodgy water heater and rusting enamel tub. Rhiannon-of-the-dreams had blonde hair now, and her face was lined. I was still only twenty-seven but at that time thirty felt really, really old. None of our Oxford mates seemed to be in that much of a hurry to reproduce. Maybe it was yet again the anxiety of exile, the need to set down properly and have children who would have a nation they could claim as theirs by right of birth.

After seven months I realized I had missed a period. Two weeks later I allowed myself to believe I was possibly pregnant, after hourly looks to see if it was yet another false alarm. When you try for a baby, your body plays these wicked tricks on you all the time. Three long days after I excitedly took a urine sample on a bus to the clinic, the pregnancy was verified over the phone by a nurse with a warm Caribbean voice.

Happiness like a multitude of butterflies danced around me in the light, yet beyond them, in the shadows, shivered unseen qualms. I imagined all those things that could crush the possibilities ahead. I played Joni Mitchell's *Blue*, my best-friend album, always good on the dark side of life, to contain the breakout of excessive joy, which refused to be contained. By the afternoon of that day in May 1977, I had stuck up notes on the walls, doors and windows, pinned them on to towels and the cork message board in the kitchen, announcing the news again and again to myself and all who came in.

Nabil, my beloved Lebanese student, was the first to know, and he rushed out to buy me my favourite Cadbury's milk chocolate (one and a half glasses of full-cream milk) and then wished me a healthy, bonny boy: 'No, no, no, no, Nabil. It will definitely be a girl, I know it, and she will be named Rhiannon from the song by

Fleetwood Mac.' 'Why you want a girl? They are too much trouble. A boy will take care of you when you are old. Girls go to their husbands, no good to you.' TL hugged me so hard I thought my ribs would crack. Joy passed from me to him and back again, and we danced. The Blaschkos were delighted; our families were too. My mother-in-law, Khatibai, was the most elated. TL was her pride, her handsome fourth son whose devotion to her was unwavering and unconditional. Over the years, she and I had bonded too, so closely that we could only ever bawl on the phone, tears drowning our words in the vast expanse between here and Toronto. I so wanted her to be nearer so she could spoil me now that I was with child.

Khatibai sent me a bright new *tasbi* and food parcel with Bill, our Canadian friend at Linacre, a Voltaire scholar. He was like a super-tall skinny latte with a gentle, easy way. The plastic box contained *khari puri* and *gund pak*, an impossibly rich sweetmeat with raw *gum copal*, to strengthen the back for pregnancy and rein-force the fragile womb, a kind of edible adhesive you could say.

Gund Pak

1 lb best ghee (I warned you)
9 oz small pieces of gum
1 tsp ground cardamom
White poppy seeds
1 cup water
½ tsp nutmeg

12 oz wholemeal flour
½ cup evaporated milk
Almond flakes and slivered pistachios
1 lb granulated sugar
½ tsp saffron

- Fry the gum in a small amount of hot ghee until it makes popping sounds. Remove and add rest of the ghee.

- To this add the flour and stir as it cooks, until it is a rich brown colour.

- Stir in the milk and cook for three minutes, then remove from heat.

- Pulverize the gum in a grinder. (This is a hard recipe and shows love and care if you make it for a mother-to-be.)

- Add the gum, spices and saffron to the flour mix.

- In another pan, melt the sugar in the water, boiling until it turns into a thick syrup. It should form threads if you pick up a little (careful you don't burn your-self; my mother in law had fireproof skin).

- Add the syrup to the dry mix and beat well – again arduous, this bit.

- Spread the mixture flat on to a greased baking tray and sprinkle with many nuts and poppy seeds.

- When cool, cut into squares and eat.

I was warned this was for pregnant females only – men were meant to avoid it as the glue, it was feared, would clog up their vital tubes. It was wickedly good and eventually banned by my husband, whose own body was sculpted perfection. TL had always affectionately called me 'Chubbs' and said he liked my peachy body, but as my belly grew and cheeks filled out, he feared I would end up one of those fat, Southall begums who roll from side to side, puffing through each step they walk.

In the years after my marriage, a kind of working peace had settled between me and my brother's family. My sister-in-law had softened towards me because her kids loved me. Besides, I wasn't a burden on them any longer, and they were fast coming up in the world. We all seemed eager to cut off from the frightful past and move on.

Britain had in the meantime been taken by Heath into the Common Market but was still ill at ease with its continental neighbours. Jim Callaghan was Prime Minister, affable but ineffectual. Unions were getting ever more unpopular, and the Labour Party was proving to be hopelessly out of touch with the public and even more out of sorts with itself. Its policies on immigration and race were at best contradictory, at worst a capitulation to the nationalist right.

In 1976, during one of the hottest summers in living memory, the mother of all industrial disputes broke out in North London, at the Grunwick film-processing plant owned by an Anglo-Indian, George Ward, who refused to let his workers form a union or to give in to demands for better working conditions and equal pay. Most of his workers were female and Asian – many of them from East Africa – who had never participated in the labour market before their move to the UK. They complained that they were being exploited, denied basic rights, and being paid £28 per week when the national average wage was £72. Their leader was Jeyaben Desai, a small, feisty woman in a sari who unexpectedly found herself at the forefront of the first-ever strike initiated by non-white workers. They did get some support from white Britons. Mass pickets gathered, including miners brought down by Arthur Scargill; Shirley Williams, a Labour minister, joined in. However, the workers never had the full backing of the TUC or the power bloc within Labour. The strikers, who had just cause, came to believe race mattered less to these left-wing bastions than class, and their conclusions had some validity.

The Grunwick dispute contained all the volatile elements swilling in the land: poor labour relations, race, immigration, union duplicity and political betrayals. Immigration was a burning issue, with the press running incendiary (often fabricated) stories. When Asian 'flood warnings' appeared, racial abuse and attacks significantly increased. In 1977 Gurdip Singh Chaggar was murdered by a racially mixed gang, and the British fascist leader Kingsley Reed said publicly, 'One down, a million to go.' Judge McKinnon, who tried Reed, wished him well and said in open court, 'Goodness knows we have a million and a half or more unemployed already and that all the immigrants are going to do is to occupy the jobs that are needed by our local population.'[2]

Primary immigration had dried up as a result of tightened laws of entry, and attention shifted to families of immigrants joining those who were already settled. There was an outcry over 'virginity tests' carried out on young Asian women to verify their claims of marriage. The Anti-Nazi League was born to combat the rising xenophobia. It was mostly a white organization promoting justice and anti-racism though peaceful means.

Surveys confirmed that racial discrimination was rife in the job and housing markets, and in the provision of goods and services. Pressure grew for legal redress. UK civil-rights lawyers tirelessly lobbied to protect Britons of colour. Roy Jenkins, one of the most enlightened of British home secretaries, pushed through new legislation in 1976. The Liberal Party supported the new law, and the Conservatives, guided by Willie Whitelaw, did not oppose it. These progressive policies modernized Britain's structures and laws, but their beneficiaries rocked the nation's sense of itself. Unemployment was rising fast; Europe seemed to be in the doldrums, while Japan was the rising sun. As ever immigrants were blamed for all ills.

During the Jubilee celebrations in 1977, the country rallied briefly and felt great again. People were determined to be jolly, to beat the national blues. WI types came out with cakes and pies to reassure those who feared the sexual revolution. I made a pot of chilli con carne (Sloppy Joes really) for the Park Town residents' garden party and even wore an apron with the Union Jack, just to show willing.

Chilli con Carne (and Sloppy Joes)

1 lb low-fat minced beef

1 tin chopped tomatoes

1 tbsp powdered cumin (my addition, this)

1 tsp sugar

2 onions, chopped

1 cup water

2 tbsp sunflower oil

2 tbsp tomato purée

2 tsp crushed garlic

1 tbsp paprika powder

1 tsp chilli flakes or powder

Salt

- Heat the oil in a lidded pan and cook the onions until translucent.

- Add the garlic and spices, and continue to cook while stirring.

- Add the meat and let that cook over low heat for ten minutes.

- Add the tomatoes and purée, water, salt and sugar to taste, and cook partially covered for thirty minutes.

⊙ Serve with rice or crusty white bread. For Sloppy Joes, you use soft baps sliced
open. Slop some of the chilli over them and eat as the bread gets deliciously
soggy. If using paper plates, they too dissolve into mush. You can put a dollop of
sour cream on top.

In 1977, I was still dutifully attending the tedious, interminable meetings of a feminist group I had joined in 1974. One of my housemates had introduced me to the
collective, and I had been welcomed with excessive enthusiasm, their initial dusky
member who could talk from first-hand experience about Africa and India and the
rest of the unfortunate Third World, and advise on various rescue schemes they had
in mind for brides in arranged marriages.

The meetings were held in a damp school hall – one of the founders was a history
– sorry, herstory – teacher. The sisters found total inspiration in Kate Millett and
Andrea Dworkin and Virginia Woolf's *A Room of One's Own*, and were totally
committed to the cause. Unfortunately many of the most mocked stereotypes turned
up assiduously. There really were women in our group with curly-haired armpits
and beardy fuzz on their legs. Some were proudly overweight and smoked constantly
(drugs and cigarettes), and the most radical sought to exterminate men. Their
extreme politics were making their necks thicken and voices deepen to a masculine
growl. Or so I thought, probably unfairly. (I respect the women's movement for
changing lives but not the daft militancy.) Besides, they were adamantly opposed

to the institution of marriage and 'oppression' of child-rearing. Some particularly self-indulgent sessions brought me out in hives. Laura, a comrade, applied beeswax to the lumps with her long, artistic fingers. I let her. She had a tender touch.

I didn't think it was wise to own up that I was in love with TL and had chosen to marry him. I could collect more Green Shield stamps of approval if I carried on letting them believe I had been forced into wedlock when too young. I loved lipstick and high heels, halter necks and garish earrings. At meetings I had to leave that woman back home, turning up with a scrubbed face and in fetching dungarees and a striped T-shirt. Made me look like Felicity Kendal in *The Good Life*, said Mary Blaschko.

The choral gripes, the songs of censure, made little sense to me then. African women back home had appallingly few resources and burdens that white Western women couldn't even imagine. Here, feminists had food, water, education, autonomy and cash enough to be free of dependency on men. They lived in a society where they could fight for rights and even get some. My mum, who had struggled all her life, kept her good grace. Some of her best friends were men; she had manipulative skills which seemed more effective than the shouty tactics advocated by the sisterhood.

Since I had little else to contribute, I served the conclave, saw to their comfort and needs. Everyone, even a feminist, loves a wifie. After meetings we would drink a few glasses of Rose Belle Cup or Cider Cup and eat buttered cream crackers with faux-cheese triangles. I happily made up the drinks in large plastic bowls while they planned their crusades.

 Rose Belle Cup

2 bottles cheapest rosé   **1 medium-sized bottle fizzy lemonade**
Ice

- Mix the wine and lemonade and serve with ice cubes.

 Cider Cup

- Same as above, but you use soda water instead of lemonade.

Audrey K was the hardest and cleverest bitch of all, and she seemed to be able to listen in on our thoughts. She knew I was pregnant long before I was ready to confess and explain. She broadcast the news as if she was denouncing a spy right in the middle of yet another discussion on the tyranny of penetrative sex and procreation. There was silence first and then a crescendo of noise. I felt more of a fraud than a traitor. They asked if I was going to have an abortion. I replied, 'Of course not.' Would they pin me down and whip out the foetus? I panicked. Stupid and unfair, that momentary fright, for they were kind and non-violent. Then someone found the relief button. It was my culture obviously. Poor me. They hugged me charitably. It was the last time I went to a meeting.

My face, belly, arms, all got plumper and rounder as the months went on, and I noticed TL gazing at those girls in short skirts on bikes again. And, even more ardently, at a particular waitress at Brown's Restaurant. She had a pert bum under a frisky apron, and the name Bo was pinned on her small breast. Mine were now so big they jiggled like overfull water mattresses even when I was sitting perfectly still. From America a friend sent over a baby carrier (not available then in the UK), and TL tried it on often as if to convince himself that it was all happening. Real men then didn't walk around with babies tied to their chests, but my real man with his very hairy chest couldn't wait for his progeny to fill the silly-looking blue-corduroy sack. And when that small head did finally nestle close to his heart, dappled tenderness spread across his face, and his eyes never looked up, not at the shortest skirt in town.

Remember – try to understand what I don't and can't – that this father then walked away as if the child was one of those unfortunate little mistakes one makes, easily erased from the book of life. There were signs, perhaps, that I should have heeded. Why did he join some evening course (I don't remember the useless subject that couldn't wait) just as the antenatal classes started up? The rest of the mums decided I was a sad, single mother-to-be pretending that I had a husband at home. The other men gallantly took it in turn to be supportive dads for the role-plays. Resting back on strangers while they told me to breathe right was not what I needed. TL was unrepentant. He was reading it all up, he said, and would do the right things when the time came.

Then I think of the way he became a hyper-sportsman around this time, thrashing opponents on tennis and squash courts for hours and hours, as if he was trying to beat time and age, his biggest demons.

At home serious money worries hovered, the buzz of an invisible menace in my ear. I worked until I really couldn't any more, stopping three weeks before the baby was due. The private college I worked for had no provision for maternity pay and expected me back in the classroom a month after the delivery. We could no longer stay with the hospitable Blaschkos – a crying baby above their heads would have ruined their peaceful retirement.

A few weeks before our baby was due, TL applied for and got a job teaching biology at a private school for boys, Radley College in Abingdon, a few miles outside of Oxford where there was a thriving car factory. Rent was paid for as part of the package, and we found a four-bedroom suburban Barratt house with two bathrooms and a riot of amazingly awful carpets. The kitchen was carpeted in slimy algae green; mud brown and yellow swirled on the living-room floor; red with brown splodges jumped at you in the hall and up the staircase; olive-green leaves lay all over the bedrooms, a depressing autumnal pile you couldn't sweep up and pack into a bin bag. But the house was big and warm, and had a fabulous tall plant with saucer-shaped leaves in the hall. We were adults now, with our own washing machine and Hoover. Jena thought the house was marvellous, a new-build, not one of those old, damp abodes which the English loved and which made her shiver. Dead skin was everywhere, she said, in those places, and the breath of old ghosts. She even liked the psychedelic carpets: 'Dirt is never showing, good for the babies. Vomit will look like the design.'

Radley College had far too many boys with undemonstrative parents. Divorces and deaths came and went, and the boys had to carry on with business as usual. At our house they found plenty of tea and sympathy, and fab pop records instead of madrigals. Soon several boys became our groupies, always eager to please, offering to help in big ways and small. But even though I could make cakes and sew costumes and warm up confused and sad boys, I was not cut out to be a master's wife.

The worst day for the poor mites was Sunday. Parents dropped in, but the encounters were as brief and awkward as prison visits. Sensitive young boys needed extra care afterwards. One never forgot. In 2002, he wrote to me care of my newspaper, 'You were very good to me when I was at Radley. My parents were separating and you helped me cry when I needed to. I remember your Bob Marley records. You also made delectable spicy roast chicken sandwiches. I write to thank you and to ask if I can have the recipe.' He never married and works as an independent financial advisor.

Spicy Roast Chicken

A whole skinned chicken

Chilli flakes to taste

2 tbsp lime juice (freshly squeezed; keep the shells – you will need them)

1 tbsp pomegranate paste (available from Arab shops)

2 tbsp crushed ginger and garlic

½ tsp each *garam masala* and ground cumin

Salt and a little black pepper

2 whole peeled onions

- The day before, wipe the chicken with kitchen paper.

- Stuff the cavity with the lime shells and onions.

- Mix all the other ingredients to make a paste.

- Slash the fleshy parts of the bird and smear with this paste, really pressing hard and working it in with your hands.

- Cover with foil and leave overnight in the fridge.

- The next day, heat the oven to 375°F, 190°C, gas mark 5 and bake the chicken, still wrapped, for fifteen minutes.

- Then tear open the foil about 12 inches at the top and cook for a further twenty minutes, basting and turning the bird over a couple of times.

- Check with a knife that it is cooked – you pierce the fattest areas, and the liquid should run clear.

- I like to cook it until the liquid has been burned off.

For the first time in our lives, TL and I had some regular and proper money rolling in. As I grew bigger and more fed up (in both senses), my true and tender lover bought me the most beautiful dress in the whole world. It was from Anna Belinda, the bijou boutique financed by the erstwhile criminal Howard Marks, who used the shop as a money-laundering house for his lucrative drug deals. (We didn't know that then.) I had been there countless times, looking, fingering, trying on clothes so perfectly lovely that they scared me – what if one of the handmade buttons fell off, or I stepped on and tore the hem? I have my dress still – soft wine-coloured velvet with an Elizabethan bodice and the sweep of a monarchical gown. It made me feel and look like a fertile goddess. Jena almost had one of her fits when I told her we had spent £60 (I think it was) on a maternity dress in my seventh month: 'Looks like a curtain. Spending three thousand shillings on such a thing? I could have made you one for £10 – velvet so cheap in Shepherd's Bush market. Come with me. Three thousand Ugandan shillings – could have kept whole family for six months in Kampala. You are going to be a mother. Return it and buy some premium bonds for your child.'

On the last day of work before taking my (unpaid) maternity break, I was travelling back exhausted on the bus from central Oxford to Abingdon. My students had bought me a lovely baby quilt, and I had other stuff I was carrying. I had to get across a young white man to take up an empty window seat. My bulge hit him in the face. It was the end of the day, and he shouted at me and my unborn, increasingly restless child,

'Fuck your bastard. Don't touch me again.' I burst into tears as I sat down, and everyone else turned away or buried their faces in books and papers. Nothing new there, but it felt as if I had been given an electric shock.

Safely back home, incoherent and trembling, I said I would never again step out into the world. TL was relieved I hadn't shouted back or lost my temper, as I was wont to do. He told me I didn't have to go back to work ever again if I didn't want to. Jena piped up: 'No, she must work. Woman must have own money and what was all the education for? That man was foolish. How many times such things happen to me? Do I cry? Remember that driver who told me on the bus I was smelling? Don't cry, *beti*. Show them one day.'

None of us had planned or arranged for it to happen, but Jena had more or less joined our household and was happier than I had seen her for years. Her presence in my brother's household had become intolerable for both sides. (This is a story so fraught that I dare not tell it in full; her ghost would chide me for revealing what had been going on. Some matters, she always said, should never be seen or heard of after they had passed on.) In sum, she was tired of being a supplicant. One stormy night we drove to London and brought her back with us to the house of many-coloured carpets. In two old suitcases, handmade in Kampala, were packed her clothes, shoes, long johns, hot-water bottles, perfumes, fabrics and threads, all her weird Indian herbal cures, two bottles of Remy Martin brandy, three bottles of fat-busting cider vinegar, her *tasbis*, photos of the Imam with his gorgeous wife, tatty albums with a few of our old pictures, a bank savings book, some premium bonds, and her umpteen heart and blood-pressure medicines. Oh, and a sewing machine. I didn't know it then, but over many weeks she had quietly packed all she owned. She was fifty-eight.

TL treated her as one of his own, and I was happy for her to become the supervisor of my impending motherhood. We had in common now the second heartbeat that starts up when a child is expected and never stops, a ticking reminder of a mother's perpetual fears and unending duties.

Everyone wanted a girl. TL and I did, obviously; the name was waiting on our tongues, ready to be called out as she was delivered, then to be embroidered on the towels and painted on the cot. My mum did because girls were considered a blessing from Allah. Khatibai, my mother-in-law, did because she had only ever had one daughter, and then, one after another, five boys had followed to her dismay. Until TL was three, she had dressed him in dresses and tied ribbons in his curly hair. People in mosque paid good money for her hand-smocked dresses, and she promised me a dozen, after the baby was born, not before, because that would be to presume and tempt bad luck or the wrath of Allah.

TL and I paid scant attention to these superstitions. We were confidently occidental now and had learned to organize the future, map it out, not leave it solely in impetuous divine hands. In the first three weeks of January we prepared the smallest bedroom for precious Rhiannon. I beautified an old white cot with a lace canopy, hand-painted flowers and woodland creatures (including a vole). The matching cupboard was stuffed with girlie cuddly toys. I designed and made Victorian-style dresses, bonnets and pantaloons festooned with satin ribbons.

Our child was born at the John Radcliffe Hospital on the coldest day of the year, 30 January 1978. A week earlier, there had been one false alarm in a cinema, halfway through Ingmar Bergman's *Autumn Sonata* with the incomparable Ingrid Bergman playing a selfish concert pianist unable to attend to her daughter. I never did see the end. Six days on, my waters broke yet I shaved my legs and washed my hair before heading off to hospital. Things didn't go smoothly at all. Even with an epidural – newly available – I couldn't bear the excruciating long spasms. It took twelve hours, and the baby was showing signs of distress and weakness.

My mother waited all that time in the waiting room, unable really to understand why her son-in-law was in the birthing chamber when it should have been her. I didn't know if I wanted to be a thoroughly modern mother or to creep back into her

arms, into the warm folds of what we once were. I felt washed up between two shores.
TL was panicky yet everything he did was exactly right. He soothed me, talked me
out of my rising fear that Rhiannon was going to emerge beautiful and dead. He
held me the way I needed to be held, just enough so I didn't feel he was intruding.
He kept sane when I was losing myself. Then the doctors decided on an emergency
forceps delivery which tore me terribly, and I didn't heal for many months.

My baby was beautiful – I thought so, even though he was most definitely cross-
eyed, bruised and loudly masculine. We had no names for a boy. I said we could call
him after TL's father, which made me favourite daughter-in-law at a stroke. So we
called our boy Karim. TL seemed besotted. He babbled with joy; tears filled his eyes
as he imagined the future, father and son, hand in hand, buddies forever.

While the playboy charmer metamorphosed into a brilliant new dad, I went into
decline, was felled by a typhoon of conflicting feelings and a sense of paralysing
inadequacy. Postnatal depression hits you in the tenderest parts. Karim stole my
sleep, and I am monstrous and inept when tired. There were some nights to
remember. When I used up six nappies because my hand was so unsteady and he
peed straight up into my face. Or when I dropped a glass of water because he was
crying so loudly and then walked several times over the shards of glass, unaware that
my feet were bleeding profusely. Or that time when I wouldn't stop crying hysterically, to the irritation of the district nurse, who was big, butch and a bit like Hattie
Jacques: 'What's wrong with you? Stop this wailing at once. Stop it, I say. Why is
your mother always holding the baby? And why is she rubbing cooking oil over
the boy? Really, such filthy habits.' Jena was doing what is always done with

Asian newborns, massaging Karim gently after his bath with warm oil to which had been added some mysterious and smelly herbs. These days such 'filthy habits' are highly recommended by the National Childbirth Trust and posh North London mums.

Why was I in this state? I was deeply in love with my child. Yet I couldn't carry him without feeling I would drop him, and when I touched his soft skin I feared it would leave a bruise, a mark to show I couldn't be trusted with his innocent and vulnerable life. Perhaps it was something more than the simple anxiety of a first-time mother. As Karim fought not to be born, then finally emerged from my body, a part of me was afraid I was ejecting him from where I could protect him into a place where his colour would precede him and determine all that he wanted to do. Enoch Powell had entered my subconscious. The man on the bus had said it all. My son was the next generation of the unwanted.

TL cheerfully took over the toughest household chores – shopping, hoovering, washing and drying clothes, stuff Jena found hard to do. He came home several times a day to make sure I hadn't topped myself (or smothered the baby, though he was too kind to say that this worried him). Jena mothered both my child and me through these months, even though she couldn't understand what was happening and why. Gradually, tentatively, I got myself up again from the pits of enervating desolation.

Meanwhile Thatcherism had arrived on the scene, still embryonic yet forceful enough to shift the tectonic plates. The indomitable leader of the opposition was eager to grab power, which she finally did in May 1979. On the very day Karim was born, she had stirred the nation with her comments on national identity. During an interview on Granada TV, she said she sympathized with indigenous Britons who felt they were being 'swamped by people of a different culture'. She went further. With four million non-white Britons expected by the end of the century, politicians had to respond to the fears of the majority. It was a cunning act of political populism, wrote the perceptive *Guardian* columnist Hugo Young. Thatcher regurgitated Enoch Powell's warnings in the guise of a clucking, protective mother hen:

These statements, regarded by the ethnic communities as shamefully provocative, were not followed up by a serious policy commitment to intro-duce a more repressive regime of immigration control. Whitelaw, the shadow home secretary, would not allow it. But the text encouraged anyone who wanted to believe that Mrs Thatcher was a repressor of immigrants...[3]

We were breeding too much and too fast for this leaderine too. My breasts were bursting with milk as those unforgivable words resonated through the land. She meant my boy and me and his father – who played croquet like an English gentleman. I was so angry that I invited my white British friends over to meet the baby and tuck into a curry. Like my ancestors I made it so hot they burned. Too polite to refuse or too addicted to stop, they ate and cried. I made them cry, paid them back for Thatcher's words.

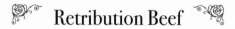

Retribution Beef

2 lb braising steak, cut into small chunks	1 tin chopped tomatoes
3 tbsp tomato purée	2 tsp ginger/garlic mix
3 onions, sliced	3 tbsp oil
1 tbsp chilli powder	3 dried whole hot chillies
1 tbsp *garam masala*	Salt

- Fry the onions until light brown in the oil.

- Add the tomatoes, ginger, garlic and spices (except *garam masala*).

- Cook for five minutes over medium heat, then add beef.

- Stir and cook for three minutes.

- Add water to cover the meat and cook (covered) over medium heat for an hour. Check to see if it is drying out; add water if it is.

- Add *garam masala*, purée and salt, and cook for another half hour or until the meat is tender and you have a thickish gravy.

Three months after Karim was born, TL got the job of his dreams, a lectureship at Bedford College, University of London. The buildings were in Regent's Park, right there at the epicentre of the capital, which until then we had regarded with colonial awe and provincial timidity. Within weeks I too had a job teaching English as a foreign language at a reputable private school in a converted grand house in Holland Park.

We had nowhere to live. My brother offered us a one-bedroom flat in a dilapidated property he had bought in an auction. I remain truly grateful to him for coming to our aid, and I am not being sarcastic. The place was small, had a bathtub next to a makeshift kitchen and rats under the floorboards. Jena had to be with us so I could go to work, and she lived in dread of the vermin, which left calling cards: slivers of shit in the kitchen, in a circle around the baby sterilizers. She slept in the living room on a broken sofa while the three of us were in the stuffy bedroom. The baby cried all night. Jena and I swept the floor every few hours so he could crawl without picking up the beastly droppings. We put down sheets, sprayed the walls with anti-fungal wash, and that brought on my asthma.

Yet, like other hard-pressed incomers to the capital, we found the oddest reasons to be cheerful. In the flat upstairs lived a widow, also from Uganda. She and Jena had known each other in the old days. The hardships fell quiet when the two met, and all you could hear were peals of delight as they reminded each other of lost people and places, and then exchanged tips and tales of the London only a poor immigrant ever gets to know, one level above the vermin and even busier.

Shepherd's Bush Green was hardly a park but was still grassy enough for us to eat al fresco on warm evenings. As cooking was hard in the kitchenette, it was often Kentucky Fried Chicken and Dunkin Donuts (sold cheap just before closing time). Super-delicious we thought them, just like the native Brits who were already well addicted to fatty American junk. We were saved by Jena's boundless energy and culinary explorations. She found a stall in Shepherd's Bush Market run by a Kenyan Asian who had been in the UK since 1963. He sold shrivelled *bhindi*, ageing aubergines, garlic, ginger and green chillies. Fast, improvised, one-pan Asian recipes were now added to Jena's repertoire and, eventually, to mine.

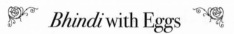

Bhindi with Eggs

1 lb fresh or frozen *bhindi* (which I often use these days)

1 tsp crushed garlic

1 level tsp sugar

1 tsp powdered cumin (*jeera*)

1 tsp turmeric

Juice of a lime or lemon

4 tbsp sunflower oil

1 finely chopped onion

1 finely chopped green chilli

1 tin chopped tomatoes

Salt to taste

1 tsp powdered, dried coriander (*dhania*)

4 eggs

- Heat the oil to medium-hot in a wok and stir-fry the frozen *bhindi* with lemon or lime juice. (If using fresh *bhindi*, wipe with wet kitchen paper – don't wash as it makes them soggy.) Then cut into rings or sticks.

- Stir often for about ten minutes. This frying gets rid of the slimy stuff that oozes out of *bhindi*.

- Then add the onions and garlic, and fry for four more minutes.

- Add the tomatoes and all the spices, salt and sugar, and cook until the sauce thickens. It should not be runny.

- Beat the eggs and add them, stirring until they are softly scrambled.

- Serve with wraps, *roti* or bread.

Three weeks before Karim's first birthday in January 1979, my cousin offered us a flat to buy in Ealing Common. It was in a Victorian house he had bought to develop but hadn't because the 'damn, bloody sitting tenants will not listen and let me buy them out'. One lot of the damn, bloody sitting tenants are still there. The flat became vacant when a ninety-year-old widow who never left her home died that Christmas, a Miss Havisham figure who left behind a pile of blank diaries, forlorn, torn lace curtains and stale heat. The first weeks felt creepy; the old woman's stifled spirit seemed determined not to leave. It did when we finally wrenched open the windows and the door leading to the wild garden with a morbidly distorted quince tree, its arms flailing as if it was being flogged.

TL said the place had real potential – large rooms, high ceilings, a veranda with a swing made of rope and a plank of wood. I was less enthusiastic. It needed a lot of work, which would cost money. Jena hated it but stayed. My asthma got decidedly worse; skin flakes of the dead, said Jena, were getting into our lungs. Relatives – including my now rich brother – gave us furniture and other stuff. I still live there, save and mind the memories, the phantoms and the histories. It gives me a sense of continuity and an affirmation of settlement.

Other hopes took less time to materialize. TL took up DIY and bit by bit made the home our own. Knotty pine-wood slabs were cheap so were used liberally, at times to mock and wreck the authenticity of the period flat, but what did we understand about such things then? Some bad mistakes were made. Polystyrene tiles were glued on to the beautiful bedroom ceiling, and the lino on the kitchen floor was ugly and irredeemably sticky. But none of that really mattered. What did was the contentment of a regular life. At last we could expect the same life to be there the following day, month, year on year.

Outside, the world was neither soothing nor predictable. In April 1979 a multi-racial demonstration was organized in Southall against the presence there of the National Front. The SPG (Special Patrol Group) – the vicious guerrilla wing of the Metropolitan Police – arrived, spoilers to provoke violence. Many blameless protesters were injured, and a white teacher, Blair Peach, was bludgeoned to death by some SPG officers. I was there, fists in the air, chanting in unison with my comrades until suddenly we found ourselves facing a line of helmeted, shielded, faceless men who rushed at our orderly column. I ran into a house owned by a Sikh family, who provided shelter for at least forty of us. For the first time since moving to Britain, I felt an old terror rising. Policemen in the UK could turn into enemies of the people just as they did in Uganda. The trusted, cheery bobby on the beat died that day.

Meanwhile the SPG were storming homes and looking for 'troublemakers'. Mr Singh got his five children to crowd the windows and wave at the bastards so they didn't come in, and we were safe. In an enormous saucepan, his mattress-sized wife made sweet *masala* tea to calm the hysterical marchers. Those of us who stayed on until the crowds and the SPG had dispersed got to eat cauliflower *pakore*, freshly fried and served with hot chilli ketchup.

Cauliflower *Pakore*

1 large cauliflower broken into small sprigs

Batter

8 oz gram flour	Salt
Bicarbonate of soda	½ tsp cumin seeds
1 tsp chilli powder	½ tsp *ajwain* seeds
1 tsp turmeric	Half a lime
Cold water	Oil to deep-fry

- Sieve the gram flour into a bowl and break up any lumps.

- Add all the spices, then lime juice and water a little at a time until you have a thick pancakey batter.

- Stir in cauliflower, then leave for an hour.

- Add a pinch of bicarbonate of soda.

- Heat the oil and test that a drop of batter rises quickly.

- Spoon dessertspoons of the mixture into the fat then turn over several times for about three to four minutes.

- Drain on kitchen paper.

There were other protests against the National Front in London, many ending in shocking violence again, partly because of poor and unfair policing. Black and Asian communities grow increasingly mistrustful of officers, too many of whom were members of extreme right-wing parties. A number of black men died in custody, and no one was held responsible. We felt that our lives were considered worthless.

The gloom did not touch TL, who was still incredulous and strutting proud that he had a job teaching zoology at a prestigious university. He was good at it too. Within a short time he became a popular lecturer and got into substantive research which was noticed by eminent people. On warm, long summer days when the sun seemed loath to leave the pink skies, I used to take my boy to TL's college in Regent's Park. On the way we smelled the roses and fed the ducks. Bliss it was to be alive. When we arrived, TL would show off his son to adoring students and at times introduce me as well. Never, though, to a tall, shapely young woman with a square, masculine jaw and cascade of wavy golden hair down to her waist who was often just leaving his office. I remember thinking her hair made her look like Rapunzel. She was to be my nemesis; her hair would call him, and he would one day climb up that tower to her.

Teaching English to young adults from around the world is about the most enjoyable job ever. They adore you, want to learn (and if not are terrific fun anyway). Imparting to Spaniards, Italians, Arabs, Japanese and the Swiss the structures, tools and infinite vocabulary of the rich and mellifluous English language was extraordinarily fulfilling. The first week of each course was always a challenge for me and for the only other teacher who wasn't white, Shobana Jeyasingh, originally from the Indian subcontinent, now a famous choreographer and director of her own dance company. Pupils were sullen, thought they were being cheated because we were patently not 'really English'. I used to pre-empt any tedious grumblings by telling them I was like them, a foreigner who had mastered English. They too could do it. It usually worked. Flirtation was also effective.

At home my darling boy was picking up language too, even more miraculous. I was already singing to him the songs I had learned at the youth club run by Miss Garvie back in Kampala. Jena, who had once been an infant teacher, taught him numbers and the alphabet. Then there was the wonderful *Sesame Street*, which awakened his curiosity and imagination. We could have lie-ins again while he was with his new friends Elmo and Cookie Monster. He developed a very peculiar English accent – part Indian, part RP, part American – and was starting to pick up a little Kutchi too, our home language, Jena's and mine.

As TL was becoming professionally more confident, he also was becoming personally too adventurous. That old talk of open marriages had started up again. Then he went further. Why did I agree? Was a part of me turned on by the obvious danger? Was I so desperately in love I couldn't deny TL anything? Was I too seeking some freedom to play around because the responsibilities of parenthood seemed so enclosing and final? Was I overconfident? Was I plain stupid? Did I think having affairs made us modern and fascinating? Was it a political choice? I can't answer any of these questions. I went along with it, and TL was most enormously grateful and appreciative.

He always made sure I knew when he was going to visit the blonde. What an honest chap. Truth was more important than fidelity in marriage. My emotions rioted. I caught the whiff of her on him, and blonde hairs twinkled on his clothes, but I behaved impeccably. He returned from a field trip to Kenya with two identical T-shirts for her and me. On the front were printed leopards with hard, green stones for eyes. He showed them to me, and I didn't flinch or make a scene. Cool, I said, why not? He isn't lying to me. That's what matters.

The polls showed that there hadn't ever been a leader other than Margaret Thatcher with such poor ratings. The election was just a year away, and we would be rid of her, I thought, hugely cheered up by the idea of her fall, the repulsive little English nationalist with her sprayed hair and icy eyes. The release didn't come. The Falklands War saved her, lifted The Lady to new heights. She was their Boadicea, the millions of my compatriots buoyed up by jingoism. Karim developed a sudden passion for guns as the drama played out on the small screen. My nephew gave him his old arsenal – ignoring my no-toy-guns rule – and my boy was in heaven, shooting everyone in sight, including the old aunties visiting Jena.

Karim was enrolled at a Church of England primary school because we wanted him to have access to Christianity and, through that, to understand better the soul of this nation. A Shia Muslim with devout grandparents and families, he was never in danger of being converted away from that heritage. At the age of four he could already read parts of the *Guardian* and was great at sports. His teachers adored him, even though for some reason his father and I never dressed him in the proper uniform. We stuck to the colours, but that was all. Maybe we thought it was clever or a way of asserting that he was not really one of 'them'. So he is conspicuous in all the group photos, looking self-conscious and bothered. By this time he was having to wear glasses too, so we got him wacky, bright-coloured frames, making him feel even more weird. The things you do. But those were also the most secure years of his life.

As TL became more entangled in Rapunzel's hair, I changed jobs, went to work for the Inner London Education Authority, teaching English and job skills to immigrants and refugees in their homes and workplaces. This was when the right-wing press and the Tories were in perpetual and sometimes comical battles against the imagined windmills of 'loony' policies, seeing equal opportunities as creeping Communism. Admittedly, the boroughs of Brent and Islington and some others *did* have some hot Trot fanatics, the mullahs of their day, but the hysteria stirred up by Thatcherite papers and ministers was to block any progressive policies.

My new job was serious, hard work, and nobody played around. I saw daily evidence of social and racial exclusion, the way hard-working black and Asian Britons were treated by their supervisors and managers. Racism expressed itself in unexplained actions, not abusive words as it had in the 1960s. Working with wives and mothers, I also witnessed cultural control and suppression of women and children within families which had relocated to the West but denied its essential freedoms.

For one couple both of these injustices came together in a volatile mix. He was a Punjabi factory worker, she was a very quiet, very lovely housewife who had been brought over in 1982, happy as a lark. She would always have a snack waiting for me, some *pakore* or *channa chat*, cheap stuff they could afford. He was bullied at work, racially taunted, denied overtime and generally emasculated. One day it all got to him, and he quit his job. When he came home his wife was out, next door as it happened, but he didn't know that. By the time she came back, he was in a rage. He beat her up, accused her of being disobedient and 'English'. He broke her arm, kicked her in the stomach and then left the house to get drunk in a pub. By the time he returned, she had miscarried their first baby.

In 1985, TL's college merged with Royal Holloway in Egham, Surrey, and moved to that site. He now was too far away for me to turn up unexpectedly with our son. Rapunzel was gone, and we were trying to put all that behind us. That same year my reformed husband, now exceedingly solicitous, had to go off to Kenya for fieldwork. At the airport our son closed his eyes and prayed aloud, 'Mighty God – save my dad from air crashes and all the other people too.' TL cried as he waved goodbye. He wrote often, repetitive letters that always said he loved and missed us, a mantra perhaps to convince himself. I was bereft without him, more than ever before. Two months later, my son and I went over for a holiday and the three of us found ourselves and each other again in the stunning game parks and on the lovely beaches. It was like scrambling on to a safe platform after too long in tumultuous waves.

Personally we had reunited, but politically we were being pulled apart. Thatcher's Britain was ever more racist and xenophobic. I was Ms Agitprop, always whipped up about this or that. Many Saturday afternoons were taken up marching against the deaths of black men in police detention, against virginity testing, against unfair immigration laws, against apartheid and Pinochet. Sometimes I took my boy with me. His father preferred to chill out, munch on popcorn, watch sports on TV while downing a beer or two. Sometimes he went out to play tennis or squash with someone good enough.

Then his spine started to give him trouble, slowed down the master racquet sportsman, then forced him off the courts. He was devastated. Games on TV made him feel 'a useless cripple'. Nothing comforted him. Physical perfection and strength defined his core identity, meant much more to him than his intellectual achievements. The bad back brought up an even deeper crisis which had no name. Eventually he confessed that he felt trapped in his job. He wanted to be an acupuncturist, this tenured zoologist with access to the greatest minds and chances to go on expeditions, this man who was popular with students and got weeks off in the summer. None of it made him happy any more.

TL found a reputable training college in Leamington Spa. We agreed that we could use our meagre savings, that I would try and write freelance articles so we could manage the finances and pay for his course, books and equipment. For three years he would be going off virtually every Friday, returning on Sunday evening.

My first small journalistic breaks came through – an article published in the *Guardian*, another in *New Society*. I did a short course in radio journalism and got some contract work at the BBC World Service and Radio 4's *Woman's Hour*. How many hours did Karim spend with me in dark little studios on Saturdays while I mastered the art of editing tape with a blade? How many books did the poor mite get through over those weekends? One night in November, we looked out at 10.30 from a dingy room in Broadcasting House and saw an incredible fireworks display in the skies. 'It's not as good as the ones Dad used to do in the garden, is it?' asked Karim. 'Why does he have to do this stupid course?'

TL's devoted wife had agreed to this arrangement – three years of weekends as a lone mother. I never doubted his word, trusted him completely. His back got markedly worse, and he looked white and drained when he walked through the door on Sunday evenings. Yet there we would be, Karim and I, playful, laying before the returning warrior something delightful – tempting foods, tricks to make him laugh, handmade gifts and cards, rehearsed songs, dances and sketches, puppet shows with Karim's many cuddly toys stuck on sticks and acting out wild and wonderful adventures. These were happy hours. Dining was made special too – a written menu one day, dozens of flickering candles the next, strange new dishes: squid cooked to a melting softness, Iranian kebabs served with thick, garlicky yoghourt.

Greek Squid

Serves 4

1 onion	1 tin chopped tomatoes
1 lb squid, cut into small rings – you can use the other bits too	3 cloves garlic
	1 glass cheap red wine
Lots of parsley	Lemon juice
Salt and pepper to taste	2 tbsp olive oil

- Heat the oil, then fry the onions until translucent.
- Add the finely chopped garlic, and cook for a couple more minutes.
- Add the tomatoes, wine, lemon juice, salt and pepper.
- Cover, lower the heat and cook for five minutes, then add the squid.
- Cover and simmer for twenty minutes.
- The Greek cook who gave me this recipe told me you either cook squid very fast or very slowly for a long time.
- Add chopped parsley; serve with crusty bread.

Iranian Kebabs

1 lb minced lamb, the best quality you can buy (my halal butcher minces mine fresh from lamb chunks)	2 finely chopped spring onions
	1 tsp chopped garlic
	Salt and pepper

2 slices white bread soaked, then squeezed so water is extracted, leaving a wet dough

Gormeh sabzi – mixed dried Iranian herbs

Ayvar (a red pepper paste you can find in Iranian shops)

A little sunflower oil

- Mix everything together well, then press into thinnish sausage shapes.

- Impale on metal skewers and bake in a hot oven (400°F, 200°C, gas mark 6), turning over every ten minutes until cooked.

And here is one favourite I have never been able to make since.

Melon, Avocado, Kiwi and Mint Salad

- Cut, mix, add lime juice and serve in pretty glass bowls as a refreshing starter.

9 The Longest Year, 1987–88

Schedules and routines tidy up restive emotions and wayward thoughts. The three of us grew accustomed to the weekly timetable, adjusted well to the new arrangements, lost touch with a problem building up, the way you do with stretchy trousers when weight piles on. Calm prevailed. Somewhere in the outer reaches of my psyche, when all else was quiet, I sometimes sensed rumbles, slight quavers. They were unheeded as I kept busy, kept order, kept faith.

At the age of eight, Karim, smart and super-confident, passed the entrance exams for Colet Court, the prep school at St Paul's, the best public school in London. It was a moment out of fiction – our son born with few advantages was about to become a little English gent. My papa, if alive, would surely have forgiven me then, gone straight to his City Bar mates to show off. In his trilby.

On the day we got the letter of admission, the three of us went to look properly at St Paul's. We wandered through the green acres, along the gorgeous riverbanks, as slim, long boats with fit rowers passed fast, then around the playing fields, counting the number of tennis and squash courts. The campus was much bigger than Entebbe's botanical garden, and the upper and lower schools had vastly better facilities, books and equipment than Makerere University.

Money was tight, but we would do whatever was necessary to get Karim that assured entrée, get him into places someone like him was never meant to infiltrate. It worked too. That priceless hauteur of privilege rubbed off on him; he acquired the silken tongue and cold logic, joined the Bar, dresses in pinstripes, knows his fine wines and relishes the best fois gras. He understands and can negotiate the intricate system, what Anthony Sampson memorably called the anatomy of Britain.[1] And I have no regrets at all about this choice at least.

I know, I know, I was and am a leftie, with an almost religious faith in public good and the NHS and equality and social engineering. But on the education and future of my child, the ambitious Asian immigrant in me drove out all guilt and shame. Hypocrisy tasted bitter but would be swallowed.

When we dropped Karim off at the imposing gates, he sauntered through them with upper-class nonchalance, made sure he didn't look amazed or thrilled. Within weeks, mates shouted out to him; he belonged. Good at many subjects and a natural-born sports kid, it was easy, and it felt subversive. What's more, he was never embarrassed to bring home friends whose parents lived in Eaton Square and had Harrods accounts. After they were picked up by the chauffeurs we ate our cheap and cheery fare. Different lives.

Lentil and Potato Soup

Serves 6

1 cup red lentils

1 onion, chopped fine

1 lime

1 clove garlic, chopped fine

1 Knorr chicken stock cube

2 tbsp rapeseed oil

5 potatoes, chopped into tiny squares

½ fennel bulb, chopped fine

2 tsp *jeera* powder

Heaps of chopped fresh parsley,
mint and coriander

- Warm the oil and gently cook the onion, fennel and garlic until soft.

- Add water to come up to about 2 inches above the vegetables.

- Add salt and stock cube, cover and cook for about six minutes.

- Throw in the potatoes and washed lentils, lower the heat and cover.

- Cook until the lentils are mushy and the potatoes are done.

- Squeeze in the lime juice, and add the *jeera* and herbs.

- Warm through again, then serve with crusty white bread.

- You can add chopped chilli if you like it hot. I do.

Jena by this time had moved to a small council flat near us. TL loved her, he said, but we needed to be on our own to rebuild our relationship. It made sense, though I felt guilt and shame asking my mother to go off to live alone after all she had done for our son, been a second mother to him in fact. She was upset, of course she was, but being Jena soon saw the bright side too. For the first time in her life, she could get her own money – never was income support received with such grateful elation. And in her flat she would be queen of her own life, not obliged to anyone and free at last. From this time to the day she died, she said those years of autonomy were the happiest she had known. Karim was always there, after school, when we were out or when he felt like seeing his nana. She made him *roti*, *puri*, what he called 'yellow pancakes' – *pudla*, which are indeed yellow pancakes made of gram flour, one of the best Indian snacks ever.

Pudla

1 lb gram flour

1 tsp *ajwain* seeds (you can use coarsely broken cumin seeds instead)

½ tsp chilli powder or 1 finely chopped green chilli

A pinch of asafoetida

3 tbsp oil

2 spring onions, finely chopped

½ bunch fresh coriander, finely chopped

1¼ pint water

1 tsp salt

½ tsp black pepper

- Mix the dry ingredients, then add water to make a pancakey batter.
- Leave to rest for an hour.
- Heat a flat griddle, frying pan or pancake pan, and spread a little oil on it.
- Using a spoon or jug, pour a little of the mix and spread it out with a wooden spatula so it thinly covers the pan (in a circle if you can manage it).
- Cook for about a minute, then turn over (you may need to flip over twice).
- Serve with yoghourt, pickles or chutneys. My son ate them with ketchup.

I felt oddly lonely and vulnerable without my mum, even though when she was with us there had been rows, too many, as she and I both grew older. She folded her knickers neatly, and lined drawers and cupboards; I was, well, wildly disorganized and to this day stuff my drawers like a bad teenager. I think at times I was jealous of the ease of her relationship with Karim. He and I were too much alike, too argumentative, and she always took his side. Karim was perfect; I just didn't appreciate how lucky I was to have such a child, she said. My mum was always kind and generous, but she made me prickle, perhaps because she was too generous and kind. There were other sites of conflict. Two women cannot easily share a kitchen without constant irritation, and I wanted to be a cook in my own right, not always the daughter of that Jenabai whose cooking is still praised across continents. Yet when she moved away, the kitchen felt more, not less, alien for a good while.

She had her own cookhouse and, at long last, all the gadgets and widgets she could buy and had collected. This is typically East African Asian. We cannot resist contraptions, especially cooking appliances, devices which promise magic and sometimes even deliver. Pressure cookers had been given away as part of girls' dowries in the 1960s. I remember the day one was delivered to our home back in Kampala – Jena was as thrilled as the day her British passport arrived. One of her nephews had sent it over as a gift from Tanganyika. They made magic in those whistling pots, the ladies back home. Dhals, pot roasts, various dried beans and steamed puddings, made with butter not suet obviously. The most delicious had pineapple and jaggery topping, sweet-and-sour gloop with small nibbles of fruit. I never asked my mother for the recipe and wish I had.

Even in the early days, soon after we landed here from Uganda, when there was hardly any money, Jena and I would wrap up in huge shawls and coats and waddle off to Edgware Road or Shepherd's Bush markets, always arriving back with some tricksy contraption sold by a fast-talking cockney whose words flew by but whose hands performed petty miracles. Jena had eleven onion choppers, each promising saved time and tearless eyes. I have even more. And an impressive collection of market-stall lemon squeezers, garlic presses, ironing-board covers, pepper mills, Moulinex food crushers in three sizes, little pointy things to de-pip tomatoes (a con, but I swear I saw the magician who sold it to us doing exactly that), fantastically useless plastic juicers, hard-boiled-egg slicers, apple corers, carrot and parsnip peelers (six different varieties), an almond splitter, a special knife to cut through a thick chocolate bar, a nutmeg sling which your bang against a wall to weaken the nut so it yields up more generously, a long comb to separate sticky strands of vermicelli, a pretty wooden spade to dig into and soften butter. More outlandish items lie quiet in the bottom drawer.

Missing Jena more than I cared to let her know, I invited TL's parents over from Canada to get to know their grandson and be with their favourite son, whose back pain was making him morose. Maybe there was some wishful thinking too. Being with them would take us back to the old world, now so far away. Their marriage was an example of what could be endured.

We were shocked to see how my father-in-law had aged. He was still as stubborn as ever and as trying, but he had shrivelled in size and was so furiously fussy about eating that it indicated early anorexia to me. TL resisted the diagnosis – an old man getting a young woman's disease seemed utterly improbable to him. Bapaji developed an endearing attachment to me over those months, and every evening when I returned from work, he would be waiting, in a clean shirt and tie, to go round the block. The two of us walked slowly, him grasping my arm so tight it hurt. Sometimes he went on and on about how we could have been rich if we hadn't wasted our lives. Pointing to fancy houses, he would say, 'See that, that is called a house. My father had one twice as big. Huh. After all these years and becoming a doctor from Oxford, you live like *maskinis*, beggars, in a flat so old it is like a grave.'

With Khatibai, I started going to mosque on Fridays again, just like the old days when I was trying to impress my boyfriend's clan. I taught Bapaji to make tea – he had never before been seen in a kitchen and had certainly never boiled water. At first he was shocked at my impertinence, then he agreed to learn. At dawn, when I was in the kitchen, typing slowly on my Brother typewriter, working away on articles commissioned by the *Guardian* and *New Society*, he brought me cups of tea, sloshed all over himself and his pyjamas. He cared but was always brusque: 'You are working too hard. Go to sleep, keeping me from sleeping, this nonsense of yours. You have no sense.' Jena always said I had collected many godly points for the tender care I extended to Bapaji. Maybe it was an offering of penance for failing to have any connection with my own father.

TL seemed quieter, ill at ease, but always perked up when his mother cooked piles of *samosas* and fried *mogo* sticks. More cooking oil was used up in a week than we had previously consumed in three months, and the house was infused with the smell of frying and spices. The odours even got into books left open and woollen hats. TL didn't object. Jena and my mother-in-law went off, the best of friends, to Southall and Alperton Asian shops, sometimes taking Karim with them so they could buy, buy, buy and have six arms to carry the bags. The boy and I grew plump on love and familial joy and the constant supply of fried snacks. My mother-in-law taught me how to make *urad* dhal, one of the hardest in the subcontinental repertoire which Jena had never bothered with. It added variety to the lentil menu, but it took a good deal longer than my other recipes. All those years ago when TL and I used to go back to his house for lunch from Makerere, this dhal had been one of his favourites, eaten with perfect small *rotis*.

Urad Dhal

Serves 6–7

2 cups black lentils, unhulled
Salt
2 green chillies, slit open
2 tbsp tomato purée (optional)
2 tbsp whipping cream (optional)

2 pints water
2 tsp crushed garlic and ginger
4 oz butter
1 tbsp *garam masala*

- Soak the lentils overnight, then drain and boil in water (three times the quantity of the lentils).
- To this add the ginger, garlic and chillies.
- It takes at least an hour and a half, perhaps more, for the slow cooking.
- Then add the *garam masala* and butter, stirring all the time.

- It will turn into a shiny, thick, dark porridge.

- You can stir in tomato purée and cream at this stage if you want to.

- Just before serving, squeeze in the juice of a lemon or serve wedges of lime or lemon for people to add at the table.

- This dhal shouldn't be eaten with rice – too heavy. Thin *roti* or *parathas* are best. Japani's Lemon, Chilli and Ginger Pickle works really well with this.

Old friends and acquaintances from mosque came to visit my in-laws, some with the all-healing *khichri* to help Bapaji recover from his strange ailment. It was Kampala again, for a few months. TL was getting moodier, the light on his face autumnal. He often found a full house, noisy with overlapping voices speaking Kutchi, when he returned from his weekends away. We would take Bapaji to a nearby Nepalese restaurant – he liked that a lot. But the fuss, burps and loud ramblings of the old man made my punctilious, perfectionist husband uncomfortable and unhappy. He couldn't bear the decomposing personality, the proud father falling to bits.

My man was always attractive, beguilingly so. He had called himself Sky for some years, had erased his old Muslim name like so much else. Celestial, blue, free and open, such connotations. His parents were the only ones now to use his birth name. To us he talked a lot about the acupuncture course, brought in books and needles, practised on me, told me hilarious stories about the younger students, so naïve, he said, so ignorant. When his parents left after four months, they were both even prouder than before. Their best son was going to be a real doctor after all, perhaps even one day curing the affliction that was destroying his father.

TL was popping in to Leamington to look in on the course, that much is true. But really his weekends away were needed to set up a new life with Rapunzel, who had moved to Cambridge. They had an immaculately worked-out, phased programme of withdrawal from the old life and into the new, and he extricated himself slowly so as not to cause himself too much sorrow. He needed time enough to adjust to his decision before he set himself free from his teenage sweetheart and a son he adored.

By this time I had given up my teaching job and joined *New Society*, a unique publication which disseminated to readers detailed information about academic research, public policy, activist campaigns and the arts. I was elated. In my late thirties, I had finally alighted at that place which had always seemed on the horizon and never come nearer. David Lipsey (now Lord Lipsey) was the editor, the most nurturing and tough master I have ever worked for. I couldn't even type fast, and for many months the lexicon of journalism baffled me. I had to pretend I knew it all and hold my own. Some of my colleagues must have seen through the twittering brown girl in their midst, but they were kind and never let me know they knew I knew nothing about the business and was winging it.

Once a month I got to edit a supplement – 'Race and Society' – and to commission young journalists who were keen and cheap. White aspirants rapidly progressed and got coveted jobs on the nationals, whence they were fast-tracked to the top. Those blessed with less – darker skin and hair – stayed on my pages, and many just gave up. I never did. One part of our game plan had worked, mine and TL's; now we only had to wait for the acupuncturist to start up, and we would be well away.

That summer, TL's eldest niece was getting married in Canada. So extremely sorry, choking with regret, TL confessed that he had to go to Zimbabwe to join a new field project for an international environmentalist organization. It had come up unexpectedly, and his professor wanted him to grab the opportunity. It was very important that Karim and I should represent our side of the family. The night before we were to go our separate ways, I made an old favourite, lamb curry with potatoes. TL left all the meat on one side, and ate only the potatoes and sauce, said he had problems with red meat suddenly, it upset his digestive system. 'Since when?' I asked crossly. You ate your mum's lamb *sag* happily enough.' 'I know, but I couldn't upset her, could I?'

 Lamb with Potatoes

Serves 5–6

2 lb meat, cut in small pieces from
 a leg of lamb

2 onions, thinly sliced

½ tsp turmeric

Salt

1 tsp chilli powder (less if you like it mild)

1 tsp *garam masala*

½ cup plain, full-fat yoghourt

1 lb potatoes, peeled and cut into large pieces

2 tsp crushed ginger and garlic

2 tins chopped tomatoes

3 tbsp sunflower oil

2 tsp ground coriander/
 ground cumin mixture

Five each of cardamom pods, whole
 peppercorns, cloves and small
 cinnamon sticks

- Heat the oil in a pan with a lid and add the whole peppers, cloves etc.

- Then add the onions and fry until they brown.

- Add ginger/garlic and the meat. Cook for three minutes.

- Then throw in all the spices except for the *garam masala*.

- Lower the heat and cook for ten minutes, stirring from time to time.

- Add the tomatoes and cook for another ten minutes.

- Add yoghourt and enough water to cover the meat.

- Cover and cook for forty minutes.

- Add the potatoes and cook for another twenty minutes.

- The meat and potatoes should now be cooked; if not, give it another ten minutes. Uncover for the last five minutes.

- Add *garam masala* and serve with rice.

When we met up again that autumn, TL's moustache, which he had had since 1972, had gone. He looked younger and unguarded without it – also weaker. When we kissed and there was no familiar brush of the thick hair above his lips, it felt as if I was kissing a stranger. He said he was trying to become a vegetarian – what? No more kebabs and samosas? No. But dhal, yes; he was dying, he said, to eat my dhal and vegetable curry. Then he said he really wanted to learn how to make the two dishes so the next time he was away he wouldn't have to miss them so. I taught him how to make perfect rice, dhal and cauliflower, pea, potato and carrot *sag*. He wrote the instructions in a brand-new notebook. And he joked, 'You know I will never leave you because I love your food so much.'

Cauliflower, Pea, Potato and Carrot *Sag*

Serves 5–6

1 medium-sized cauliflower	4 potatoes, peeled and cut into
2 carrots peeled and sliced or	walnut-sized pieces
½ cup frozen carrots	1 cup frozen peas
3 tbsp sunflower oil	2 cloves garlic, chopped
2 tsp cumin seeds	1 dried red chilli
1 tsp black mustard seeds	1 tsp turmeric
2 tsp cumin/coriander powder	1 tin chopped tomatoes
½ tsp chilli powder	½ tsp sugar
Lime juice and salt to taste	½ tsp powdered cinnamon

⊙   Steam the cauliflower for five minutes, and boil the potatoes for ten minutes.

◉ Heat the oil, then throw in the seeds and dried chilli. When they splutter, add the garlic and stir for thirty seconds.

◉ Add tomatoes and all the spices, and cook for six minutes, stirring from time to time.

◉ Then add the vegetables, cover and cook for ten minutes or until the potatoes are done.

◉ Remove the lid and let the liquid boil off a little.

◉ Add lime juice, sugar, cinnamon and salt.

◉ Serve with rice or pita bread and plain yoghourt.

Twenty December 1987. I had bought tickets for us all to see *The Wizard of Oz* at the Barbican. Karim loved the theatre. I had taken him to see plays and musicals – Shakespeare included – from the age of four; this was a regular pre-Christmas treat. I remember what I was wearing: a bright blue satin jacket and black trousers with silver flecks. While parking the car, TL crashed it violently into a lamp post. He was never ever that distracted and careless when driving. He got into a vile mood, kicked the car and told us to go in. During the show his face remained fixed, a photograph of panic.

The next morning he brought me coffee, and as I was sipping it, still trying to cheer him up about his dented car, he blurted out that he had never stopped seeing Rapunzel and that he was tormented, confused, suicidal even, hated himself more than I could imagine. They had been together for all those sunny weeks in Zimbabwe while Karim and I had been in North America. I remember a kind of flash and brief blackout; all my organs seemed to collapse at once into my stomach. I threw the coffee cup away from me as if it was on fire, and the brown stains spread across the carpet, the bedcover, my beautiful faux-Victorian Laura Ashley nightdress.

Jena was off to visit my brother for a few days, and TL persuaded Karim to go too, told him not to worry his sweet head about that silly little fight. Then the red mist came down. All I recall now of those hours of turmoil is that at the end he begged, cried, begged, cried some more, trying to convince me and himself that our marriage was going to survive, that he was going to do whatever it took to get back my trust and our old lives, which had been incinerated by his admission. By the next morning I had surrendered yet again to his entreaties, his excuses and my fantasy that we could make things work. In Les Deux Alpes on Christmas Day, we sat down to dinner in an isolated ski chalet, with many candles and a small roast chicken, cheese, wine and bread. Swiss chocolates and Christmas cake were brought out by our boy, tired after a day of great skiing . All seemed recoverable. When Karim went to bed, we heard him turning off the light, leaving the door wide open as if that would make us behave. Then his father softly broke the news that he was leaving. Karim came rushing out when he heard my scream, his eyes heavy with sleep. Then my poor nine-year-old had to witness his mother's undignified collapse and his father's abject, stiff endeavours to explain.

TL had brought us all that way to give us an idyllic final holiday before the sad ending. We should carry on with the holiday surely, after coming this far and paying for the chalet. Was he crazy? I guess so. I couldn't eat or sleep. TL ate and slept remarkably soundly, with relief, I think, that it was all in the open, over and resolved.

The exhilaration of skiing made him look fresh and eat well, brought quick repose when he hit the sack. Meanwhile I was vomiting blood and warned him that I would simply walk out into the snow and have done with it. Karim was getting angrier and angrier with me —I was spoiling his first-ever skiing trip. They both had hot chocolate and *pain au chocolat* for breakfast, went up and down the sunny slopes together.

On the fourth day, I walked a couple of miles to the nearest hotel and, using a credit card, got through to Feriyal, my best friend in Pittsburgh. She promised she would fly over to London immediately, take charge because I clearly was falling apart. TL craved her good opinion and agreed to drive us home. I had tried to numb the pain I was feeling by drinking glasses of wine on an empty stomach. Come to think of it, maybe it was wine and not blood I was chucking. The effect was still pretty dramatic, and that eventually scared him too.

There followed more weeks of torment as TL vacillated between leaving and staying. I finally told him to leave when Karim was safe in school. Ten days before our son's tenth birthday, TL ironed his clothes, packed his bags carefully, checked his long list and went. I sat on the sofa, silent and strangely unruffled as I watched his movements, determined and self-conscious. The act had gone on too long; the play needed to end. I was exhausted.

That night I cooked Jena's fish and chips, an ensemble I had refrained from making for many years. How TL moaned if we left spicy smells lingering too long, and fried food had more or less been banned since his parents had departed. The house filled with the forbidden aromas, and felt less empty and abandoned. I was clumsy and blinded by periodic bursts of tears, nearly burned myself. What a terribly

Asian end to a bad marriage it would have been if I had caught fire. I didn't have that kind of death wish, though. Karim ate lots. I tried but couldn't; a boulder seemed to have been rolled up to block my throat. Clearing up afterwards took the longest time; oil had got into and on to everything. It was a useful displacement exercise.

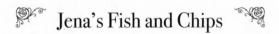 Jena's Fish and Chips

Serves 4

2 lb haddock or cod fillets, fresh, frozen and thawed

Marinade

1 bunch fresh coriander	**1 lime**
½ tsp crushed garlic	**2 green chillies**
¼ tsp salt	**3 tbsp water**

Batter

1 egg	**4 oz plain flour**
¼ pint half skimmed milk and half water	**½ tsp salt**
½ tsp paprika powder	

Chips

2 lb potatoes, peeled and cut into large chips	**2 tbsp *garam masala***
2 tbsp tomato purée or tomato ketchup	**Oil for deep-frying**

- Whiz the marinade in a food processor.

- Dry the fish by patting it with kitchen paper then cover well in the marinade, cover and chill for three to five hours. It should take on a lovely, fresh green colour.

- Meanwhile make the batter.

- Add the salt and paprika to the flour and then the egg.

- Stirring with a balloon whisk, add in the liquid; there should be no lumps.

- Cover and leave.

- Peel and cut the potatoes, and soak in water.

- Spread potatoes on clean tea towels, and let the water soak out.

- Heat the oil in a wide vessel suitable for deep-fat frying. The oil needs to be very hot. (This is hazardous, so best not to do it when you have just been dumped.)

- Throw in some dried-off chips and step back, for there will be some spitting.

- Cook until light brown and drain on kitchen paper.

- Keep warm in the oven at a low temperature.

- Take each piece of fish, shake off excess marinade, dip in batter, and fry quickly in the oil, turning over three to four times until the batter crisps up.

- Drain off excess oil on kitchen paper.

- Take the pan off the cooker.

- Into a frying pan, transfer a tablespoon of the hot oil and boil the remaining marinade until it thickens.

- Add the *garam masala* and tomato purée or ketchup.

- Serve fish on a large plate with slices of lime, surrounded by chips over which the masala sauce has been poured. Live to tell the tale.

———

The days and nights that followed passed mostly in a natural or an induced coma interrupted by violent outbreaks of emotion. I couldn't hear Karim's constant questions and entreaties; the silence and eruptive noises in my head were deafening. He moved into my room, into my bed, into my arms, and talked feverishly through the night. A large bottle of cheap whisky was brought in by a Mexican friend whose heart was also breaking, and soon I was slugging lots to knock myself out. For the first time in my life, I bought cigarettes and started smoking.

One night – a night I wish I didn't remember as clearly as I do – Karim woke up suddenly and demanded to speak to his dad. I tried to calm the little boy for hours – he ran round the house just as he used to when pretending to be an aeroplane, but instead of the vroom the house reverberated with sobs and howls. At 3.00 a.m., worn out, I gave Karim my journalist's tape recorder, told him to go into his room and talk to his dad on tape. He did. Using exact metaphors to describe his loss and panic and needs and desires, and proffering the effortless love of a son for his father. And tears.

When he and TL met two days after this cathartic session, TL refused the tape, politely handed it back, apparently told his son: 'Life is hard sometimes, darling, everyone goes through hard times. We all have to learn to deal with it.' Then he took Karim for a whopping big hamburger, his favourite treat at the time. For Karim's birthday we went for tea to Harrods, a joyless afternoon marking the start of a hopeless new year. His father gave him an outrageously expensive ski jacket, handed over with much gush the following day. He also made a nefarious promise that he would be back and we would be a happy family again. He just needed six months to live away from home. Karim carefully circled the date on his wildlife calendar. On 17 June it would be six months exactly. Seventeen June was our wedding day.

Have I held on to what really happened then or to any of the other memories set down in this book? Or have the years of storage caused gradual corruption? The controversial Egyptian feminist Nawal El Saadawi has written: 'Truth changes, is never the same, like the sea, like the movement of water, of air and soil.'[2] My beloved son, will, I hope one day write his story. It will contradict mine on every point, that much I know for sure. Not because he is naturally contrary (though he is that), but because he was ten and I was thirty-nine, and what happened in 1987 and has happened since has taken us along two very long and different roads. Perhaps TL will write his version too, recounting struggles as he broke free from us and my unending malevolence. I will not find it easy if and when he breaks his story. But then I imagine it has been tortuous for him these long years when I have written about us. Never wrong a writer.

As weeks turned into months, we navigated the chaos as best we could, and then came the first bad fight, the first of the thousand and more small, painful cuts that come with family disintegration. TL wanted to take Karim to Cambridge for their weekends together, to be with his amour and get to know her. Over my dead body, I said. That woman, *that grasping witch* who had broken us up, was now turning her attention on my son. Karim would go to Cambridge, I informed my husband, but not if she was there. It was not dignified. TL acquiesced to these conditions for a while, and with grace, while the juices of guilt were still coursing through his veins.

In those in-between days, our pet gerbils, beautiful, long-haired creatures, were found crushed and still in their box. The mystery of these deaths remains just that. I called TL at work, and he came over, genuinely distressed. Nobody could ever say of TL that he didn't care about animals. We buried them together solemnly in the garden, and as we stood over the small heap of turned earth, Karim held his dad's hand tight.

I asked him if he wanted something to eat. As if awakened from a sweet reverie, he looked startled at the suggestion, and apologized, said he needed to get away as he and Rapunzel were going to a college do, as a couple, official now. I threw him out again. Karim and I cooked an omelette and ate silently. What might I have made for TL? Probably spicy stir-fried vegetables with noodles, a store-cupboard-and-freezer dish to please the newly converted veggie man.

Spicy Stir-fried Veg and Noodles

Serves 4

1 packet thread egg noodles
1 lb mixed frozen vegetables and/or
    finely chopped fresh vegetables
    – anything you have
½ tsp crushed ginger
¾ tsp sugar
2 eggs
1 cup salted peanuts, broken up in a
    food processor

1 chopped onion
1 bunch spring onions if you have them
2 tbsp soy sauce
¾ tsp red chilli flakes
A handful of sesame seeds
2 tsp plum sauce
3 tbsp oil

- Beat the eggs with a little salt, then add finely chopped spring onions if you wish.

- In a wok or frying pan, heat 1 tablespoon of oil and fry a thin omelette, turning over when the bottom is set properly.

- Take out the omelette and let it cool.

- In the same pan, heat the rest of the oil to a medium temperature and cook the onions for three minutes.

- Add ginger and cook for another two minutes.

- Increase heat and chuck in all the veg, stirring briskly all the while.

- After six minutes or so, when the vegetables are cooked but still crunchy, add the sesame seeds.

- After a minute, add the sauces, sugar and chilli flakes, and cook for a further minute or so.

- Boil water in a kettle and pour over noodles in a bowl (the water should be at least an inch above the noodles).

- Cover and leave for five minutes.

- Drain and mix with the vegetables.

- Cut the omelette into thin strips.

- Add to the noodles and vegetables, and (finally) mix in the peanuts.

- You can also add some chopped green chillies at this point.

———

When TL rejected my food, that should have shown me I had lost him forever. By March 1988, his guilt and shame had evaporated and been replaced by a militant sense of entitlement. The adulterers were furious that I wasn't following their script and were impatient to get on with their new lives – who can blame them? TL rejected the contact conditions I had laid down for my son, soon persuading himself that these were the actions of a vindictive and vengeful wife who couldn't let go. They were, but at that time, when I was as near as I have ever got to a breakdown, and my ten-year-old boy was so confused and full of trepidation that you felt he was afraid of touching his own skin, the preservation instinct took over. If I had succumbed to TL's disgraceful demands, Karim would have lost two parents as he had known them.

After a number of exhausting rows, I told TL that Karim was mine, that I would manage the money and the care, do it all. I would never phone his new home, nor ask him for any help from then on. I never did; I never have. He picked up Karim on the appointed day and time from my mother's flat. She was still coming to terms with the bust-up; her son-in-law had deceived her too with his bountiful charm. After all those years, TL had become for her a kind of domestic god, the perfect man, husband and father. She loved him and was a little in love with him too. She aged ten years in that year, never believed he would ever leave his family, his firstborn, his only son. No men in our community ever did that, not even her wayward husband, who always came back home. After the break-up, all her affection went to Karim. From the fifth-floor windows of her council house she would watch the boy run to the car where his dad stood waiting. The hugs between them, said Jena, made her cry. TL's own parents and siblings were even more bewildered. We were the perfect couple, he the perfect son. TL had strung them along for a while, telling then not to worry, that all was well with us. I had to break the news to them. My mother-in-law was convinced the mistress had used black magic. A brother, one we all respected, came over from Canada to drum sense into the prodigal one, to no avail. TL came home for three days for his grilling, said nothing much and left mumbling vague apologies. All four of his brothers promised they would stand by me and treat my son as their own. My ex-in-laws have always been brilliant assuagers. They didn't mean it really. Karim, their own flesh and blood, had no place in their pantheon. But it was good to have their declarations of unstinting support at the time.

Allah did bring TL back for another three days a few months after he had left. His father died, and my husband was distraught. So much had remained unspoken between them. I too was very affected. My relationship with Bapaji meant a lot to me – it was uniquely honest. I couldn't bear the thought that he had slowly and agonizingly withered away. TL wept in my lap, rivers of salty tears, held me like a scared child, slept in our bedroom again (on the floor), undressed in front of my eyes, so close but not close at all. As he stood there naked before me, he looked like cold stone instead of flesh, and I saw his beauty but as one would see a statue. He returned from the funeral bringing gifts, a top with many sequins, I remember, and then was off, back to Cambridge, his grieving done. He left behind a pair of underpants.

TL was a man of those times, one of the first wave of the me, me, me generation of young adults who wanted it all with no regard for the consequences. Our personal drama played itself out against the backdrop of the confrontational mid-1980s. In 1985 we had had the Brixton riots, which had led to a further deterioration of trust between the state and black citizens. The Scarman Report, written after the 1981

Brixton uprising, had warned of further unrest unless racism and underlying causes of disaffection were dealt with by those in power. In retrospect, it is clear Scarman was largely ignored by the centralized authoritarian state, and that caused immense frustration among black Britons, who had been led to believe the state was ready to tackle racial disadvantage. Thatcher, not interested in their demands, set about disabling the local authorities that had implemented policies recommended by Scarman. Powellite on immigration, she could also confound expectations, proactively inviting some ten thousand Vietnamese refugees into Britain, using her power with the press to turn this rescue operation into a positive story about the West offering asylum to the victims of Communism.

British Gas, British Telecom, electricity and water had all been privatized, and small investors got a taste of shareholder power. The sale of council homes had proved popular among the working classes and racial minorities; unions had been weakened by laws and public opinion. As the playwright David Edgar wrote,

The achievement of... Thatcherism has been to weld together the instincts of individual greed and collective self-righteousness into a coherent model of the world, in which the rhetoric of freedom can co-exist with the reassertion of virtue. Put crudely, the new authoritarianism allows people to vote in their own narrow interests and feel good about it.[3]

In 1987, Thatcher won a third term. It was a triumph for the first-ever women PM of Britain. Four months after TL left, in April 1988, at Bristol Temple Meads train station, I looked into the face of a man and was enchanted. He had blue eyes, infinitely generous and bottomless, I thought, an earring too and lots of floppy hair. It was instant; I knew. Strangers at a station, a cliché materialized.

The man was Colin Brown, a race researcher at the Policy Studies Institute, a respected think tank that had considerable influence on public policy. He had written a book, *Black and White Britain*, a study of race discrimination proving beyond doubt that in Thatcher's land of hope, glory and opportunity for all, black and Asian citizens were systemically held down and out. That book was on my desk at *New Society*, used often when I wrote on race. But in my head the author was a middle-aged, radical Caribbean man, someone like C. L. R. James, not this boyish white bloke who might have been gay – clearly possible, I thought, given the earring and the fact he said he lived in Islington.

We had both been invited to Bristol to take part in a BBC TV debate on race and were in the taxi queue. We had drinks and talked as if we were continuing a conversation we had started a long time back. We were ideological soulmates. He told me I should never again wear the curious culottes and daft woolly hat I had on. Such liberties taken so soon. We came back together on the train and had another drink at the Paddington Station hotel. He told me he was living with someone after leaving his partner of many years and that I appeared an avenging angel, reminder in flesh to treacherous men. (I was about to make him behave even more treacher-ously.) His current partner had been his lover off and on over several years. He went back to Islington, and I went home feeling just a little less sad. When we met again at a conference a couple of weeks later, he was distant and his eyes grey-cold. He had decided to be good.

But I pursued him, though he denies this, rang him often for professional 'advice' just to hear his voice, invited him to the Young Vic for lunches and flirted. His resistance was weakening. So what was I doing playing the femme fatale, wearing down his good intentions, hurting another woman? The first reasons are excuses I make to myself. I was wounded, afraid of being alone, tending my self-esteem, so low after the separation, punishing an unknown woman who had destroyed Colin's previous long and stable partnership. She was a surrogate for Rapunzel, whom I hated more than hell itself. The truth is somewhat grubbier. I acted selfishly and didn't care. I was little better than Rapunzel and sought to secure my own nest. I honestly couldn't have done what I did if there had been kids involved – how do you live with anyone who abandons their children? Yet this unknown woman's pain will have been as deep as mine, and my indifference to that makes me ashamed of what I had become.

He says he knew he had to be with me, that there was no turning back one day in early June when he sat in my cheap pine kitchen watching me make small *chapattis* on a creaking table, still drawn and frightfully neurotic. I told him the whole sorry tale, properly and in too much detail. She was younger, obviously, and, worse, much slimmer. He looked startled. I was unbearably thin by then. 'You don't know what I looked like then. I wasn't fat but always round, like a plum.' As if to show them both, the plump flesh which had gently settled over my contented frame had burned away.

Initially I'd looked dead glam and elegiac, but all too soon I was way beyond svelte. My breasts melted down; clothes flapped; straps slid off bony shoulders; I thought I could hear my thighs clicking. Food made me either choke or throw up. I was starving for love and food and reassurance that I wasn't old junk asking to be chucked away.

On this evening, with Colin, sweet desires were reawakened. I wanted to eat again and, even more miraculously, to cook again. I did both. And I did not cry or heave. *Chapattis*, I decided, spread with real butter, and something hot to burn my tongue – perhaps those quick, zingy Zanzibari prawns, plus comfort food, *moong dhal* with spinach.

Colin was dispatched to the corner shop, to Mr Khan, who sold comatose vegetables and out-of-date goods, always with a broad, shameless smile. Mr Khan had come down in the world. In Uganda he had run a successful business making suits for bank managers and my father, who, remember, liked to be dressed like the best of English gentlemen. Mr Khan had long ago forgiven Papa for dying before settling his overdue tailoring bills. In the back of the corner shop there was a store-room where slightly fresher foodstuffs were kept for his *Indian* customers. Colin was not given access to the special supply even though he told Mr Khan he was a friend of mine. The Englishman was fleeced. So he arrived back, feeling a failure, carrying wilted spring onions, puckered green chillies, a bunch of yellowing coriander, butter, yoghourt and cream which smelled sharp and looked untrustworthy. Never mind, no fret. The ladies in mosque always say a really good cook can bring alive old, special-offer, even dead ingredients. 'Won't kill me, will it?' Colin laughed nervously, pretending it was a joke.

I ran water through the dhal in a sieve, put it to boil in salty water, a tomato, green chilli and chunks of garlic. It would take twenty minutes to cook the grains so they still had a bite. Meanwhile the *chapattis* needed to be started – they would take the most time. The dough I made up and kneaded was soft and pliant: sieved *chapatti* flour seasoned with salt, with a little vegetable oil rubbed in and then bound with warm water. I divided it into ten small pieces, rolled them into balls, flattened those a little, enclosed some oil and flour in each (helps to make the *chapattis* flaky) and shaped them into patties.

I delicately worked on the patties one after another with my slender Indian rolling pin, painted chilli-green and red. Nimble, graceful, it is a rhythmic dance of the hands. You lightly roll, then turn the disc leftwards with your palm, stroking it gently as you would the top of a child's head. A perfect round soon appears which you sweep up with a floury hand and lay gently on to the hot *tawa* to smoulder. Two *chapattis* puffed up perfectly. The third blistered and died a black death as he kissed me. I left flour handprints on the back of his black linen suit which he must have found later, to remember again this improbable coming together. Smart move, girl, you might say, leaving my mark. Fourteen years on and this delicate rolling and turning and appetizing smoke which makes my eyes water can still produce an erotic charge in my old man.

From his pocket, Colin shyly produced a present – a volume of Wendy Cope's poems, *Making Cocoa for Kingsley Amis*. I told him I had once dreamed of England and had so wanted cocoa, dressing gowns and warm slippers in Kampala (how he laughed) and that I despised arrogant master-race men; they were, like Amis, cynical and dismissive. I had had my fill of them as an Oxford postgrad – intellectually wasted years. He agreed, then teased that he was not Oxbridge material even in his dreams because he was only the son of a second-hand car dealer. He babbled a lot that night – between other delightful distractions – mostly about how grateful he was that we had come along and brought aubergines and chillies and colour to his country, which had become dreary.

The aroma of spicy prawns and dhal filled the kitchen as I served the food, even more intoxicating than the smell of jasmine on a warm evening. After so many lonely and famished months, I lunged at it, dared to eat with my own childlike hands whose nails had been bitten down to bleeding rawness. We never eat with our hands in front of whities, don't want them to think we are backwater *desis*. We do it less and less in front of each other; we are so civilized now. But forks and knives corrupt the taste of South Asian cooking, make it taste metallic and cold. On this evening, primal urges took over. I needed that old intimacy we once had with our food, the feel of it warming the skin, the soothing memories of safer times. All through childhood, my mother and aunts (real and adopted) had, with their hands, fed me *chapattis* and yoghourt, rice and dhal, hot meat pies, cake slices, Huntley and Palmer biscuits dunked in sweet tea, patiently teaching me the care you had to take so you didn't look like a greedy piglet emerging from a trough.

He watched. I broke a bit of the *chapatti*, held it with the tips of four fingers and the thumb, gently picked up a prawn and wrapped it up quickly without getting any sauce on my hands and placed the morsel delicately into my wide-open mouth. Then, without making an idiot of himself, he dropped his tools and followed suit. Within minutes the plates were clean (so were we; he was a fast learner), and we were bonded, two people from different, long-conflicted worlds.

 ## Zanzibari Prawns (Love Bites)

Serves 4

I lb large frozen or fresh peeled prawns
1 tsp each crushed garlic and ginger
4 spring onions
Chopped fresh coriander
I tsp *garam masala*
1 tbsp vegetable oil

3 tbsp tomato purée
I thinly sliced hot red chilli
Juice of half a lime
Salt to taste
3 tbsp crème fraîche

- Heat oil in a frying pan.

- Add chilli and spring onions, and fry for two minutes.

- Add tomato purée, garlic and ginger; cook and stir for three to four minutes.

- Add prawns and cook from raw for five minutes or for a couple of minutes if already cooked.

- Add lime, coriander, crème fraîche and *garam masala*, let it all bubble a little, serve and eat immediately.

Spinach Dhal

Serves 4

A mug of *moong dhal*

3 cloves garlic, roughly chopped

1 green or red chilli, slit open

1 packet frozen leaf spinach

1 tsp black mustard seeds

1 tsp turmeric

1 tsp *dhania* powder

Lime to taste

1 large fresh tomato or a couple
    of tinned ones

Salt

2 tbsp oil

2 cloves

1 tsp *jeera* powder

½ tsp sugar

- Add the *moong dhal*, tomato, garlic and chili to a saucepan and cover with water which must reach ¾ inch over the dhal. Bring to the boil, then reduce the heat and simmer for fifteen minutes.

- Check to see if there is a need for additional water (you don't want too much as this is a dry dhal). The cooked grain should not feel mushy.

- Add the spinach and let it melt into the dhal.

- In a small pan, heat the oil, add mustard seeds and a clove.

- When they splutter, add spices and cook for three minutes.

- Add to the dhal, stir, cook for a couple more minutes, and season with lime and sugar.

Seventeen June came; promise rose like an early summer sun. His dad, thought Karim, would be back before the day ended. It was half-term, and my son washed his hair without a nag and dressed up in trendy clothes – recent presents from his father – and I dropped him off at Jena's. The night before he had made a welcome-home poster with a picture of a red car. His face looked polished, shone with happiness. I wasn't sure I wanted my son's wish to be granted. Six months on, I had regathered my self-respect, and then there was the man with the blue eyes I thought about every day, almost as much as I thought about the one who had left us. But I knew for the sake of our child that I would agree to a reconciliation. I had to really.

I hear the father and son went to buy socks first. Then the man sorrowfully told the boy he wasn't coming back, not then. Perhaps in August. He gave Karim a recording of a Phil Collins song, something about being there, looking over his shoulders, stuff and nonsense. Jena described my distraught son when he rushed up to her after his daddy dropped him off: 'He was like a mad child, like a child who had been bitten by a mad dog.' I knew then that we had to stop this game.

In those first months after I met Colin, there were moments when he was querulous and unsure whether he was ready to pack up and move on again to another woman. One day, he definitely was absolutely sure he shouldn't, just couldn't. He decided to dismiss me from his life. His voice was unyielding, the blue had vanished from his eyes again, and he had a carrier bag filled with yummy *satay*, chocolate and wine. We often met for delicious romantic trysts in London parks – Victoria Park, where the dogs were savage and growled at kissing couples; Regent's Park, with its roses; Holland Park, where he once left me a note in the hollow of a tree proclaiming his infatuation. The picnic was the longest goodbye that turned back even before we had got to the chocs.

Soon afterwards he moved into one room in a house near us. All his life, all his stuff was there. As soon as TL knew there was this man lurking somewhere, he turned into a jealous beast, a typical non-domiciled husband who still believed we belonged only to him, had to. I let him stay in our flat on some weekends with Karim while I went off to Colin's room, smaller than college digs. The ex-husband became a mean spy, started to look for signs of a cohabiting male. I always locked my bedroom – a symbolic gesture – so he got on to a ladder to peep in through the window to discover my 'perfidy'. He threatened me, blackmailed his son and warned he was no longer going to be Mr Nice Guy. The level of aggression seemed out of character, and a part of me still wanted the old times back. However, I was becoming more detached, and weekly sessions with Jafar Kareem, a gifted psychotherapist who died too young, helped me to find peace and strength through the next, disputatious stage.

Karim had for years been going to the brilliant acting school in Islington run by the indomitable Anna Scher. She told me my son was traumatized and that she was using role-plays and improvisations to help him manage stormy, complicated feelings as best a child can in these situations. His regular class work had suffered so much that he had been downgraded in his various sets. Like most private schools, St Paul's was supremely unconcerned about the emotional fallout of divorce and the financial difficulties that could follow unexpectedly. No one offered any kind of pastoral care.

New Society was taken over by the *New Statesman*. I kept my job, but money was tight. The fees at St Paul's were impossibly high, and TL, now vengeful, was talking of taking Karim out and putting him into a state school. That, I knew, would not happen; I wouldn't let it. The child had lost enough of his old life already. In spite of the official indifference to his emotional needs, Karim loved being at St Paul's. His mates were there, and the teaching was undoubtedly exceptional. My brother was not forthcoming – told me to get the father to pay up. I asked Colin to help us out with the fees for a few months. Without missing a beat he said he would, for as long as we needed.

I saw TL one more time that August, asked him to come back for the sake of our son, and told him that if he didn't we were finished. He looked very sad and said he couldn't, not just then. So that was that. I gave him back his rings and went home, told Karim I had tried, but it was time to go on with our lives. I never spoke to TL again.

When my ex-husband departed in 1988, he took our history, irreplaceable memories of those early tentative years, hard times and good times, as we struggled to belong. That bereavement left me cut up and grieving for too long. You cannot forgive, but, as the years pass, you can look back with some tenderness. These low-fat kebabs are dedicated to old TL, the fastidious one who soaked up oil with kitchen paper from the tops of curries, samosas, even fried eggs. The man I thought I knew would have loved them, but they were made up long after he flew the nest.

Baked Kebabs

Serves 4

1 lb minced chicken	Bunch fresh coriander
1 green chilli	1 tsp crushed ginger and garlic
½ tsp salt or to taste	1 tsp *garam masala*
1 egg	½ cup unroasted cashew nuts
1 tbsp sunflower oil	

- Mix all the ingredients together except for the oil.

- Cover and chill for three to four hours.

- Line a baking tray with parchment paper and lightly grease the top.

- Have ready a bowl with hot water, and start making sausage shapes with the mixture, dipping your hands in the water from time to time – they don't need to be perfect shapes.

- Brush the shapes with oil, then bake in a medium oven (350 °F, 180 °C, gas mark 4) until they brown.

- Test to see the insides are thoroughly cooked.

- Eat with Greek yoghourt, which you can pep up with chilli powder, or with black pepper or cumin powder and salt.

Colin hails from Brighton in the South Downs, descended from people who for generations have lived and died in those parts. He knows his firmly rooted, sturdy family tree, his birthright is uncontested, the soil is his which once flowed with blood as savage wars were fought in the making of fearless England. His days as a child were spent walking miles in these hills with his mates, diving, swimming in the cold sea and working as a butcher's boy, as a newspaper boy and, later, drawing pints in the pub frequented by his dad, Doug, and uncle Alan. Both brothers eventually moved along the coast, leaving rowdy, multifarious Brighton for the safe charms of clean bungalows and samey people in Shoreham-by-Sea. I could never stand English bungalows, their jumpy occupants and twitchy curtains.

Before I turned up, the years had passed in the Brown household without much contact with black or Asian Britons. But then, until we met, Vera confessed, she hadn't personally encountered anyone who had been divorced either. None of this mattered; she and Doug opened their hearts to us the moment I went to their tidy home with my ten-year-old boy. There was not a flinch, not ever a shadow of doubt that their only son, unmarried, clever and attractive, was embarking on a possibly destructive new relationship with a dark stranger, an Asian, Muslim divorcee and lone mother. I returned this love by cooking them Indian food. Vera is now a widow living in a flat in a complex for the elderly. When I can, which is not often enough, I take her some dishes that her son has grown to love. They stimulate her tongue too and bring back the old sparkle. This is one of her favourites.

# Melting Roast Lamb

Serves 6

4 lb whole leg of lamb, fat removed

Marinade

1 large tin tomato purée

1 large full-fat yoghourt (not Greek-style)

1 tsp paprika powder

1 tbsp *garam masala*

2 tbsp crushed ginger and garlic

1 tsp chilli powder

1 tsp ground cinnamon

Garnish

Mint and pomegranate seeds

- Mix the marinade ingredients.

- Make deep slashes in the meat and spread the thick paste all over, using it all up.

- Wrap in three layers of thick tin foil and chill overnight.

- Roast in a slow oven (325 °F, 170 °C, gas mark 3) for up to five hours.

- Open up the top of the foil, increase the temperature, and cook for another forty-five minutes.

- The meat should fall off the bone. Pull the chunks into shreds and transfer on to an ovenproof dish to serve.

- Pour the sauce over this and return to the oven for another ten minutes.

- Sprinkle with pomegranate seeds and fresh mint leaves.

- Serve with pita bread.

It has been ever thus. Exotic food is erotic, a powerful stimulator of ardour and adoration. More than any other indigenous tribe in Europe, the English have been wonderfully receptive, promiscuous even, when it comes to foreign food, and also adventurous lovers with wild stories to tell. Knowing this, did I deliberately ensnare an innocnet I found at a station? Who knows, but he didn't resist. To have an Englishman fall in love with me, to have him in my hands, may have been settling a score with those ineffable snobs, the colonial administrators who made us feel so insignificant and uncivilized back in Kampala. Ha, maybe I am saying to them, what do you feel now, now that so many of your heirs are falling hopelessly in love with us natives and their grub which you were so sniffy about? Remember those rules you haughtily pasted up in the school halls in red? 'No Vernacular in School.' 'Malodorous Lunches Not Permitted.'

There have always been maverick Britons who refused to keep to the distance placed between themselves and the subject peoples of their country, even in the most arrogant days of imperialism. Why, the incorrigible Queen Victoria herself transgressed rules of race and class decorum and developed a passion for her handsome Indian Muslim servant Abdul Kareem. She moved him into a palace suite, had his portraits painted, learned Hindustani and spent much pleasurable time playing games with him (some seen, others private to this day). I wonder what they ate together.

10 *The Sun Also Rises, 1988–2006*

THE SENSE OF FRESH, dewy beginnings made my skin bloom and my eyes shine. Crying Hindi songs by Mukesh and Lata Mangheskar no longer brought forth fresh supplies of tears from an endless well. The walls of my home were no longer humid with sorrow. A new woman was stepping out, shaking herself dry. My hair was cut short and sharp. Startling post-separation haircuts are par for the course; ask any divorcee and her stylist. I knew that the tow of the past would drag us back from time to time. When such unexpected crashes happen, you find yourself watching several movies of your own life at once, crowding the screen and driving you crazy. Images from the past persist and at times feel palpably present; the present presents itself and is unfamiliar and unsteady; and the future appears sometimes as the recovered old life or another country with possibilities not yet imagined.

Karim was still sure his father would return one day and that we had to save him his place. He adored Colin yet kept back most of himself. Then there was my mother, who had not yet been informed of the new man. Jena by then was resolutely anti-men; none could really be trusted, most especially those who struck you where you couldn't see them, snakes in the shoe. Charmers were the worst. On and on. The long-ago bitterness of her own marriage surfaced again, although now she said that though Kassim was bad, my ex-husband was the worst, the *badmash*. I knew I had to introduce Colin to Jena. My divorce was making her turn against the country she loved.

I took Colin with me when I was driving Mum to the local mosque. He was in the back, wearing a hot-pink shirt, the colour of Dolly Parton's lipstick; his hair was floppy and long, and then there was that little hoop in his ear. He looked dissolute and too young, was speechless with nerves, scared of this little round woman in her sari and layers of many cardigans. Usually when she met strangers, her face was gentle, her eyes playful. On this day she looked fierce and ugly, like a jowly guard dog. 'Who is this?' she snapped in Kutchi without saying hello to the conspicuously silent passenger. 'Why is he here? You have a son, growing up. Can't behave like a teenager yourself now.' Only the word *teenager* was in English, as we have no term in Kutchi for trying young things. As I walked her to the mosque entrance, gossips were staring so she went into an elaborate explanation. That man in the car was nobody, just the estate agent helping me renegotiate my mortgage because my faithless husband had abandoned us. 'What to do? In England our men are behaving like the English, hopping in and out of families.'

I had promised my child that without his approval no man would join our depleted, vulnerable household. I meant that. By then Karim seemed chastened and wistful, suddenly grown up too. There was no more childish wishful thinking. One day, my son simply said that Colin could come to live with us on two conditions. One was that he should definitely not bother if he thought he too might one day walk away. And the other was that he could only sleep in my bed every other night. Karim himself had been sleeping in the double bed since that day in January when his father had finally packed up and left. He was happy to share me, but the terms had to be reasonable.

Yes, agreed to both conditions, said Colin. He said something then which did him enormous credit: 'I'll be your friend, help you, Karim, be with you and your mum. But I don't expect you to love me or see me as a kind of borrowed dad. I can't be your dad, you have one already.' And so it started, strange bedfellows switching places every night, building up trust. Within four months of Colin moving in, Jena had found another perfect man to adore. When Colin was referred to as his father, my son would issue an immediate correction: 'He's not my dad. My dad left. He's my good friend.'

Ex-TL discovered that his son was now with another man all hours of the day; my ex-husband had allocated time, and was restricted to 'activities' with beginnings and ends. Imagine how emasculating that was. I still would not let our son spend time with the blonde paramour. I accept that my stubbornness was not reasonable. It was vindictive. I wanted her to hurt. I still do. Far, far worse was the effect this constant provocation and guerrilla sniping had on Karim, our wretched go-between. His father and I continued not to have direct contact. That was what I had chosen. But I did it in a way that must have disoriented my boy and scraped his own grief, kept the wound open. I am more sorry about that than any other bad mistakes I have made as a parent. Karim, who loved us both, was forced to fight us both.

One Friday night at about 10.00, the doorbell rang. It had been eight months since Colin had moved in. We were chatting, sipping tea in our dressing gowns, and, oh, Colin was ironing my skirt. At the door stood the religious leaders of our local mosque, their wives and Jena. 'I have brought them to see how you are all living together, not married, and that I know, so the gossips will stop their bitter-lemon tongues, saying such ungodly things straight after prayers. I am telling them wait and see, you never know what will happen next, could be your turn. Nice Ismaili boy, your husband, what good was he? Come in, go make tea.' Everyone was embarrassed except for my mum, who then made this startling assertion in Kutchi: 'A boy and girl must live together before marriage – then they can know the real person, good habits, bad habits. After marriage it is too late. Look this man is ironing. Will any of our men do that, lift a teacup even?'

Nobody spoke for many minutes, and poor Colin looked as if he was lost in translation. Then one of the women, a respected lady in her sixties, piped up: 'So true. My husband was like Dilip Kumar, filmy hero before we married, so kind and caring, singing me songs from his veranda. Two weeks after wedding, then *bas*, *khalas*, all finished. Became like his father, silent and hardly looking at me. Now he is better but too late, too old now.' Her husband nodded indulgently and took this unexpected insolence. Another guest suddenly confessed that their daughter, a teacher, was living with a black man. They sat up, all of them, and even Jena found her tolerance stretched to breaking by this news. The member of the mosque council spoke for them all: 'Don't worry, sister. Pray. Times are bad. Did we leave Africa to give our girls to them over here? Bring her to *khane*, here, my wife has some holy water in her purse, just put it in her tea or Coca-Cola.'

Mum had brought with her *sak dhokri* in a large Tupperware box – a spicy vegetable stew with flat pasta-like squares made of gram flour, an all-in-one meal from Gujarat. Unlike most of the people in mosque who looked down on the *Banyanis* (Hindus), my mum had many close Hindu friends who had taught her to cook sophisticated Guju food. Colin loved the dish, and this, said Jena, was further proof that in his previous life he was most definitely an Indian. We all tucked in, and the gang of muttering worthies went off persuaded that Jena was both a matchless cook and wise.

Sak Dhokri

Serves 6

4 large potatoes, cut into smallish chunks

1 tin chopped tomatoes

½ lb fresh young *goowar* (they look like runner beans, but you eat them whole; they can be found in Asian groceries)

2 aubergines, cut into small chunks

2 tbsp sunflower oil

Juice of 1 lime

1 packet frozen *toower* (pigeon peas)

2 tsp grated ginger

1 onion, finely chopped

¾ tsp chilli powder

1 tsp turmeric

2 tsp *dhania jeera* powder

1 tsp sugar

Salt to taste

For the Dhokri

½ mug each gram and plain white flour

½ tsp chilli powder

½ tsp mango powder

¼ cup sunflower oil

Salt

½ tsp crushed garlic

½ tsp *ajwain* seeds

Water

- First make the *dhokri*.

- Mix all the dry ingredients.

- Rub in the oil and then a little water until you have a stiff dough.

- Cover and leave aside.

- In a wide saucepan with a lid, heat the oil, then cook the onions and ginger over low heat until the onions start to brown a little.

- Add the tomatoes and spices, and simmer for ten minutes, stirring from time to time.

- Add sugar and lime juice.

- Add a mug and a half of water and the potatoes, then cook them for ten minutes.

- Take off the heat and cool.

- Remove the potatoes. Mash four pieces, leaving the others whole.

- Roll out the dough until it is as thick as a 10-pence coin (you will need sprinklings of white flour to stop it sticking).

- Cut into squares with a sharp knife.

- Returning the pot to the cooker, get the stew broth to reach boiling point and add the other vegetables.

- After five minutes, carefully place the cut squares into the cooking stew. Cover, lower the temperature and simmer for twenty minutes.

- Check that the *dhokri* are cooked through; they will have turned lighter and should taste like spicy dumplings.

- Return the potatoes – mashed and cut – to the stew and reheat briefly. Eat in bowls with a spoon.

I had chosen to share my life with an Englishman, and that shocked many of my old equality warriors: I was sleeping with the enemy. We were simple then, preferring clarity to messy complexity. In her novel *Beloved* Toni Morrison writes, 'There's no bad luck in the world but white folk.' We really, really wanted to believe that. Never mind Idi Amin and Bokassa, Mao and Gaddafi. It was white power that blighted our planet and its peoples. A lot in that but never the whole truth. Soon after the news spread, I was shouted down at a meeting by people I had known for years. I was, they shouted, a 'coconut', a 'Bounty bar' – meaning brown on the outside and white on the inside. I was also described as mulligatawny soup, a Raj vegetable slop, a mishmash of nothing identifiable or honourable, using something the *goras* like to call 'curry powder'. Yuk. Note that all the insults used food. Some were laughing, teasing they said, but too many of their teeth showed.

Who cared what they thought? My mind was made up on that night of the hot *chapattis*. And though I never, ever cared for the original served too often in my college in Oxford, I created my own mulligatawny soup recipe, a joke and a riposte in one pot.

Yasmin's Mulligatawny Soup

(an invention of defiance)

Serves 6

4 carrots, sliced	4 potatoes, cut in chunks
2 sweet potatoes, cut in chunks	3 sticks celery
4 skinless chicken thighs	1½ tsp crushed ginger
2 tbsp red lentils, washed	2 onions
1 oz butter	2 tsp ground *jeera*
Ground pepper	Ground cardamom
Salt to taste	A couple of sliced green or red chillies

- Boil everything together until cooked.

- Take out the chicken thighs and shred the meat, then return to the pot, throwing away the bones.

- Remove and mash some potatoes and sweet potatoes.

- Return to the pan – the mash is a thickener better than the floury thickening used in the Raj recipe.

- Get to boiling point again.

- Remove from heat.

- Sprinkle chillies and lime juice over each serving.

Soon after we got together, Colin and I went shopping to Alperton. The street food entices and stops you just as it did back in East Africa. One stallholder was a very lovely Hindu lady with enormous eyes the colour of chocolate Minstrels. It was a day cold enough to crack the bones, but she was happily humming songs in a bright pink cotton sari, an embroidered cardigan and a matching pink *bindi*.

Colin lingered, tasting each one of her special chutneys on bits of *khari puri*: Date and Tamarind, Cashew and Coriander, Lemon, Turmeric and Burnt Sugar. A white bwana loitering at her makeshift stall was causing a flutter. She took to him. Minstrel Eyes asked me in Gujarati, 'Where did you find him? Are there any more out there? Any brothers?' Forty minutes later she was still telling us her life story, how she had never felt appreciated in her marriage, about her divorce. Sadly Colin has no brothers. He did manage to get a couple of recipes out of her, though. 'Must have a good chopper Mister Colin, remember. Go to Popats General Store, cheap over there. But this should not be a job for a gentleman, sir. Your wife must be doing it, her job to keep you happy. Or come to me any time.' The hussy.

 ## Ramilla's Best-selling £2 Coriander Chutney

I juicy lime

1 tsp sugar

2 tbsp water

1 teacup cashew nuts

2 bunches fresh coriander

Salt

4 green chillies

½ tsp *jeera* powder

- Blast the whole lot in a whizzer until chopped, not pulped (use the pulse button).
- Can be frozen.

Choppers, liquidizers, electric grinders, skillets, grills, the most expensive Kenwood machines have replaced sturdy old pestles and mortars. East African Asians, proud of their modernity, happily move on to every invention that comes along, just as my mother once did, except in her case she could only afford low-grade plastic gadgets and Formica. When they watch programmes about cooking in India, they fall about laughing to see how those peasants still grind pastes on stone slabs using smaller stones and their weary hands, and don't appear to know anything at all about non-stick pans. Aga cookers, beloved by British natives, also bring on the giggles: 'What is wrong with these *goras*? Can get top-class ovens, faster than aeroplanes, *yaar*, and they want these ugly things that take one month to boil water, stupid they are really. Like wanting their grandmother's old shoes.'

So nouveaux are we, we would turn Windsor Castle into a shopping mall and parking area without a qualm. Some sharp-suited young gals running the cookery section of a big publishing company once informed me that the only thing they were interested in was 'slow cooking' – that was the trend, what people wanted. 'Bollocks,' I thought, just as my mum and aunties would have. 'You think we came all this way away to toil for hours in the kitchen? What next? Shall we be growing the food and keeping cows in the garage? Making our own flour and spices like our grandmothers used to do – killed them young they worked so hard in the villages of India. Want us to be *desis* again? We are in Britain not Jamnagar.'

This explains why all Asians love the microwave cooker – the most expensive arrive as part of the dowry and are now expected back in the smallest villages in India and Pakistan too, where probably no electricity will ever appear, just for show, proof of a good family well connected to Western fads. A growing number of microwave recipes are joining the vast repertoire of South Asian and East African Asian cooking styles, old and new.

Microwave Date *Halva*

(Our people are getting worried about sugar and fat,
and this a 'healthy' sweetmeat, made in England)

1 lb dried, stoned dates (not the block)   **½ pint whipping cream**
Peeled, unsalted cashews or pistachios

- In a glass bowl combine dates with the cream and cover, then zap the mixture for five minutes.
- Stir and zap again for three minutes.
- Do this twice more.
- Add the nuts and zap for three more minutes.
- Press into a greased tray, cover and freeze for three hours.
- Defrost and cut into diamond shapes.
- Sprinkle with desiccated coconut.
- Store in a sealed box in the fridge.

I was now at the *New Statesman and Society*, an amalgam that never worked. The *Statesman* was the dominant big boy, and it could barely disguise its contempt for the weaker partner. I hated the job, the atmosphere was ruthlessly misogynistic – a new experience this, for me. As the *Satanic Verses* row broke out, I realized there was also among many of my peers a gross intolerance of Muslims who were expressing quite legitimate opposition to the book, which they felt had set out to demean or malign them. That was their view – a view I didn't share – but hadn't we been told that in this free country it was OK to dissent? In the first months after publication, dignified protests were organized in Leeds and Bradford. The media were deeply uninterested. I was then the only person in the mainstream press who came from a Muslim background. My editor swept aside any suggestions that we should, as a left-wing magazine, cover the unfolding crisis, give the objectors a voice. Meanwhile, I was being assailed by bewildered and hurt Muslims who wanted me to tell their side of the story.

Salman Rushdie's book had been published in London on 26 September 1988. In the following two months, there were protests against the novel in India, South Africa and some Arab states. People were enraged by the coarse language used when describing a fictionalized Prophet Mohammed and his wives, and by the disrespectful characterization of the Messenger, deeply revered by the faithful. Before the book had been published, some eminent pre-publication readers had warned that millions of Muslims would feel it was a deliberate provocation and that there was a risk of violence in the streets. The most respected of these was Kushwant Singh, an Indian journalist, liberal and Sikh, as it happens, and an indefatigable campaigner for a free press. The warnings were not heeded. Muslims asked the publisher, Viking/Penguin, for a disclaimer to be inserted to indicate that the book was an imagined world and not an alternative history of Islam or an attack on the faith. These requests were ignored, even though there exists a convention for novels to include statements dissociating real characters and events from fictional ones, to fend off libel actions. A disclaimer would have protected the principle of freedom of expression and placated sincere people who wanted to know their views also mattered. Thatcher had banned Peter Wright's book *Spycatcher*, so the non-negotiable stand taken by Rushdie's defenders appeared unfair to Muslims. Those who protested were all regarded as illiterate fanatics who obviously didn't read or understand books. Some serious Muslim intellectuals joined the protests, yet this did not affect the stereotype.

It was also well known that Rushdie himself had apologized publicly in the High Court to India's Indira Gandhi in 1984 for 'a cruel attack' on her and her late son Sanjay in *Midnight's Children*, the novel that had brought Rushdie much acclaim. That he would not apologize for or compromise when it came to *The Satanic Verses* caused many to feel that the writer was being inconsistent and hypocritical. In January 1989, the novel was set alight in Bradford during yet another demonstration. The maddened protesters stirred the European consciousness, awakened old memories of Nazis and book burnings. That image became a symbol of the confrontation that lasted more than a decade and a half. Worried governments took preventive action. The book was banned in India, South Africa and other countries. Then on 14 February 1989, encouraged by the hard-line Muslim spokesperson Kalim Siddique, the Ayatollah Khomeni issued a death threat against Rushdie, and some British Muslims (a vociferous minority) came out in blind support of this execution order issued by a leader who had little respect for human rights. So started the long and still-continuing clash between Western liberalism and the most illiberal Muslim factions. A year after the book burning, the writer Anthony Burgess wrote, 'The stupidity of the Islamic death mongers burning a book they do not have the intelligence to understand... portends a situation Chesterton foresaw at the beginning of the century – the renewal of an ancient and basic struggle which the distraction of the Cold War occluded.'[1]

The modern crusade had arrived. The list of liberals turning against Muslims and Islam grew long – Fay Weldon, Michael Foot, Hugo Young, Paul Theroux and many others. Even Roy Jenkins, with his commitment to diversity and equality, and his impeccable liberal values, bemoaned the presence of too many Muslims in Europe. Learned and temperate Muslims like Zaki Badawi tried to reduce the rising national temperature. They were disregarded by militant Muslims, for whom this had become an unholy jihad. A new breed of self-selected Muslim leaders hatched during these heated days, with the aim to promote, some would say, a separatist Muslim agenda. Intellectual Muslims – only a handful – began to find a voice and mediate between those who sought conflict, including Rana Kabbani, Ziauddin Sardar and Tariq Modood.

I came out as a Muslim at this time, just when the row turned into a war of words between liberal fundamentalists and fanatics. It was arguably the worst time to declare such an allegiance, but I have never been a strategist. Something stirred inside me – something often does when there is an imbalance of power and patent injustice. It was a political label, embraced for political reasons and, I think, because of innate loyalty. So many of the people who had loved me unconditionally throughout my life were Muslims, from Mama Kuba to my mum to my cousins to the many beloved family friends who have appeared in this book. I wanted to disabuse Britons who assumed that if you were educated and Europeanized, you had to anoint *The Satanic Verses* and despise Muslims. There was another reason too. I sensed a silhouette forming, a contour, a hollow – in Rushdie's own beautiful words, a 'god shaped hole' – a dissatisfaction with the world where nothing seemed sacred except the right to upset and offend.

This may sound contrived, but I did feel doubly bereft at the time. The break-up of my marriage was caused by the cultural jostling between who TL and I had once been and who we had become. The hostile responses of the white British intelligentsia to Rushdie felt like the same clash writ large. Britons I trusted and liked had turned against an entire faith (knowing nothing about it), old civilizations and connections. We had to surrender totally to the hegemonic West or be damned. Or we could withdraw into the angry Islamic ghettos and be damned that way. Loiterers, ditherers, self-doubters were left wondering where we could get a sense of belonging without losing ourselves. We were mental and emotional wanderers without homes.

I left the *New Statesman and Society*, resigned and felt this absurd sense of liberation. I had no job and a child to bring up, but still it was good not to breathe the malevolent air in those offices. A couple of Muslim writers had finally been allowed to publish their thoughts on the crisis. Rana Kabbani wrote an essay in the *New Statesman and Society* at this time – a poignant response expressing better than I ever could what it felt like to be a European Muslim then:

> Coming from a world just beyond Europe's borders on that same Mediterranean with which you are so culturally familiar. Yet almost nothing is known about us, as though we hailed from a different planet altogether. If it was merely ignorance that separated us then that would be a bridgeable gap, but prejudice, preoccupation and even hostility have created a huge gulf between us.[2]

I never gave into anti-racists who thought the personal had to be the political at every level, even in the choices you made about who could be invited into your heart and bed. But around this time I did wonder to myself whether such relationships can survive when there is so much history blocking possibilities and new confrontations bursting forth like weeds in newly turned soil.

Twenty years on from when I threw in my lot with Colin, there are still days when race, religion, the Empire and immigration walk into our home and invade our privacy. He laughs at me because I sometimes get colloquial English wrong; I fly into a terrible temper and ask him how many words of my various home languages he has bothered to learn. For an Englishman never needs to adapt to others; his ignorance is superior to Eastern knowledge. Or if it has been a week heavy with racist abuse directed at me, I can sort of blame my husband for coming from that heritage where foreigners are held in contempt. He is gentle, has never paid me back in kind. His methods are less direct and more subtly wounding. And though he would surely deny it, an old supremacy raises its head sometimes. He beats me with facts and rationality, logical argument, red rags to my bull within. I use emotional weaponry. Sparks fly. But we always make up, and without malice, then I, feeling soiled by my temper and guilty, banish myself to the kitchen and make amends or try to, often by choosing dishes I know are easy to get wrong. The one that wins him over completely is *parathas* with potatoes. That motion of my hands with the dough and rolling pin works again and again.

Potato *Paratha*

(the redemption method and the easier way)

5 waxy potatoes, peeled, cut and boiled until soft enough to mash

3 tbsp fresh coriander and 1 green chilli, finely chopped

1 tsp crushed garlic

½ tsp turmeric

Salt to taste

½ tsp *garam masala*

For the dough

4 cups *chapatti* flour, white or mixed with whole wheat

Warm water to mix

Salt

2 tbsp sunflower oil

½ cup oil for frying

- Mash the potatoes with the herbs, spices and seasonings.

- Rub the oil into the flour and salt.

- Slowly add the water and mix with your hand until you have a dough that is pliant like Blu-Tack.

- Leave both covered for an hour at room temperature.

- Break off bits of the dough slightly smaller than a tennis ball.

- Roll into balls in your hand and flatten.

- Cover again.

- Roll out each circle to the size of a saucer, and place a teaspoon and a half of the potato mix in the centre.

- Fold over the edges so the circle gathers in the centre like a flower.

- Press down and turn over. You must roll on the smooth side.

- Using flour to dust the surfaces, roll gently and turn without breaking the surface – it's hard to do this so you may need to chuck a few failures.

- Roll out all *parathas* and keep covered with tea towels.

- Heat the frying pan until it is hot but not sizzling.

- Carefully place a *paratha* into the pan (dry not oiled), and let it cook for a couple of minutes.

- Turn over and spread a little oil on the top with a spoon then drop a teaspoon of oil on to the pan. Cook for a minute and flip over.

- You will need to do a couple more turns then press down to make sure the dough is cooked.

- It should look light to reddish-brown with some dark spots.

- Drain on kitchen paper, and eat with yoghourt.

Easier method

- Roll out the balls into thinnish circles the size of smallish plates.
- Spread the potato mixture on one and then cover with another, sealing edges with a little water.
- Fry as above.

The personal is the political.

Karim's schoolwork was seriously slipping by 1989, and again St Paul's was remarkably unconcerned. Bad marriages and divorces were as common as colds in the high and mighty Establishment, so they couldn't see why I should think I was special in any way. The staff were, at times, most alarmed by this hyper mum who walked too often through their vast and imposing doors. So un-English. One teacher said, 'Mrs Alibhai, may I advise you to cool it a bit? I fear this hysteria may be why your son is slipping in his work.' He meant well. Perhaps he was right. As TL had said to me when we had met for the last time, 'Everybody is doing it; it just happens.'

My son was approaching his teen years, a child born and raised in Thatcher's Britain, where self-gratification had assumed the potency of a prayer. City bonuses were sky high, the rich young were unabashedly free with cash and the seeking of pleasure. Colin gave Karim quiet affection, cooling comfort, just what he needed during those tempestuous days and nights. Unlike Karim's father's mistress, Colin had played no part in the destruction of the marriage; he made no demands, never pushed himself into a part in the tragedy that was still playing itself out. Karim needed that uncomplicated love. To this day, I think he feels Colin will always help keep him safe and steady when the winds blow too hard and the rest of us around him are weak or wild.

That spring, Doug, Colin's dad, died, in an instant, while watching football on TV. We were away in the Alps and found out on our return. Just as Colin was becoming a surrogate dad to my son, his own father passed away, a man who had never failed to love, provide or comfort, an unassuming working-class man who had received us into his heart. The death took away my mother-in-law's only consistent, life-long companion and organizer. Her childhood had been hard, and then this young and lovely woman had met her lifeguard on Brighton Beach and that had been that, blankets on the ground, love and marriage forever. She had never had her own chequebook, knew nothing about how to change light bulbs. At the funeral she apologized for crying a little in the taxi. I was baffled by the restraint among the other mourners, their silence and stillness, the English upper lip, trembling but never letting go. I am glad Vera has never been to one of our noisy, wailing send-offs.

All changed in our home too. In November 1990, my decree nisi came through, a dull brown cheap envelope dropped through a letter box, so banal, so final. I knew

I wanted it but never knew how much I didn't, even then when there was nothing left. Grief returned, and once again I lost my appetite completely. Colin brought home exquisite figs, red and sexual, and softly coaxed me until I ate one, tasted of nothing, then two, and eventually five, by which time my tongue woke up to sweetness again. When the decree absolute landed on the mat, the torment was over.

Three days later, after apparently plotting with Karim, Colin proposed to me, on his knees in the house of my friend Anne, who had been my crutch during the broken days. He wanted us married before Christmas, four weeks away. Many candles flickered on the dining table and mantelpiece, and a golden glow emphasized the shadows on the walls. I had no intention of ever marrying again. I never wanted a stepfather for my son; I couldn't trust a man to behave for the rest of his life.

I accepted the proposal without any hesitation. The candles, hope and love shoved away caution. It was too soon, yet I couldn't refuse the lover I'd found at a railway station who bought me all the figs I craved.

Karim was the most elated, a surprise that, for me. He yearned for a reconstituted family, proper ties that this time would be secure. The children of divorced parents often turn ultra-traditional, maybe to atone for the sins of their fathers and mothers. And so we had the wedding, with our many friends present (asked to contribute champagne, otherwise we couldn't afford to invite them all). The reception was held in the same hotel in Paddington Station where we had had a drink the first day we met. Jena's friend made some dead-cheap biriyani and kebabs; the room too was given to us cost price as the owner was from our Ismaili community, and a complimentary room for the night. Diasporic loyalty can be a godsend. Anne and I went to a market to buy flowers and set up the room while Colin met up in Alperton with Chutney Ramilla, who helped him negotiate a good price for a box of *jalebi*, orange-coloured coiled sweetmeats bursting with syrup.

Two hundred guests were expected, hopefully bringing at least eighty bottles of champagne. My relatives and family friends would never follow the no-gifts injunction and would most certainly not bring booze even though most liked to drink it. From them I expected gadgets in their cardboard boxes with their names written in felt-tip pen, trinkets wrapped in used paper (why not? bloody waste of money, they would rightly say), gold jewellery and premium bonds folded into silky scarves. The richest distant uncle who had stormed off at my previous wedding brought a glass figurine, a Bo Peep shepherdess. The price tag was on, £2.99. He didn't get where he was by spending money.

It was bitterly cold, and there were cinematic snowstorms. A coach full of guests was held up in Birmingham unable to get through the drifts. Good thing too as it turned out; the food was just enough for the ones who did make it. White Brits really can put away biriyani. My Muslim girlfriends had insisted I should buy this rainbow-hued wedding outfit, sparkling with glitter, straight out of Bollywood, not at all appropriate for a reject woman just turned forty. Maybe I should have worn sober dark blue or quiet grey, colours of the sky which foretold possible downpours. Glad I didn't. These unreal colours of a carnival or funfair captured the fear and reckless thrill of the decision to marry again. Lord Bhikhu Parekh, a Hindu, was chosen to be my adopted father. My son, only twelve, was the best man, and his speech made the guests cry, even the hardened hacks. Goodwill danced around us, unseen spirits wished us well, and the crowd collectively blessed this unlikely marriage. A handful of anti-racist comrades were invited, and they behaved.

I was by this time a freelance journalist writing for the *Guardian* and *Observer*, and was also working part-time training unemployed Bangladeshi and Somali adults in the East End of London, a job that opened my eyes to ghettos, real and mental, and utter deprivation half a mile from the Bank of England. Invited into the homes of my female trainees, it was at times impossible to swallow the tea they served without feeling guilty. So down were these families, they had merged into the thick dust building up around them and the melting warmth blasting from dodgy gas heaters. The huts of the poorest in Uganda were kept pristine. Here filth was accepted as a by-product of penury.

A year after our wedding, I conceived. It was certainly not planned, and suddenly a new desire surged, dormant hitherto. We wanted a baby. There were two miscarriages one after another at around twelve weeks, followed by inconsolable sadness. From thinking I should never have another child, I was filled with fear that if I didn't have one, Colin would definitely leave, and with good reason. Then after a holiday in Turkey, a third pregnancy was confirmed and, as the weeks went by, seemed to settle.

On 11 April 1993, my girl was born – another horrid delivery, again helped by an epidural, much better than they used to be. She was perfectly beautiful with what looked like a flight of brown hair and the most incredible mouth, sculpted by the gods. My sister's sensual lips had been reborn. A preternatural attachment formed between niece and aunt from the first moment they met, even though my sister's mental illness makes her communicate in bite-sized morsels. Leila's other features are definitely more from the Brown clan, but her colouring is Asian. She wishes all the time that she had blue eyes and straight hair like her dad.

At a party to welcome Leila into our lives, I served chilli-cheese toast. This grocer in Wembley had started to import Mombasa giant prawns and was testing the market. So we bought five boxes ridiculously cheap, and I made them as they are made in coastal areas in East Africa, barbecued. Sitting out in the garden, lush in spring, the guests had to learn to eat these with their hands. They threw the shells into the bushes over-eagerly, taking authenticity further than was necessary.

Chilli-cheese Toast

Sliced white bread
Thinly sliced green, orange and red chillies

Lots of grated Cheddar cheese
Butter

- Butter the bread.
- Mix cheese and chillies.
- Press a lot on top of each bread slice.
- Grill until the cheese bubbles.
- Cut into small squares and serve.

Barbecued Giant Prawns

The largest prawns you can buy with the shells on

Filling

Tomato purée	**Lime juice**
Crushed red chillies	**Crushed garlic**
Butter	

- Make a paste with the filling ingredients.

- Cut each prawn open to make a butterfly, still connected along one edge.

- De-vein.

- Spread filling thickly on one side and close the prawns up again.

- Wrap in foil and either place on a grill on a barbecue or cook on a tray in a hot oven (425°F, 220°C, gas mark 7) for about ten minutes.

- Serve on leaves of iceberg lettuce with thickly sliced onions.

Jena was of course ecstatic: another grandchild to nurture, bathe and massage, to sing to and spoil. She looked years younger again. No other woman I know had so much surplus love; no other gave it so freely to her own and others who came into her life, however briefly.

Like my in-laws, Ugandan Asians adored Margaret Thatcher – of course, a low-tax lady, daughter of a grocer, who understood corner shops. Some were among the first to dash to Russia when the Berlin Wall came down, made so much money they could pipe Muzak into every bathroom in their Kensington homes. The taps were of course gold-plated and the walls best marble. One wealthy Asian acquaintance shed tears when Thatcher left Downing Street: 'What kind of people are these? She was their greatest treasure. She promised me, you know, one seat in the Home of Lords, when I met and promised to give her a cheque for the party, big cheque, bigger than anything.' I argued with him – we were in his big house in Surrey with a dried-up moat and a sour-faced butler who looked down on his master and was paid for his disdain: 'She left millions of people out of work, children living worse than in Africa. Don't you care?' 'Silly girl. These English don't want to work, did somebody tell them to stay at home? We, who came with nothing, look at us today.' 'You had many bank accounts, Uncle, you even sent some cash with me when I came over for Papa's funeral. Remember? You were not penniless.' Jena usually had to intervene when such gatherings threatened to blow up and spoil the food.

This family to the manor loaned prided themselves on their 'non-*desi*' cooking. They were better than us because they had moved on from strong, embarrassing food. The lady of the dried-up moat produced a pasta invention that day to impress upon us how fusion they were, how subtle and sophisticated were their taste buds: 'We don't eat the rice any more. He is liking pasta so much, better for you. So today having my special dish. I'm making new styles all the time. Not too much masala. Today beef and coconut macaroni. I made it when the English High Commissioner came to our house in Kampala.'

Beef and Coconut Macaroni

Serves 6

1 packet macaroni

1 chopped green chilli

2 tins good-quality coconut milk

4 tbsp tomato purée

½ tsp chilli powder

2 tbsp sunflower oil

2 tsp *garam masala*

3 each whole cinnamon sticks,
    cardamom pods and cloves

1 tsp turmeric

Salt

1 lb good braising steak

2 tsp crushed garlic and ginger

2 chopped onions

Water

½ tsp mango powder

- In a casserole dish, heat the oil and add the cinnamon sticks etc.

- After a minute, add the chopped onions and cook until they start to brown.

- Add the meat, garlic, ginger, chilli and water until it is an inch above the meat.

- Stick into a medium-hot oven (350°F, 180°C, gas mark 4) and let it cook for an hour and a half.

- Meanwhile boil the macaroni in salted water for four minutes, then drain.

- In the same saucepan, simmer the coconut milk with all the other ingredients for about eight minutes.

- Add the macaroni to this, and cook slowly for another five minutes. Leave on one side.

- When the meat is cooked, pile the pasta on top of it, cover and return to the oven for five minutes.

- Serve with a green salad.

It actually is rather good, but I can't stand such brown sahibs and memsahibs, descendants of the old élite of the old Empire, ever ashamed of their own cultures and greedily grasping anything they understand to be European.

Jena hated Thatcher so much she had said special prayers to get Allah to smite her down. I had never known my mum not to find in her big heart to forgive and sympathize with anyone. It was the subject of many rows between us – I couldn't stand her capacity to forgive even those who had been unkind to her and caused her undeserved grief. By this time, for example, her relationship with her daughter-in-law had been bleached and ironed out so none of the creases and marks were visible. They got to treat each other with kindness, not too much to expect after so long. But Jena could not excuse Thatcher and relished the moment when the Iron Lady seemed to cry as she left Downing Street.

Around this depressing time, my brother, Jena's only and most beloved son, decided to move back to Africa but to the south. He had never really been happy in this country and sought new pastures. Jena let him go, but from that moment to the day she died, she missed him more than she had ever missed anyone in her life. She hung on in hospital until he flew over from South Africa, saw his face and then peacefully left. Our son too was away at university, and I understood for the first time what it felt like to have a child leave the family home, fly to his own future.

In 1994, I too was pulled back to the old continent. It was meant to be a short trip to make a radio programme for the BBC on what it feels like to return to places left behind. The drive from Entebbe Airport to Kampala seemed so familiar, I felt I had never left; it had all been a delirious dream. I went to buy papaya from a street vendor and spoke to her in Swahili; her child shrieked with the sound of an ear-splitting police siren. The shy mother looked down and then explained to our driver in her indigenous language that her daughter had never seen anyone with brown skin before, and she couldn't understand what I was saying.

Within two days I was a mess. My hometown was slummed down; bullet holes and wrecked buildings reproached the eyes. Shops, streets, schools were all crumbling like the rotting teeth of a tramp. Even the grass in the fields had aged and yellowed. The daily rains had no reviving powers any more, it seemed. My old school in Shimoni seemed to have been asleep for years, and our beautiful white mosque stank of animal dung. After the expulsion of Asians, it had been used to keep goats.

The biggest shock was Makerere, so dilapidated I cried. The stench of piss was everywhere, even in the grand graduation hall. A few hundred Ugandan Asians had returned after President Musevini had taken over. With help from the Tanzanians he had finally driven out Amin and invited us back to help rebuild his shattered country. But Amin had expunged us from national memory, and we were strangers. I did meet some Asians who had never left, but they had survived by purging themselves of past identities. They tell me it is all very different now, buzzing and growing and happy. I hope all of that lasts. The poor folk of Uganda have suffered too long.

Britain then seemed to going through its own nervous breakdown. By 1997, the country had decided to punish and banish the Tories. Tony Blair – this young, persuasive, good-looking, anointed man who spoke with conviction (we had learned nothing from the Thatcher regime about the perils of conviction politicians) – had a wife who was a human-rights lawyer, a brilliant QC and a mother of three. They were us. The day New Labour won the election, Colin and I danced in the streets of Covent Garden, joined by many others. The sun blazed; God smiled; we had been set free.

The immigrant teaching project in the East End ended. While carrying on with the exhausting business of freelance journalism, I took up a part-time job at the New Labour think tank the Institute for Public Policy Research, a place stuffed full of men and women with whom I sometimes felt stupid and politically unconnected. They were bright, intellectual and tribal. I would never be that. Their time had come. I sensed those old Oxford blues coming back, the cracks of uncertainty, that feeling I was intruding. The day after the election, telephones rang all day, as the favoured policy wonks were called by Downing Street and government departments to be offered top jobs, just like that, no need for applications, equal-opportunities proce-dures, level playing fields. Corruption? Of course not. A new establishment was carrying on the old tradition, of 'understandings'.

Still, with a very supportive colleague I worked diligently on a report on the role of government in influencing public attitudes on race and the nation. The book was published, and the IPPR boss got Blair and Jack Straw to launch the report in the Commons. I was asking the Blairite magic circle to take the lead, change the long British tradition of condemning immigrants – needed but never wanted by this self-regarding nation. Blair uttered platitudes, and I was flattered. Understandably. This was the first time I had been so close to the heat of real power. Jena couldn't under-stand why TV didn't show this moment when her daughter met the always-smiling

Prime Minister. She was getting less mobile, but she had still insisted on casting her vote for Labour and that excellent Mr Blair.

Princess Diana died that summer, and Blair picked up on the depth of the nation's shock and sorrow with words that could not be bettered. Jena had Diana's photo stuck up next to one of Bob Geldof, close to a painting of Mecca on velvet and a family picture of her beloved Aga Khan. Diana was the victim of an oppressive arranged marriage, bad in-laws, a faithless husband, the stuff of Jena's favourite weepy Hindi films. I had to go Kensington Palace, be in the sea of flowers, share the pain. Leila was in her pushchair; Colin was baffled by the scene, so outlandish, so un-English (he understands better now). Under one tree about ten Muslim men, women and children were praying and swaying around a candle and some incense. There were many other unlikely mourners – some hairy white bikers, near them a clutch of black bouncer types in suits, willowy Chinese women, drunk and maudlin Sikh men, Caribbean gospel singers, Hindu widows in white, all gathered lamenting the lost princess who had ended up with the son of the most hated Arab in England, the Merchant of Cairo. You heard a unifying melody in the murmurs and chants, the various tongues converging in grief.

We cried together for several days, Jena and I. Then, on the tenth day, we made a pudding, invented one in Diana's name, took it to mosque. It is a glittering thing, lovely and delicate, surprising and glamorous.

 Diana's Pudding

You need to have a beautiful glass bowl for this.

Serves 6–8

2 lb curd cheese

8 oz caster sugar

2 tbsp blossom honey

2 cups almond slivers, broken, unroasted cashew nuts and split pistachios

Sheets of edible gold leaf

The ripest, reddest pomegranates you can find

1 pint extra-thick double cream

Rind and juice of two oranges, not too sweet

1 oz butter

Red rose petals without any trace of pesticide

- Melt the butter in a wide frying pan and pan-cook the nuts fast on medium heat until they start to turn light brown.

- Cool.

- Mix together the sugar, curd cheese and double cream.

- Divide into two in separate bowls.

- Into one add the orange juice and rind, into the other streak in the honey without mixing it in completely.

- Put the nuts into the bottom of the serving dish.

- Top with the honey/curd/cheese mix, then smooth on the next layer of the orange/curd/cheese mix.

- Chill.

- Wash the petals in cold water to which you have added ½ tsp of salt.

- Dry on kitchen paper; freshen in cold water just before serving and dry again.

- Sprinkle the pomegranate seeds, gold-leaf shards and rose petals over the top.

Two months after Diana's death, I got a weekly column on the *Independent*, beyond anything I had ever allowed myself to imagine. I was the first non-white Briton to get to this privileged position. I started timorously but was soon off. Opinions come out of me like eggs from well-fed chickens. This was what I was born to be.

Not everyone agrees. Hundreds of letters arrive each week from around the world. The missives have made me think, laugh, cry, scream and sometimes shiver fearfully through the night. Like any respectable nerd, I used to count the positives and negatives and drown in pathological anxiety. Not any more. Although it is enraging to hear from racists, Muslim Stalinists, unwavering ideologues and extreme Zionists, it is important they do write in and I am getting tougher.[3]

These conversations are an essential part of the job I love. Ted writes in with alarming frequency to tell me to shove off to where I came from. Ted, you are an American, from Texas. It is one thing to be invited to leave this island by the fans of Norman Tebbit, but what gives you the authority?

Then there's Edward, who longs to rip my clothes off and do me over: 'You Pakis with your shaved off clits, need to be fucked senseless by English patriots and thrown to the sharks, like in those James Bond Films.' There's no stopping Sharon or Michael either, oh no. Since I wrote I was going to boycott Israeli goods, these two have been accusing me of being an anti-Semite, 'the most dangerous sort, who claims to love Jews'. Egocentric Americans furiously demand a blind and unconditional approval of their nation. I must mention the O'Dwyers and Maureen and Milo (who likes to call me a 'trashy girlie'), hysterically opposed to black and Asian immigration, for whom I represent Beelzebub.

A confused ex-BNP supporter wrote that he was madly in love with Lisa, a jet-black Zimbabwean asylum seeker he met on a packed coach to Manchester. He had his wallet nicked; she gave him a fiver, and they have been seeing each other ever since. She has no idea what the BNP is, and he doesn't want her to find out. What do I think? I was reminded of Ross Parker, the poor white teenager who was murdered in a racist attack in Peterborough by three young men of Muslim origin. Ross was attacked with CS spray, a hammer and a foot-long knife. His story was not on the front page of too many newspapers. There was no demonstration. I did not write about him. I failed.

The vast majority of my Muslim respondents agree that we need to reform ourselves. These people help to stop me going mad, not to capitulate to the dozens of fanatics who write emails like this one:

Moderates like Yasmin Alibhai-Brown are our eternal enemies. Allah hates these people… her face is like a dog's backside, she denounces true Muslims who have taken the trouble to fight for true Islam, Wake up ms Apostate Brown. Allah shows us how to recognise these traitors Alibhai-Brown has even supported the adulteress in Nigeria when all true Muslims know fornicators must be punished. She supports sodomites, she has Jewish and Christian friends. The only reward for these people will be death, crucifixion.

The millennium came just as reality hit us. The spiky, planet-shaped Dome was illusory and alien, an apt symbol of a government that believed its own propaganda. We had never had it so good in so many ways. Yet many of us knew it was too late for idealism. Tony Blair was the proud son of Thatcher, charming and therefore more effective than she ever was. By 2000, the dancing on the streets in May 1997 seemed foolish, as absurd as those jubilant crowds who came out to shake their bottoms on the day Uganda became independent. What is it with us people, so ready to swing and sing when history always teaches us to be chary? I had been a member of the Labour Party for a while. The same politicians who said Tory immigration rhetoric and asylum policies were racist and unjust turned into demagogues. I was incredulous that a progressive-left party was going with Bill Clinton's policy on Iraq. Abominable sanctions were being imposed on the poor; children were dying for lack of medicines; some had had mysterious fatal illnesses since the first Gulf War, and we were punishing them. Their dictator and his cronies had never had it better. I left the party, announced it in my column, gave the reasons. It was no longer possible for me, a displaced person who sought safety in this country, to stand by and watch New Labour starve and punish others in the same position. It was the end of an affair.

The following year a letter arrived, asking if I would accept an MBE for my services to journalism if I was offered it. I threw it into the bin and was forced by Mum and Colin to retrieve it. Jena by then was in a state of fervent paranoia. The hostility to immigration was getting to her and her friends. What if we were thrown out of this country too? 'That daughter of yours, making too much trouble in the television, talking so much with her big mouth. Tell her, Jenabai, to keep quiet. We are guests here, she is giving us a bad name. Tell her, too much like Kassim she is, too much like him.' She told me again and again to show more humility, go along with things, maybe go back to teaching? Safe job. The MBE, she thought, was a kind of certified promise, an assurance we wouldn't be moved on from here even though her daughter was a major national irritant. Unlike me, Mum never mourned for Africa. Myths of return held on to by so many of her friends from India, Pakistan and East Africa were as foolish, she thought, as longings for youth flown past. She was so keen on this bauble. Colin was too, oddly maybe for the same reason. His wife the hell-raiser was being brought into the fold; she was safer than he had feared.

It was bizarre in Buckingham Palace. I was shuffling with embarrassment and shame that I had surrendered to this system. Her Majesty was diminutive and white all over. Her voice seemed pre-recorded. 'I hear you on *Woman's Hour*,' she said, allowing one sentence per punter. I didn't curtsy, was not overcome with awe. I was delighted to see how proud my children and husband were. Again Jena was disappointed that TV didn't show her daughter getting royal blessings. Workaholic Colin couldn't come to a fine repast at the Savoy, insisted on by my son. It was a good lunch, and even though I never cared about the bauble, Colin will never be forgiven for not joining us.

In the evening Jena made a celebratory meal: pink *pillau*, to thank the pinko-white nation, and mince cutlets.

 Pink *Pillau*

Serves 6

2 mugs basmati rice

2 chopped onions

2 hot green chillies, chopped

1 tsp each cumin seeds and mustard seeds

3 aubergines or courgettes, cut small

4 tbsp oil

6 cooked beetroots (they make fresh blood, Mum said)

¾ tsp turmeric

2 tbsp broken cashew nuts

Five curry leaves

Salt

- In a saucepan with a lid, boil plenty of salted water.
- Wash rice and cook in the boiling water for six minutes.
- Drain away the water, cover, turn the temperature right down, and leave for seven minutes.
- Meanwhile, heat the oil in a pan and throw in all the seeds.
- After three minutes add the curry leaves and chillies. It should all sizzle.
- Add the turmeric and cook for a minute.
- Then add the aubergines or courgettes. (I never bother with salting these, it doesn't seem to matter.)
- Stir-fry for a few minutes, turn down the temperature, cover, and cook for another seven minutes.
- Uncover and add chopped beetroot, cashew nuts and salt to taste.
- Cook only for one more minute.
- Mix the vegetable with the rice gently so the colour of the beetroot stains the rice.
- Cover and leave for five minutes before serving.

 Mince Cutlets

1 lb very lean minced beef

2 medium-sized onions, chopped
small or grated then squeezed

2 slices of bread, soaked briefly in
water and squeezed

2 eggs, beaten with a little salt and
1 tbsp water

1 tsp ginger paste

½ tsp garlic paste

1 tsp *garam masala*

2 green chillies, finely chopped

A handful of chopped fresh coriander

Salt to taste

Oil for shallow-frying

- Mix all the ingredients except for the eggs and oil (use your hand to do this so it mushes together properly).

- Cover and chill for a couple of hours.

- Break off small amounts and shape into patties, not too thin, like small hamburgers.

- Heat the oil until a small bit of bread dropped in rises quickly to the top.

- Have the egg near the pan and dip each patty into it, then fry, turning over three times to make sure it is cooked.

- Drain on kitchen paper.

My son had graduated and left Edinburgh with a degree in politics, and was dallying with the idea of becoming a chef, much to my consternation and Jena's horror: 'What, he is going to be a *pishi*? A cook, *hai hai*, what is happening to him? Clever boy, university-trained, going to cook? In a *kitchen*?' He soon saw sense and qualified as a lawyer as expected. But around this time when he was searching for and finding himself, there was some kind of upset with his father via email and he was cut off by his dad, told never to make contact again. History repeats itself, and I don't know where and when it will end.

In spite of the perfidy of politicians, the colour of England was changing, its tempo too. I allowed myself to believe that the various tribes of these isles understood and liked each other more than in the 1970s, 1980s and 1990s. Immigrants were here to stay, and millions of old Britons wanted nothing better. As our daughter grew up, a part of me had to commit to this nation; now our blood was mingled. We were not guests, we were family, and would quarrel and love forever and beyond.

I wrote a book on the soaring levels of mixed-race families in our cities, that story now in ascendancy. Half of Caribbean kids in this country have one white parent or grandparent; a third of Asians were in the same situation. My son married a beautiful blonde Englishwoman born in Cheshire to a family with much land and many lakes, gentility and generosity. They keep horses, and some apparently have been known to go fox hunting. It was a challenging wedding for this urban, leftie immigrant. Their side wore hats with beautiful feathers, ours garish Indian clothes. The Unitarian minister was gay and American and open to the world. I spoke in church and told them about Thatcher's speech on swamping the day my boy was born. The feathers quivered. I promised their daughter would be our *amanat*, our precious. She is. And they have taken in my son as their own too, given him a stable family lost long ago. Jena sat drinking champagne in the gorgeous garden, beaming and delighted for her Karim. Samosas and smoked salmon were served.

Some of my old black radical purists had since married out and smiled sheepishly when I reminded one of them of mulligatawny soup. One married a Swede and fathered lovely toffee-coloured babies: 'Was just a joke. Anyway looks like we are all eating olive oil now, in the simmering pot, melting into each other.' I don't think people can or should melt down into monochrome slush, but he was right about the olive oil. Even Jena and her mates were now olive-oil converts, and soon learned to infuse theirs with garlic and chillies.

Asians had discovered good health. They wanted to live forever like whites, slim down too. So they went all low fat and low cal. Sugar substitutes were bought in sacks, but the *mithai* never quite worked as well. Food was baked, grilled and steamed more and curries made with good olive oil. (White chefs meanwhile were eagerly going for the old killer recipes, chicken and biriyanis made with lashings of butter and ghee.) Old ladies started 'jogging', walking less slowly with trainers on and tracksuit bottoms: 'Must be eating healthy food only, really too much ghee before, look at us, bodies like sofa set.' A new repertoire of recipes emerged, of course.

Spicy Salmon

1 large salmon, filleted and cut in
    half lengthways
3 tbsp olive oil

2 fresh chillies, a chunk of ginger,
    ground *jeera*, lime juice, a little
    black pepper and ground
    coriander whizzed to a paste

⊙   Mix the oil and paste, and spread it liberally over the fish.

- Wrap the fish loosely in foil.

- Chill for a few hours.

- Bake for fifteen minutes (375 °F, 190 °C, gas mark 5).

- Open the package and return to the oven for five more minutes.

- Serve with healthy baked potato – NO BUTTER; use the juices from the fish.

- Serve with carrot pickle. So healthy.

I may have felt less restless in some ways, but there were many aspects of twenty-first-century British society I feared and detested. The boundaries between childhood and adulthood have been worn away by commercial interests to make bigger bucks. The selfish gene has entered the DNA of the population. Wealth is the new piety. Drink, drugs, teenage pregnancies, sexual incontinence, divorce, adultery, grotesque TV shows have coarsened Britain. Bringing up a girl in this climate is hard and scary. As my daughter handles teenage life, I compare it with mine in Africa and wish I could whisk her away to there, where we were safe.

Meanwhile Muslim girls and women around the world are being stifled by their families and mullahs, in Britain too. Some women themselves are willingly surrendering liberty for religious discipline. The revivalists are partly responding to globalization, which leads to more permissive societies, bedlam in their eyes, with increased alcohol consumption, sexual freedoms and no self-restraint. I noticed the rise of, first, the *hijabi*, then the sanctimonious *jilabi*, and all too soon the streets of my city were full of black-shrouded women whose eyes pierce the soul. I hate it all, the meanings behind these garments, the mark of evil placed upon femaleness; how many have had to die because they refuse these burial shrouds? My mother's generation had fought against such cloths of insult; our Imam had freed them in the 1950s. The Koran makes no demands on women to wear these garments, which deny them a place in the world.

On 10 September 2001 I wrote a column condemning the Taliban for their violence against girls and women, and the denial of their rights to freedom, education and self-sufficiency. The West, I argued, needed to intervene. On 11 September those planes went into the Twin Towers in New York, and the West screeched, swerved and fell into an abyss. Muslims like me couldn't condone what was done in the name of our faith, but we also couldn't side wholly with the Americans who wanted to claim that it was the worst tragedy to befall the world since the Holocaust, that nothing else counted as much, not Rwanda or the genocides in the Balkans, finally stopped by NATO intervention. I tried to explain these complicated reactions on a BBC1 *Question Time* programme three days later. All hell broke loose. I was denounced and a number of death threats ensued. Police protection was provided, and I have not slept easy since.

Then came the build-up to the war on Iraq, the lies, the torment felt by those of us who were from the Third World, now of the First. The war made us guilty, culpable. People I respected (some I cared for very much) turned into warmongers, while others who were right wing became anti-war protesters. The long marches to nowhere at least revealed that we were integrated when it came to important national choices, could coalesce across divides even though we were powerless to stop Blair siding absolutely and insanely with George W. Bush. I handed back my gong as we went to war, partly because I should never have accepted it, mostly because a new empire was being launched and the medal celebrated empire-building.

When the allies destroyed Fallujah, an act of merciless collective punishment, I felt responsible. In a democracy you have to. My country – now irreversibly my country – was acting with such dishonour, it was agonizing. How much easier it was when I could talk about 'them' and 'me'. It got worse than even my deadly pessimism could have predicted.

Added to this is the unending struggle of a reformist Muslim, which is what I am. We crouch nervously, sheepishly, as packs of wolves try to blow our house down. At the front door are the Muslim fanatics, growling and exacting, these days as likely to be teachers, doctors, scientists, students, salesmen and social workers as one-eyed maddened imams. Most Muslims came to Europe to escape tyranny, economic failure and ignorance. Today their children seek tyranny, economic failure and ignorance. They hate Muslims at home in the West even more than they hate the West. We stand for a composite, fluid, open and evolving society. They want to drag us into the Bora Bora caves. At the back are white, liberal and neo-con Muslim-baiters and haters. The Rushdie confrontation, then 9/11 and the bombs in London have turned them into the new crusaders.

In the autumn of 2007 Gordon Brown made his first prime-ministerial speech at the Labour Party Conference. He used the word *Britishness* about seventy-eight times. I was there and listening to the leader-in-waiting, who I thought would serve his nation better than the previous incumbent ever did. His patriotic whacks gave me a headache, though, and I took to my bed, forlorn once again. What the future holds seems as uncertain as ever. Perhaps I should keep a bag half packed. Just in case.

Epilogue

JENA DAMJI DIED ON 3 March 2006. Mother's Day was approaching – when I was both a daughter and a mum, a kid and a grown-up, a receiver with one hand and a giver with the other, delighted by both. As my excited children plotted to please me, I did the same with the same childish excitement for the best-ever mum. That year one hand was empty, and a chamber in my heart too, and Mum's small flat, once bursting with stuff old and new, the corner of the brightly patterned sofabed where she sat rolling a *tasbi*. Her companions were Sunrise Radio – the Asian station – video films and television. Sharp till the end, she followed all the soaps (*EastEnders*, she complained, had gone stale and implausible) and the news.

I never expected to feel this cavernous, echoing loss as the days passed. Sometimes heavy sleep overcame me in the middle of the day, and I awoke unable to form precise thoughts and images, but my face and pillows were awash in tears.

She was my mate, my conscience, at times exasperating, always fiercely protective of her family, and great company. She held safe precious stories of my childhood and even now, in my fifties, I wanted to hear them again and again.

She had arrived in 1970, and I had followed in 1972, when she was fifty-two and

I was twenty-two. Enoch Powell was then a national hero of indigenous Britons who wanted to keep us out, keep their country white. She tried to understand how they felt. One Christmas a group of white lads started throwing stones at her outside Woolworths, where she was headed to buy a present for Karim. She calmed the boys with her gentle voice and asked one of them to help her choose a CD. He walked her home and later left her a Christmas card. I found the card after she died.

Jena believed she had to show respect to the old citizens of Britain for sharing their small island with us. It was their home, they had let us in, she would say. In contrast I was full of youthful temper, bursting with anti-imperialist zeal and an unshakeable sense of entitlement. The Empire had exploited us; now the children of the Empire had struck back, come home to roost.

'Why do you go on so much about the past? They were not so bad, you know. Things were better than under Amin.'

'Mum, you have no sense of history. Was Gandhi wrong to fight these British? We have rights, nobody is doing us any favours. How can you stand it, whites treating us like we are second-class citizens?'

'Gandhi was never as angry as you. Yes, some people don't like us because we are brown, so what? They are stupid. Why let them spoil your life? Look what they have given me – a pension, my own independence. They didn't look at my face and refuse me that, did they? I know you are fighting for equality but life is not perfect.'

Since her death I can see what she saw, and yes, I do feel grateful that this country made Jena feel so free and sheltered. Her life had been hard, but she had embraced it with zest. She was a teenage orphan when she married my father, sixteen years older, sophisticated and brilliant but a gadfly, a bohemian. Jena had feminism thrust upon her. She had to work – teach, sew, cook – to keep us. She juggled debts, kept her head high. made many friends, ingratiated herself with family members, especially those with much cash. She pushed me into education, to succeed but with humility. Vanity and hubris were unbecoming, she said.

I have had so many calls since her death. Unknown to me, she had fans in Russia, India, Pakistan, Canada, Romania, Kenya, the US, all over this country. My mother befriended all sorts. As we emptied her flat, I found fourteen old Mother's Day cards and some cuttings of my articles wrapped in soft scarves, and unused presents – blank photo frames, a hat I bought her one year because she had developed an acute sensitivity to the sun, a beautiful cotton-lace nightdress, brand new but yet smelling of her.

We took her to some of the poshest restaurants in London. She always refused at first: 'You go, why are you troubling an old woman? You too will be old and will know how hard it is.'

'Please come, we want you to. Leila is asking...'

'Why are you forcing me? I know you love me. No need for this show. Give the money to Oxfam. Anyway, not in my *nasib* to go to such places, maybe in the next life.'

When Colin added his voice, she melted at once. She then had to be coaxed to wear one of her beautiful silk saris, but only after she had put on her thermals, tights, socks, two vests. I put rings on her fingers, gold chains round her neck, doused her in her favourite French perfumes. On most such hard-won evenings, once out, she drank much champagne, laughed and became the woman she had been.

Then suddenly in 2005, she stopped eating. Her body began to shrink. I made her soups, Indian fishcakes, cardamom rice pudding – they were all stuffed in the fridge to rot. Eight Lucozade bottles, all full, stood forlorn in the kitchen. She told me she was desperate to die; too long here already, she said. The last months were agony, her pitiful face pleading for release.

She looked beautiful in her coffin, her head framed with her favourite bright magenta sari. She was buried by men white and brown who loved her. I miss her so much, need to talk to her, quarrel with her, stroke her lovely skin. Sometimes I resented all the time she took up; when she was gone, time flapped round me like a shirt too big.

So in the summer of 2007 I took the family to Tanzania, to Dar-es-Salaam, Jena's birthplace, still languid and untouched really by the busyness of the new millennium. We walked where she must have walked as a child, imagined her as a bright schoolgirl and how she must have felt when her parents both died and she had to leave her birthplace. We went on to Zanzibar, where I spoke Kutchi to old folk hanging round the old mosque, preserved exactly in my head, and where I failed to find the holiday hostel. The Arab slave story pulses through the island, as do the tremors of the 1964 revolution, when Arabs and Indians were massacred by Africans.

Unlike my trip to Uganda, this one filled in gaping spaces, comforted and reinforced my multiple identities. But here too there was a message whispering on the breeze, passing over the ears: 'There is no coming back. You don't belong. The place has moved on.' Razi, a reader of my columns, wrote to me after I described the trip in the *Independent*:

I too made the journey back and in some ways wish I hadn't at all. All it did was shatter the happy memories I had of the beautiful land I was blessed to be born in. I cried when I saw the family home and the state of my old school... I truly felt a complete stranger in the land I thought was mine and sadly the only place I could find solace was in the graveyard where I knew everybody, literally. Having returned 'home' to Leicester, I wonder all the more who I really am and where I belong.

Unlike Razi, after my last spell in East Africa I know where I belong. A child of Caribbean migrants, the novelist Caryl Phillips, proclaimed that Britain has 'been forged in the crucible of fusion, of hybridity'.[1] London is that crucible, that national forge. The city where no one belongs is where I belong.

Notes

Prologue

1. From a collection of postcards printed for the Poet Tree Project, London Borough of Newham.
2. In his diary entry for 22 November 1663.
3. In a speech Phillips made at a conference in Paris in 2004.
4. I am indebted to Johann Hari for revealing the Lytton order in his column in the *Independent*, 12 June 2006. The forever-spun history of the Empire mostly ignores such inconvenient information. The particulars of this tragedy were a revelation to me.
5. Paul Theroux, 'Hating the Asians', *Transition* 33 (1967), p. 60.
6. Cynthia Salvadori, *We Came in Dhows*, limited edn (Nairobi, 1996).
7. Personal communication.

1 Enticing Blightie, 1972

1. Both quotes are from *Daily Nation* (Nairobi), 13 February 1967.

2 Paradise Found, AD 68–1920

1. In an essay on Anselm Kiefer in the *Guardian*, 3 February 2007.
2. Winston Churchill, *My African Journey* (1908), reprint edn (London, 1990).

3. *Periplus of the Erythrean Sea* (Goteburg, 1927), quoted in R. Oliver and G. Matthews, eds, *History of East Africa*, vol. 1 (Oxford, 1963), p. 94.

4. For a full account, see G. P. Murdoch, *Africa and Its People and Their Culture* (New York, 1958).

5. 'The Voyage and Acts of Dom Francisco', in G. S. P Freeman-Grenville, *The East African Coast* (Oxford, 1974), p. 110.

6. From Livingstone's journals, quoted in J. S. Mangat, *A History of the Asians in East Africa, c. 1886 to 1945* (Oxford, 1969), p. 23.

7. See Oliver and Matthews (note 3).

8. See Aarthi Prasad, in *Prospect* (April 2007).

9. Cambridge University Library, Hardinge papers, 29 November 1912.

10. Cynthia Salvadori, *We Came in Dhows*, limited edn (Nairobi, 1996), vol. 1, p. 160.

11. J. H. Patterson, *The Man-Eaters of Tsavo* (London, 1973), p. 15.

12. Quoted in Salvadori (note 10), p. x.

13. Richard Meinertzhagen, *Kenya Diary*, quoted in John Reader, *Africa: A Biography of the Continent* (London, 1998), p. 573.

14. M. G. Visram, *The Red Soils of Tsavo* (Mombasa, 1987).

15. Mangat (note 6), p. 38.

16. Some of this information came to light in July 1998, when Channel 4 made a programme with my son about his ancestors.

17. Esak Abdul Rehman Kana, in Salvadori (note 10), p. 9.

18. Olive Grey, *Picturesque British East Africa* (privately published, 1902), p. 11.

19. Sir Harry Johnston, FO 2/204/13 October 1899.

20. Bhanuben Kotecha, *On the Threshold of East Africa* (London, 1994), p. 63.

21. Several other such testimonies can be found in Salvadori (note 10).

22. Edward Vizetelly, *From Cyprus to Zanzibar* (London, 1901), p. 118.

23. J. A. Hunter and Alan Wykes, *Hunter's Tracks* (London, 1957), p. 22.

24. Jameela Siddiqi, *The Feast of the Nine Virgins* (London, 2001), chap. 1.

25. Churchill (note 2), p. 49.

26. Owen Letcher, *The Bonds of Africa* (London, 1913), p. 205.

27. A descendant of one of them confirmed this story to Salvadori (note 10), p. 69.

28. Government of India dispatch, 21 October 1920.

29. Oliver and Matthews (note 3), vol. 2, p. 515.

30. Jivrav Somji Vanoo, *The History of the Solar Race: A History of the Indians of East Africa* (Birmingham, 2001), p.16.

3 Born in Elysium, 1920s–54

1. Dr Shireen Walji, in 'Ismailis in Kenya: Some Perspectives on Continuity and Change', unpub. thesis, Nairobi University, 1994, describes the effect of the Depression on Ismailis: 'In the 30s and 40s business opportunities for the Ismaili traders had become limited. The first pioneering migrants were well established but the newer migrants found it difficult to set up businesses with the meagre amounts of capital they were able to accumulate as apprentices... trade became increasingly speculative and competitive. Most traders lost heavily.' Aga Khan III created new financial credit institutions and co-operatives to secure the future for his people in East Africa (pp. 5–6).

2. Quoted in Walji (note 1), p. 7.

3. Farhad Daftary, *A Short History of the Ismailis* (Edinburgh, 1998), p. 200.

4. Robert Baden-Powell, *Birds and Beasts in Africa* (London, 1938), p. 43.

5. W. Lloyd-Jones, an army commander, quoted in Cynthia Salvadori, *We Came in Dhows*, limited edn (Nairobi, 1996), vol. 2, p. 114.

6. Lady Cobbald, *Kenya, Land of Illusion* (London, 1935), p. 73.

7. Edgar Bronson, *In Closed Territory* (Chicago, 1930), p. 130.

8. Julian Huxley, *Africa View* (London, 1931), p. 42.

9. Shamsud Deen, quoted in J. S. Mangat, *A History of the Asians in East Africa, c. 1886 to 1945* (Oxford, 1969), p. 112.

10. Karen Blixen, *Out of Africa* (London, 1937), p. 15.

11. Quoted in Salvadori (note 5), vol. 3, p. 131.

4 *The Sun Drops, 1955–60*

1. Chris McGreal interviewed survivors and camp officers in the *Guardian*, 13 October 2006. The evidence is pretty indisputable.

2. Caroline Elkins, *Britain's Gulag: The Brutal End of Empire in Kenya* (London, 2005).

3. For a full account see *Guns, Gems and Uniforms: Kenyan South Asians and the Mau Mau, AWAZ*, 3 October 2006.

4. In Michael Twaddle, ed., *Expulsion of a Minority: Essays on Ugandan Asians* (London, 1975), p. 81.

5. Agehananda Bharati, *Asians in East Africa* (Chicago, 1972), pp. 155–59.

6. See Jameela Siddiqi, *The Feast of the Nine Virgins* (London, 2001), chap. 5, for a wonderful description of the dowry mania in East Africa.

7. Ibid., p. 35.

8. Joanna Moorhead, 'Milking It', *Guardian*, 15 May 2007.

9. Stuart Jeffries, *Guardian*, 29 September 2006.

5 *Children of the Revolution, 1961–67*

1. There is a fascinating book by Joan Karmali, an Englishwoman married to a Kenyan Asian, who ran a school that was racially mixed and so was an exception: *A School in Kenya: Hospital Hill, 1949–1973* (Worcester, 2002).

2. Her autobiographies tell her own version of these times. See *My Pearl of Great Price*, vols 1 and 2 (Port Melbourne, 2003, 2007).

3. Published in *Transition* 75 (1963), p. 160.

4. See Giles Foden, author of the best-selling novel on Amin, *The Last King of Scotland* (London, 1998), in an article in the *Guardian*, 24 July 2003.

5. In 2000, the National Museums of Kenya funded an exhibition on the Asian African heritage, the first in East Africa. It was a small reminder and not nearly enough to redress the historical amnesia. The exhibition booklet acknowledges the lack of interest in this history spanning two hundred years: 'The Asian African presence is neither sufficiently represented in our history books nor in our schools and universities... education and self examination by the minority as by the nation itself are long overdue.'

6. 'Hating the Asians', *Transition* 33 (1967), p. 61.

6 *Paradise Bust, 1967–72*

1. See Rickin Majithia, 'Britain's Management of the 1972 Ugandan Asian Refugee Crisis', undergrad. thesis, Queen Mary's University of London, 2007.

2. V. S. Naipaul, *An Area of Darkness* (Harmondsworth, 1964), p. 61.

3. I am grateful to our mosque in London for publishing *A Taste of Our Cooking* (1986), from which I have taken this and a few other recipes.

4. Quoted in the *Daily Mail* after the Public Record Office released key papers, 5 January 2001.

5. Foreign Office report, July 1970.

6. See press coverage at the time; they quote his lawyer.

7. Ibid.

8. Henry Kyemba, *State of Blood: The Inside Story of Idi Amin* (London, 1977), p. 15.

9. Lella Umedaly and Muneera Spence, *Mamajee's Kitchen* (Vancouver, 2005).

10. The best and most disturbing account of British policies at their most unethical is to be found in *Unpeople: Britain's Secret Human Rights Abuses* (London, 2004) by the historian Mark Curtis. There is a section on the rise of Idi Amin.

11. R. Slater to FCO, 3 February 1971, FCO 31/1024.

12. H. Smedley, Note, 27 January 1971, FCO31/1028.

13. Curtis (note 10), p. 249.

14. R. Slater to FO, 30 May 1972, FCO31/1328.

15. *Independent*, 25 January 2001.

7 *The Nation of Shopkeepers, 1972–77*

1. N. Deakin, 'The Immigration Issue in British Politics', unpub. thesis, University of Sussex, 1972.

2. E. J. B. Rose et al., *Colour and Citizenship: A Report on British Race Relations* (Oxford, 1969), p. 11.

3. Zig Layton-Henry and Robin Cohen, eds, *The Politics of Migration* (Cheltenham, 1992), p. 139.

4. See B. Smithies and P. Fiddick, eds, *Enoch Powell and Immigration* (London, 1969).

5. See press coverage of that week.

6. Trevor Grundy, *Daily Telegraph*, 2 August 2002.

7. Mahmood Mamdani, *From Citizen to Refugee* (London, 1973), p. 64.

8. 8 August 1972, PREM15/1257.

9. Read this section in Mark Curtis, *Unpeople: Britain's Secret Human Rights Abuses* (London, 2004), chap. 13.

10. For a full description, see Vaughan Robinson, *Transients, Settlers and Refugees* (Oxford, 1986).

11. Henry Kyemba, *State of Blood: Idi Amin's Reign of Fear* (London, 1977), p. 64.

12. B. Tejani, 'Farewell Uganda', *Transition* 74–5 (1974).

13. In his brilliant biography of *London* (London, 2001), Peter Ackroyd describes both these sides of the city. The quote from Thomas Carlyle is from 'The Centre of the Empire', p. 705.

14. Mamdani (note 7), p. 87.

15.   Kyemba (note 11), p. 54.

16.   In the *Independent*, 29 July 2007.

8 *Rhiannon was a Blonde, 1976–86*

1.   Foreword to 'Great Interviews of the 20th Century', *Guardian*, September 2007.

2.   See press reports of the case.

3.   Hugo Young, *One of Us: A Biography of Margaret Thatcher* (London, 1989), p. III.

9 *The Longest Year, 1987–88*

1.   Sampson wrote several books on the anatomies of Britain, the intricate connections between the powerful and institutions.

2.   Nawal El Saadawi, *A Daughter of Isis* (London, 2007), p. 2.

3.   In Ruth Levitas, ed., *The Ideology of the New Right* (Oxford, 1986), p. 76.

10 *The Sun Also Rises, 1988–2006*

1.   Anthony Burgess, *Observer*, 23 September 1990.

2.   Rana Kabbani, *New Statesman and Society*, 31 March 1989.

3.   See *Some of My Best Friends Are...*, a selection of my columns (London, 2004).

Epilogue

1.   Caryl Phillips, ed., *Extravagant Strangers* (London, 1998), p. x.

Further Reading

Rohan Candappa, *Picklehead* (London, 2006)

Jules Damji, *Oyster Bay and Other Short Stories* (Bloomington, 2006)

Richard Dowden, *Africa: Altered States, Ordinary Miracles* (London, 2008)

Caroline Elkins, *Britain's Gulag: The Brutal End of Empire in Kenya* (London, 2005)

Joan Karmali, *A School in Kenya: Hospital Hill, 1949–1973* (Port Melbourne, 2002)

Henry Kyemba, *State of Blood: Idi Amin's Reign of Fear* (London, 1977)

John Reader, *Africa: A Biography of a Continent* (London, 1997)

Colette Rossant, *Apricots on the Nile* (London, 2003)

Emily Ruete, *Memoirs of an Arabian Princess from Zanzibar* (Zanzibar City, 1998)

Cynthia Salvadori, *We Came in Dhows*, limited edn (Nairobi, 1996)

Jameela Siddiqi, *The Feast of the Nine Virgins* (London, 2001)

M. Twaddle, 'Expulsion of a Minority: Essays on Ugandan Asians', unpub. thesis (University of London, 1975)

Lella Umedaly and Muneera Spence, *Mamajee's Kitchen* (Vancouver, 2005)

M. G. Vassanji, *The Gunny Sack* (London, 1994)

—, *The Book of Secrets* (London, 1996)

Conversion Tables

All conversions have been rounded up or down.

Weights

½ oz	10 g		7 oz	200 g
1 oz	25 g		7½ oz	215 g
1½ oz	40 g		8 oz	225 g
2 oz	50 g		8½ oz	240 g
2½ oz	60 g		9 oz	250 g
3 oz	75 g		9½ oz	260 g
3½ oz	90 g		10 oz	275 g
4 oz	110 g		12 oz	305 g
4½ oz	125 g		1 lb	450 g
5 oz	150 g		1½ lb	700 g
5½ oz	160 g		2 lb	900 g
6 oz	175 g		3 lb	1.35 kg
6½ oz	190 g		4 lb	1.8 kg

Volume

¼ pint	150 ml
½ pint	275 ml
¾ pint	450 ml
1 pint	570 ml

Cups

It is best to use a 'cup' measure for ingredients listed in cups. The following are approximate guidelines for the weight of 1 cup of common foods:

1 cup butter	225 g
1 cup dessicated coconut	80 g
1 cup fresh coriander	40 g
1 cup granulated sugar	225 g
1 cup lentils	200 g
1 cup plain flour	150 g
1 cup slivered almonds	108 g
1 cup uncooked rice	200 g

List of Recipes